"Masters are often aware that they rei
the wisdom of a master who knows we all remain apprentices as we seek to
read Scripture. Yet he guides us through the scriptures with a delightful sense
that we can learn to read with joy these wonderful texts. This is a book not
to be missed by those who are charged with discerning God's word for the
Christian people."

—**Stanley Hauerwas**, Duke Divinity School

"*Hermeneutics as Apprenticeship* contributes usefully to the genre 'how to
read the Bible' by focusing on the Bible's method of appropriating and applying its own teaching. It brings home in practical ways some of the more
theoretical attention given recently to intertextuality and canonical studies.
With commendable balance, the author shows how contemporary discussions
of themes such as gospel and empire can help Christians read and apply their
Bibles more accurately and faithfully."

—**Douglas J. Moo**, Wheaton College

"David Starling's *Hermeneutics as Apprenticeship* actually makes biblical
hermeneutics enjoyable! Not only does he sample books from all major parts
of both testaments in light of key debates on biblical interpretation that fit
them well, but he writes with elegant prose and interesting examples that
make his work a real page-turner. Not only does he help readers understand
what to do, and not do, with each part of Scripture, he also makes you want
to go back and read the Bible itself with fresh lenses. This book should have
a long and productive life for theological students and interested laypersons,
but seasoned pastors and scholars can learn from it as well."

—**Craig L. Blomberg**, Denver Seminary

"David Starling's hermeneutical studies are very helpful examples of theological exegesis and biblical theology intertwined. They are attentive to Scripture itself and to the challenges—both perennial and contemporary—of its
reading. Their unifying idea is an important one: Scripture itself provides the
church's most indispensable collection of hermeneutical exemplars."

—**Daniel J. Treier**, Wheaton College Graduate School

"*Hermeneutics as Apprenticeship* serves up a series of hermeneutical vignettes
that reflect the array of Scripture. So the book is a rich menu of observations
about the different kinds of material we meet in Scripture. It is a study that
will lead you to reflect on how to read Scripture both better and well."

—**Darrell L. Bock**, Dallas Theological Seminary

Hermeneutics as Apprenticeship

How the Bible Shapes Our Interpretive Habits and Practices

DAVID I. STARLING

Baker Academic

a division of Baker Publishing Group
Grand Rapids, Michigan

Published by Baker Academic
a division of Baker Publishing Group
P.O. Box 6287, Grand Rapids, MI 49516-6287
www.bakeracademic.com

Printed in the United States of America

Library of Congress Cataloging-in-Publication Data
Names: Starling, David Ian, author.
Title: Hermeneutics as apprenticeship : how the Bible shapes our interpretive habits and practices / David I. Starling.
Description: Grand Rapids, MI : Baker Academic, 2016. | Includes bibliographical references and index.
Identifiers: LCCN 2016006541 | ISBN 9780801049392 (pbk. : alk. paper)
Subjects: LCSH: Bible—Hermeneutics. | Bible—Influence.
Classification: LCC BS476 .S753 2016 | DDC 220.601—dc23
LC record available at https://lccn.loc.gov/2016006541

In keeping with biblical principles of creation stewardship, Baker Publishing Group advocates the responsible use of our natural resources. As a member of the Green Press Initiative, our company uses recycled paper when possible. The text paper of this book is composed in part of post-consumer waste.

16 17 18 19 20 21 22   7 6 5 4 3 2 1

For my family,
who first taught me to read,
and to read the Bible.

Contents

Foreword

Dr. David Starling's fine book on evangelical hermeneutics makes a distinctive and creative contribution to current debates about how to interpret Scripture. While recognizing that Holy Scripture is a weighty, complex and multilayered unity, Dr. Starling presents a series of fourteen case studies in "inner-biblical hermeneutics" from a range of books in both the Old and New Testaments. His aim is to provide an introduction for learning the art of scriptural interpretation from the biblical writers themselves.

Instead of attempting to integrate the contents of Scripture overall or unlock all its mysteries, he focuses on one aspect of the interpretive work done by each of these biblical authors and relates it to a theological or ethical issue that has been confronted by Christians from previous centuries up to the present. This gaining of "hermeneutical wisdom" means receiving the biblical writings as Holy Scripture and knowing how to appropriate their words within our own situation.

Dr. Starling's presentation takes into account the literary, historical, and theological contexts the biblical authors address. His work is based on thorough exegesis within a salvation-historical and biblical theological framework. At the same time his chapters judiciously address the wider interpretive questions that systematicians rightly ask of the text. The answers that emerge are refreshing and challenging, whether one is learning the hermeneutics of delight from the Psalter, studying Job and the limits of wisdom, knowing Jesus as the truth from John's Gospel, interpreting allegory in relation to Paul's letter to the Galatians, or seeking to grasp the significance of empire that is integral to 1 Peter.

This important book wrestles with a wide range of interpretive issues that students of exegesis, biblical theology, and systematics have often raised. Its author is well qualified to address these interlocking, though often regarded as unconnected, fields. All can profit immensely from the "inner-biblical hermeneutics" that emerge from Dr. Starling's insightful research. Strongly recommended.

Peter T. O'Brien,
Emeritus Faculty Member,
formerly Senior Research Fellow in New Testament,
Moore College, Sydney, Australia

Preface

This book could not have been written without the generous help and encouragement of many. Much of its content was written during a period of study leave that I was granted in the first half of 2013, which I spent at Tyndale House in Cambridge. I am most grateful to the friends and fellow researchers with whom I worked while I was there; to the trustees of the Morling Foundation, whose generosity made that visit possible; to my colleagues at Morling College who covered for me during the six months of my absence; and to my wife, Nicole, and our four children, who accompanied and supported me through all the upheavals of that delightful adventure. Other portions of this book had their genesis as papers presented at various meetings of the Society of Biblical Literature, the Evangelical Theological Society, the Tyndale Fellowship, and the Trinity Symposium in Perth; my thanks are due to the University of Divinity, the Australian College of Theology, and the Morling Foundation for the part they played in enabling my participation in those conferences.

Earlier versions of chapters 3, 10, 11, and 13 of this book were previously published in the following places:

"Full and Empty Readers: Ruth and the Hermeneutics of Virtue." *BibInt* 24 (2016): 17–26.

"'Nothing beyond What Is Written'? First Corinthians and the Hermeneutics of Early Christian *Theologia*." *JTI* 8 (2014): 45–62.

"Justifying Allegory: Scripture, Rhetoric and Reason in Gal. 4:21–5:1." *JTI* 9 (2015): 69–87.

"'She Who Is in Babylon': 1 Peter and the Hermeneutics of Empire." In *Reactions to Empire: Sacred Texts in Their Socio-Political Contexts*, edited by John Anthony Dunne and Dan Batovici, 111–28. Tübingen: Mohr Siebeck, 2014.

They are included in this volume with substantial revisions and with the kind permission of the original publishers.

No work of scholarship is ever an entirely solo enterprise. In my case, I am deeply indebted to the friends and colleagues at Morling College (particularly Andrew Sloane, Anthony Petterson, Edwina Murphy, and Tim MacBride) who read portions of this book and offered feedback and encouragement along the way that was immensely helpful in the shaping and refining of my own thoughts. In the earliest stages of the project, I received indispensable help and encouragement from colleagues and mentors further afield, including Craig Blomberg, Darrell Bock, Stanley Hauerwas, Douglas Moo, Peter O'Brien, Jamie Smith, and Kevin Vanhoozer. Without their warm endorsements (and without the willingness of James Ernest and his colleagues at Baker Academic to take a risk on an unknown Australian) this book would have been unlikely to see the light of day. James Ernest, and more recently, his Baker colleague Jim Kinney and the other members of the Baker editorial team, contributed enormously to the project, not only through their continuing belief in the book's usefulness but also through their wise advice on how it could be improved.

Among those various colleagues and mentors, I am glad to have the opportunity in this preface to express my particular gratitude to Peter O'Brien, whose wise and generous advice and example were a constant encouragement to me when I was first learning the craft of New Testament scholarship under his supervision. His willingness to write a foreword for this volume is a further instance of that generosity.

Soli Deo Gloria.

Abbreviations

Old Testament

Gen.	Genesis		Song of Sol.	Song of Solomon
Exod.	Exodus		Isa.	Isaiah
Lev.	Leviticus		Jer.	Jeremiah
Num.	Numbers		Lam.	Lamentation
Deut.	Deuteronomy		Ezek.	Ezekiel
Josh.	Joshua		Dan.	Daniel
Judg.	Judges		Hosea	Hosea
Ruth	Ruth		Joel	Joel
1–2 Sam.	1–2 Samuel		Amos	Amos
1–2 Kings	1–2 Kings		Obad.	Obadiah
1–2 Chron.	1–2 Chronicles		Jon.	Jonah
Ezra	Ezra		Mic.	Micah
Neh.	Nehemiah		Nah.	Nahum
Esther	Esther		Hab.	Habakkuk
Job	Job		Zeph.	Zephaniah
Ps. (Pss.)	Psalms		Hag.	Haggai
Prov.	Proverbs		Zech.	Zechariah
Eccles.	Ecclesiastes		Mal.	Malachi

New Testament

Matt.	Matthew		1–2 Cor.	1–2 Corinthians
Mark	Mark		Gal.	Galatians
Luke	Luke		Eph.	Ephesians
John	John		Phil.	Philippians
Acts	Acts		Col.	Colossians
Rom.	Romans		1–2 Thess.	1–2 Thessalonians

1–2 Tim.	1–2 Timothy	1–2 Pet.	1–2 Peter
Titus	Titus	1–3 John	1–3 John
Philem.	Philemon		
Heb.	Hebrews	Jude	Jude
James	James	Rev.	Revelation

Apocrypha

1 Kgdms.	1 Kingdoms (Septuagint)
Sir.	Sirach (Ecclesiasticus)
Wis.	Wisdom of Solomon

Ancient Sources

Ag. Ap.	Josephus, *Against Apion*
Cherubim	Philo, *On the Cherubim*
Spec. Laws	Philo, *On the Special Laws*

Bibliographic

AB	Anchor Bible
AcBib	Academia Biblica
AnBib	Anelecta Biblica
ANF	A. Roberts and J. Donaldson, eds. *The Ante-Nicene Fathers*. 10 vols. 1867–72. Reprint. Grand Rapids: Eerdmans
AOTC	Apollos Old Testament Commentary
ASBT	Acadia Studies in Bible and Theology
AThR	Anglican Theological Review
BECNT	Baker Exegetical Commentary on the New Testament
Bib	*Biblica*
BibInt	*Biblical Interpretation*
BNTC	Black's New Testament Commentary
BST	The Bible Speaks Today
BZAW	Beihefte zur Zeitschrift für die alttestamentliche Wissenschaft
BZNW	Beihefte zur Zeitschrift für die neutestamentliche Wissenschaft
CBC	Cambridge Bible Commentary
CBET	Contributions to Biblical Exegesis and Theology
CBQ	*Catholic Biblical Quarterly*
CBQMS	Catholic Biblical Quarterly Monograph Series
CNTC	Calvin's New Testament Commentaries
ExAud	*Ex Auditu*
HC	The Harvard Classics
HS	*Hebrew Studies*
ICC	International Critical Commentary

Interpretation	Interpretation: A Commentary for Teaching and Preaching
IVPNTC	IVP New Testament Commentary
JETS	*Journal of the Evangelical Theological Society*
JSNT	*Journal for the Study of the New Testament*
JSNTSup	Journal for the Study of the New Testament Supplement Series
JSOT	*Journal for the Study of the Old Testament*
JSOTSup	Journal for the Study of the Old Testament Supplement Series
JSPL	*Journal for the Study of Paul and His Letters*
JTI	*Journal of Theological Interpretation*
JTS	*Journal of Theological Studies*
KEK	Kritisch-exegetischer Kommentar über das Neue Testament (Meyer-Kommentar)
LCL	Loeb Classical Library
LHBOTS	The Library of Hebrew Bible/Old Testament Studies
LNTS	The Library of New Testament Studies
NAC	New American Commentary
NCBC	New Cambridge Bible Commentary
Neot	*Neotestamentica*
NIBCOT	New International Biblical Commentary on the Old Testament
NICNT	New International Commentary on the New Testament
NIGTC	New International Greek Testament Commentary
NIVAC	NIV Application Commentary
NovTSup	Supplements to Novum Testamentum
NPNF	*Nicene and Post-Nicene Fathers*
NSBT	New Studies in Biblical Theology
NTM	New Testament Message
NTS	*New Testament Studies*
PNTC	Pillar New Testament Commentary
RTR	*Reformed Theological Review*
SBET	*Scottish Bulletin of Evangelical Theology*
SBJT	*Southern Baptist Journal of Theology*
SBL	Society of Biblical Literature
SHBC	Smyth & Helwys Bible Commentary
SNTSMS	Society for New Testament Studies Monograph Series
TOTC	Tyndale Old Testament Commentaries
TynBul	*Tyndale Bulletin*
UKHL	Reported Judgments of the United Kingdom House of Lords
VT	*Vetus Testamentum*
WA	*D. Martin Luthers Werke, Weimarer Ausgabe* (collected works of Martin Luther, Weimar edition)
WBC	Word Biblical Commentary
WTJ	*Westminster Theological Journal*
WUNT	Wissenschaftliche Untersuchungen zum Neuen Testament
WW	*Word and World*
YJS	Yale Judaica Series
ZNW	*Zeitschrift für die neutestamentliche Wissenschaft und die Kunde der älteren Kirche*

Other Abbreviations

cf.	confer, compare	LXX	Septuagint
ch(s).	chapter(s)	MT	Masoretic Text
e.g.	*exempli gratia*, for example	NT	New Testament
ET	English Translation	OT	Old Testament
i.e.	*id est*, that is	v./vv.	verse/verses

Introduction

Scriptura Scripturae interpres—Scripture is the interpreter of Scripture. Of course we know this self-interpretation of Scripture at all times and in all places only as it is reflected in the human exposition visible in human opinions, resolutions, and actions of every kind. But everything depends on our recognizing this latter as something secondary, as the reflection of that real and genuine exposition, as the multiplicity of the attempts more or less successful to follow in the steps of that self-exposition of Scripture.

—Karl Barth, Gifford Lectures (1930),
quoted in Webster, *Barth's Earlier Theology*, 108.

"What Is Written in the Law? . . . How Do You Read It?" (Luke 10:26)

Whenever we read Scripture we are interpreting. We do some of the work of interpreting as we decipher the inscriptions of the text and some as we reflect on and discuss it after reading. Much of the work is wrapped up already in the preunderstandings that we bring to the text before we even begin to read. Add it all up and the sum is clear: there is no such thing as "pure reading," innocent of interpretation.

This is true not only in the obscurer reaches of Daniel or Revelation but also in the plainest and most familiar places. Any doubt that this is so can be dispelled by a few minutes' reflection on one of the most familiar biblical texts of all, the commandment in Leviticus 19:18, "You shall love your neighbor as yourself" (NRSV), and the multitude of questions that arise in the process of understanding it.

1

To begin with, there are questions about the meaning and reference of the words:

- Who is the (masculine singular) "you" addressed in the commandment? Is the commandment directed exclusively to the members of the particular Israelite congregation referred to in the opening verses of the chapter? Should it also be understood as addressing the Israelite reader who encounters the commandment in generations to come? Is this commandment, along with the others within the chapter, spoken equally to all of the people, or is it directed primarily to those particular (adult, male, landowning) Israelites who own farms and vineyards (19:9–10), breed animals (19:19), plant trees (19:23–25), grow beards (19:27), and exercise authority over the sexual conduct of their daughters (19:29)?

- Should we understand the "shall" of the English translation (and the Hebrew construction behind it) in the indicative mood, as a prediction that you will love your neighbor, or in the imperative mood, as a commandment that you must?[1]

- Is the "love" that is commanded merely the absence of the vengeance and grudge-bearing referred to in the first part of the verse (along with, perhaps, the other behaviors prohibited in the surrounding verses), or does it also include a positive quest for the neighbor's good?[2] And if it does, is that orientation toward the neighbor's good to be understood as an affection of the heart, or a habit of conduct, or both?

- Who is the "neighbor" in view in the commandment? Is it (only) the fellow Israelite mentioned in the preceding line? Or does the category also include the "foreigner" referred to a few verses earlier and, in language almost identical to verse 18, in the command of verse 34? What about the neighboring nations? Does the category of "neighbor" include the enemy of the individual? Of the nation? Of God?

- What kind of relationship between self-love and neighbor love is indicated by the "as"? Is self-love assumed or commanded? And is neighbor love required to correspond merely to the fact of self-love, or also to the mode and the degree? Are you to love your neighbor the same way you love yourself? To the same degree that you love yourself?[3]

---

1. The Hebrew verb sequence (*lō'-tiqqōm wĕlō'-tiṭṭōr . . . wĕ'āhabtā*), like the English of the NRSV ("You shall not take vengeance or bear a grudge . . . but you shall love"), can function with either indicative or imperative force. It is an interpretive decision, based on the context, that opts (validly) for the latter over the former.

2. Cf. Goodman, *Love Thy Neighbor*, 18–23.

3. Cf. Wolterstorff, *Justice in Love*, 82–84, 97–99.

Second, in addition to questions of this sort about the meaning and reference of the words and phrases, questions could be asked about what the speaker intends to do in uttering the commandment and to accomplish through it in the understanding and action of the hearers—this is what speech-act theorists call the commandment's intended "illocutionary" and "perlocutionary" force:[4]

- Is the intention of the commandment to *legislate* a certain standard of neighborly love as an enforceable requirement of Israelite law?[5] Or is the commandment given to provide moral instruction that *guides* conduct, without necessarily creating legal rights and duties?[6]
- Is the commandment intended to produce in the hearer a confident, joyful obedience or a heartbroken, contrite confession of sin? Is it given (along with the whole law in which it is embedded) as a path to life? As a criterion for justification? As an unfulfillable, impossible demand, leaving us no option but to rely on divine grace?
- When we speak of the intention behind the commandment, can a valid distinction be drawn between the intention of God in giving the commandment to Moses to speak to Israel, the intention of Moses in speaking it, and the intention of the redactor of the final form of Leviticus in preserving it? Can we validly infer multiple divine intentions for the original and subsequent hearers of the commandment?

And then, third, questions arise quite specifically and directly out of the situation of the twenty-first-century Christian interpreter. Some of these are questions about how to understand the text which arise when it is read as Christian Scripture by a twenty-first-century reader. Other questions concern how to understand ourselves and our world in the light of the text. But both of these dimensions of the interpretive task are essential and inseparable if the text is to be read and understood not merely as an object of antiquarian

4. Cf. Austin, *How to Do Things with Words*, and the brief explanation in Brown, *Scripture as Communication*, 32–35.

5. In the landmark case of *Donoghue v. Stevenson*, Lord Atkin famously wrestled with the question of what the "neighbour principle" might mean if translated into an enforceable legal obligation: "The rule that you are to love your neighbour becomes in law you must not injure your neighbour; and the lawyer's question: Who is my neighbour? receives a restricted reply. You must take reasonable care to avoid acts or omissions which you can reasonably foresee would be likely to injure your neighbour." *Donoghue v. Stevenson* [1932] UKHL 100.

6. Cf. the discussion of "apodeictic laws" and their likely function in Alt, "Origins of Israelite Law," 103–32; and the reflections on the original and contemporary political functions of Lev. 19 in Bauckham, *Bible in Politics*, 20–40. See more generally the discussion of law as the shaping of wisdom in decision making in Walton, *Ancient Near Eastern Thought*; and Andrew Sloane's discussion of law as the shaping of a moral vision in *At Home in a Strange Land*.

curiosity but as a guide to Christian understanding and existence in our contemporary context. Many questions belong to this third category, but a few of the more obvious stand out:

- Should Christian readers consider themselves included, by some valid mode of extension, among the addressees of the commandment—the "you" to whom the commandment is spoken—or is the commandment given exclusively to the nation of Israel?
- What happens to the "neighbor" category (or, for that matter, the "foreigner" category of Lev. 19:34) when the people of God are no longer constituted geographically or ethnically? Is my neighbor my fellow believer? Is the concept defined by proximity, so that my neighbor is the person I live alongside or bump into, or whose actions are most directly affected by my own? In our contemporary context of economic globalization, is anyone *not* my neighbor?[7] Does the technology that extends the reach of my vision and communication expand the scope of the "neighbor" category beyond what might have occurred to the original readers of the commandment in Leviticus, or to Christian interpreters in previous generations? Should the television screen that shows me the face of a stranger on the other side of the globe or the ultrasound screen that shows me the face of a fetus in the womb give me a new intuitive insight into the scope of the biblical commandment and its implications?[8]
- In a culture that has its own collection of widely diverse (and mutually inconsistent) ways of understanding what "love" means, can I adequately understand and obey the biblical commandment without exposing and unpicking some of my own inherited assumptions about the meaning of love?[9] Does the very word "love" still mean something close enough to what was understood by the original hearers of the biblical commandment for it to serve as an adequate English rendition of the intended concept? Do we have an alternative? And even if we do, does the continuous tradition of a thousand years of English translation in which the same word

7. See especially Andrew Sloane's exploration of this question in "Love and Justice," 16–18.

8. Oliver O'Donovan pushes the question even further: "Earlier generations had perfectly legitimate difficulties in recognizing an unborn child (in embryo stage) as a human being. . . . Scientific study of embryology has laid to rest the notion of a major physiological discontinuity in human development between embryo and fetal stage. . . . Our generation cannot avoid the implications of this knowledge. Our recognition of the human face is improved, and we can now see it in the embryo, even in the invisible blastocyte and zygote, where our ancestors could not." "Again: Who Is a Person?," 135–36.

9. Cf. the comments offered by way of a "protracted introduction" in Carson, *Love in Hard Places*, 11–34.

has been used provide a reason to stay with the old, familiar, four-letter word, and clarify its meaning in the gloss rather than in the translation?[10]

The End of Interpretation

A list of questions strung together like this does not prove that the commandment is obscure or incomprehensible. Many of the questions, after all, can be readily and confidently answered, and the answers to some are so obvious that it hardly occurs to most readers to ask them. Frequently, the questions that might occur to us are marginal to the meaning and intention of the commandment, and some result more from the complexity of our circumstances than from any obscurity in the text.

But the fact remains that questions arise, and pondering the text often involves thinking of new questions as much as answering old ones. And if answering one question leads to another, the path to comprehensive and certain understanding stretches on, it seems, forever. Medieval writers played with the metaphor of an endless interpretive labyrinth, or *laborintus*, punning on the Latin phrase *labor intus* as a description of the inward labors of the interpreter.[11]

But interpretation is not an end in itself, and endless interpretation, in quest of an elusive perfect understanding, can actually work against the intentions of the author. Søren Kierkegaard depicts this perverse possibility in his parable of a royal ordinance. The king's subjects, rather than faithfully and promptly obeying the ordinance, endlessly and earnestly speculate as to its meaning: "Everything is interpretation—but no one reads the royal ordinance in such a way that he acts accordingly."[12]

Of course not all communications are royal decrees, asking for a click of the heels and immediate obedience. Some texts are sent out into the world precisely in the hope that they will become fodder for rumination. But interpretation still serves an end beyond itself, even in the case of texts that call for a fair bit of digesting. In the case of Scripture, as Augustine famously declared, the goal of interpretation is love: "Anyone who thinks that he has understood the divine scriptures or any part of them, but cannot by his understanding build up this double love of God and neighbor, has not yet succeeded in understanding

10. The tradition goes back at least as far as the eleventh-century Old English Hexateuch, which renders the commandment "lufa þinne freond swa ðe sylfne," choosing the Old English verb *lufian* to translate the Vulgate's *diligo*.

11. E.g., Hugh of St. Victor, *De arca Noe morali* 4.9, in Hugh of St. Victor, *Selected Spiritual Writings*, 151; Geoffrey Chaucer, *House of Fame*, 2103–7. Cf. the history of the metaphor in Doob, *Idea of the Labyrinth*.

12. Kierkegaard, *For Self-Examination*, 36.

them."[13] And if there was ever a text in which it was transparently obvious that this was so, the commandment of Leviticus 19:18 must surely be that text.

If we read this commandment as Christian Scripture, then we read it (at least in part) in order to be spurred on to love our neighbors and to do the good works that visibly express that love.[14] Some hermeneutical reflection is warranted if that love is to be informed by wisdom; zeal that is not "based on knowledge" may be full of works, but the chances are that those works will be the wrong works done for the wrong reasons.[15] But the time properly allocated to such reflection is not infinite; eventually we reach a point when we must put the unresolved interpretive questions to one side, adjourn the conversations, and decide at least provisionally how we will interpret what the commandment is calling for.

Under some circumstances, the interpretation adopted may be a collective understanding decided on by the consensus of an interpretive community. Sometimes it may be an authoritative interpretation handed down to a community by those who are granted the right to make such pronouncements. And sometimes the interpretive decision—for good or for ill—is made by an individual who feels at liberty (or under compulsion) to adopt an understanding of his or her own.

Because of the multiple possible meanings of the text itself, because of the diversity of motives and preunderstandings that different readers bring to the text, because of the sinful dysfunctions that distort our understanding and communication, and because of the finite amount of time that can be allotted to the interpretive conversation, comprehensive and universal consensus is an elusive goal. And even within a particular, given community, we are typically left to choose between a single common understanding, determined by an interpretive authority, and a multiplicity of understandings adopted by the various individuals and subcommunities that make up the group.

The Plight of the Evangelical Interpreter

This predicament is particularly acute for evangelical Protestants, who claim the Bible as their supreme authority for faith and conduct and approach the

13. Augustine, *On Christian Teaching* 1.36.40, 27, trans. R. P. H. Green.
14. This is not the only possible function that the commandment ought to have for a Christian reader. We also read it, e.g., in order that we might be reminded of our failures to love, provoked to contrition, driven back to the grace of God in the gospel, and increased in our thankfulness for the forgiveness of God and the renewing work of the Spirit.
15. Cf. Rom. 10:2 and the comments on "malformed care" in Wolterstorff, *Justice in Love*, 102–3.

task of Bible reading without the direction of an infallible church tradition to govern their interpretive decisions. The plight of the evangelical interpreter has been discussed often in recent years. Two realities have been highlighted in the discussion. The first is the reality of *interpretation* itself: evangelicals have been urged to own up to the fact that they are involved in interpreting Scripture, not merely discovering and restating an uninterpreted, transparent, and universally obvious meaning.

A particularly acute articulation of this challenge can be found in Jamie Smith's book *The Fall of Interpretation*.[16] One of the principal themes of the book is a sharp criticism of what Smith calls the "present immediacy model" presupposed or argued for in much contemporary evangelical theology. According to this model, as he describes it, "interpretation . . . is a mediation that is to be overcome, restoring a prelapsarian (pre-Fall) immediacy." The typical evangelical approach to Bible reading is, Smith argues, "something of a realized eschatology: the curse of interpretation is lifted here and now (for the evangelical Christian, that is)."[17]

Against this assumption, Smith argues that "the conditions of hermeneutics— tradition, culture, history"—should not be viewed merely as distortions and barriers to true understanding but rather as constitutive dimensions of created human existence.[18] We interpret not only because we are alienated, blinded, and confused but also because we are finite, situated, and human. There is no escape from interpretation, and that is a good thing.

The second reality of the plight of the evangelical interpreter is the *plurality* of evangelical interpretations. This, again, is a major theme in Jamie Smith's work:

> There is always already interpretation in every relationship, which means that there is also room for plurality, or rather, plurality is the necessary result of irreducible difference. We abandon, in addition to the myth of "objectivity," the monologic of a hermeneutics of immediacy that claims to deliver the one, true interpretation. But if interpretation is part of being human, then its analogue is a creational diversity: a multitude of ways to "read" the world.[19]

A more polemical statement of this theme as a problem for evangelical Protestantism can be found in a book by another Smith: Christian Smith's popular and controversial *The Bible Made Impossible*. After outlining what

16. J. K. A. Smith, *Fall of Interpretation*, 210.
17. Ibid., 17.
18. Ibid., 61.
19. Ibid., 167.

he understands to be the "biblicist" hermeneutics of most contemporary evangelical Protestants,[20] Smith attempts to demonstrate that the biblicist approach to the interpretation and use of the Bible in the church manifestly fails to do what it ought to be able to do, if the theory were a sound one:

> The very same Bible—which biblicists insist is perspicuous and harmonious— gives rise to divergent understandings among intelligent, sincere, committed readers about what it says about most topics of interest. Knowledge of "biblical" teachings, in short, is characterized by *pervasive interpretive pluralism*. What that means in consequence is this: in a crucial sense it simply does not matter whether the Bible is everything that biblicists claim theoretically concerning its authority, infallibility, inner consistency, perspicuity, and so on, since in actual functioning the Bible produces a pluralism of interpretations.[21]

Christian Smith's criticism of the "pervasive interpretive pluralism" that is generated by the hermeneutical practices of evangelical Protestantism is not, of course, a new complaint. It was there at the very birth of Protestantism, in the papal bull *Exsurge Domine*, which Leo XXIII published in response to the proscribed writings of Martin Luther:

> Some, putting aside her [i.e., the Roman Catholic Church's] true interpretation of Sacred Scripture, are blinded in mind by the father of lies. Wise in their own eyes, according to the ancient practice of heretics, they interpret these same Scriptures otherwise than the Holy Spirit demands, inspired only by their own sense of ambition. . . . We have found that these errors or theses are not

20. Christian Smith's concept of what counts as "biblicism" is a constellation of ten mutually interrelated beliefs: (1) that "the Bible, down to the details of its words, consists of and is identical with God's very own words written inerrantly in human language"; (2) that "the Bible represents the totality of God's communication to and will for humanity"; (3) that "the divine will about all of the issues relevant to Christian belief and life are [*sic*] contained in the Bible"; (4) that "any reasonably intelligent person can read the Bible in his or her own language and correctly understand the plain meaning of the text"; (5) that "the best way to understand biblical texts is by reading them in their explicit, plain, most obvious, literal sense, as the author intended them"; (6) that "the significance of any given biblical text can be understood without reliance on creeds, confessions, historical church traditions, or other forms of larger theological hermeneutical frameworks"; (7) that "all related passages of the Bible on any given subject fit together almost like puzzle pieces into single, unified, internally consistent bodies of instruction"; (8) that "what the biblical authors taught God's people at any point in history remains universally valid for all Christians at every other time, unless explicitly revoked by subsequent scriptural teaching"; (9) that "all matters of Christian belief and practice can be learned by sitting down with the Bible and piecing together through careful study the clear 'biblical' truths that it teaches"; and (10) that "the Bible teaches doctrine and morals with every affirmation that it makes, so that together those affirmations comprise something like a handbook or textbook for Christian belief and living." *Bible Made Impossible*, 4–5.

21. Ibid., 17.

Catholic, as mentioned above, and are not to be taught, as such; but rather are against the doctrine and tradition of the Catholic Church, and against the true interpretation of the sacred Scriptures received from the Church.[22]

Numerous similar criticisms of Luther's approach have been voiced across the subsequent centuries—for example, from closer to our own time, the searing critique in Joseph Lortz's history of the German Reformation, in which Lortz insists that "no religious objectivity is possible unless [one is] accompanied step by step by a living interpreter" and holds Luther responsible for the triumph of the subjectivism that "split up Germany," dissolved "the unity of the Church, of Christianity, of the world," and led to "the chaos of unfettered, modern life."[23]

Scripture as Its Own Interpreter

Luther responded to such criticisms by vigorously asserting the self-interpreting clarity of Scripture itself, articulating a principle that was to become a fundamental rule of Protestant hermeneutics:

> Tell me, if you are able, by whose judgment is the question settled if the statements of the fathers are in conflict with one another? Scripture ought to deliver this judgment, which cannot be delivered unless we give to Scripture the principal place in all things, which is acknowledged by the fathers: so that it might be, in and of itself, of all things the most certain, the most simple, the most clear, interpreting itself [*sui ipsius interpres*], testing, judging and illuminating all things.[24]

Answering the accusation that he was guilty of interpreting Scripture according to his own private spirit (*proprio spiritu*),[25] "inspired only by [his] own sense of ambition,"[26] Luther insisted that his desire was for Scripture to be interpreted neither by his own spirit nor by any human spirit but *suo spiritu*—by its own spirit: "I do not want to be boasted of as more learned than all, but Scripture alone to rule: nor for it to be interpreted by my spirit

22. Leo XXIII, *Exsurge Domine*, Papal Encyclicals Online, available at http://www.papal encyclicals.net/Leo10/l10exdom.htm.
23. Lortz, *Reformation in Germany*, 1:448–58.
24. *Assertio Omnium Articulorum M. Lutheri per Bullam Leonis X. novissimam damnatorum*, WA 7, 97.19–24 (my translation).
25. *Assertio Omnium Articulorum*, WA 7, 96.10. Luther is clearly quoting his accusers at this point, but the phrase itself is not taken directly from the language of the papal bull.
26. Leo XXIII, *Exsurge Domine*.

or by any human spirit, but understood through itself and by its own spirit
[*per seipsam et suo spiritu intelligi*]."[27]

The claim that Scripture is its own interpreter (*Scriptura sacra sui ipsius
interpres*, as the maxim came to be formulated)[28] can itself be understood in
a variety of senses. Most commonly, the meaning of the maxim is unpacked
in a passive sense, as a claim about the perspicuity of the text in the hands of
the interpreter. Kevin Vanhoozer's paraphrase is typical:

> Luther claimed that any Christian had the right to interpret the Bible. He also
> affirmed the "perspicuity" or clarity of the Bible, claiming that its meaning was
> clear for those who attended to the grammar of the text and to the leading of
> the Spirit. Calvin, similarly, argued that the meaning and authority of Scripture
> did not depend on the church. Rather, "Scripture interprets Scripture." By this
> latter phrase the Reformers indicated that obscure passages should be read in
> the light of clearer ones.[29]

There is support for this passive sense of the maxim in Luther's own language—
for example, in his claim that Scripture is "to be interpreted . . . [and] understood through itself and by its own spirit," and in his depiction of Scripture
as "of all things the most certain, the most simple, the most clear." The idea
that Scripture contains "obscure passages" that "should be read in the light
of clearer ones" can also find some support in Luther's writings,[30] as well as
in a long line of precedent going back as far as Augustine and Irenaeus,[31] to
which Luther explicitly appealed.[32]

27. *Assertio Omnium Articulorum*, WA 7, 98.4–6 (my translation).

28. James Bretzke claims that "Thomas Aquinas used this expression [*Scriptura sacra sui
ipsius interpres*] to indicate that one part of Scripture could be used to interpret or clarify another
part of Scripture." *Consecrated Phrases*, 127. He supplies no citations in support, however, and
I was unable to find any instances myself in the works of Aquinas. The idea that "one part
of Scripture could be used to interpret or clarify another part of Scripture" was certainly not
original to Luther, of course.

29. Vanhoozer, *Is There a Meaning?*, 171.

30. E.g., the assertion in Luther, *Bondage of the Will*, 26, trans. Philip S. Watson, that "if
the words are obscure in one place, yet they are plain in another."

31. E.g., Augustine, *On Christian Teaching* 2.9.14, 37, trans. R. P. H. Green: "After gaining a
familiarity with the language of the divine scriptures, one should proceed to explore and analyse
the obscure passages, by taking examples from the more obvious parts to illuminate obscure
expressions and by using the evidence of indisputable passages to remove the uncertainty of
ambiguous ones." See also Irenaeus, *Against Heresies* 2.10; 2.28.

32. E.g., *Daß diese Wort Christi "Das ist mein Leib" noch fest stehen wider die Schwärmgeister*, WA 23, 225: "The holy teachers had the practice in the exposition of Scripture to take
distinct and clear statements and use these to make clear the obscure and uncertain ones."
Translation in Pelikan, *Luther the Expositor*, 128.

But this passive sense of the maxim does not exhaust its meaning. Alongside these depictions of Scripture as the clear, accessible object of interpretation, Luther's prose also contains intimations of Scripture as an active subject, "interpreting . . . testing, judging and illuminating."

In part, what Luther has in mind here is the agency of Scripture in relation to the reader and his or her circumstances.[33] In the imagery of the psalm to which Luther immediately turns, the implied object of the "interpreting . . . testing, judging and illuminating" activity of the word is the psalmist and his world: "my feet" and "my path" (Ps. 119:105). This aspect of Luther's language is helpfully emphasized by Gerhard Forde: "The interpreter does not remain standing simply as subject over against the text as object to be interpreted. Rather, in the engagement with scripture, it is the scripture that comes to interpret the exegete. It is the task of the exegete to allow the Spirit of the scripture, the matter itself, to speak."[34]

There is still more to be said, however. At the intersection between the passive sense of the maxim (which speaks of Scripture as an accessible and clear object of interpretation) and the active sense (which speaks of the agency of Scripture itself in illuminating and interpreting the world of the reader), there is a third, reflexive sense—arguably the primary sense of Luther's phrase—which speaks of the agency of Scripture in interpreting *itself*.

What this third, reflexive sense refers to is not the activity of the reader in using one text of Scripture (a "clear" text) to interpret another (an "obscure" one). Nor is it principally concerned with the interpretive agency of the particular text, or the Scripture as a whole, interpreting the reader and the reader's world. In addition to these senses, and integrally connected with both of them, this third, reflexive sense of the maxim appeals to the plural, human authorship of Scripture and speaks of the interpretive work that the biblical authors themselves perform in understanding and appropriating the antecedent texts and traditions that functioned for them as Scripture does for us.[35]

Gerald Bruns makes the point well:

> The beginnings of scriptural interpretation are to be looked for within the
> Scriptures themselves. Scholars now recognize that the making of the Scriptures

33. Strictly speaking, of course, "the agency of Scripture" is functioning here as a metonymy for the agency of God as the one who spoke and speaks through Scripture.

34. Forde, "*Scriptura Sacra*," 71. See also the similar comments in Forde, "Normative Character of Scripture," 305; Bayer, *Martin Luther's Theology*, 68–72.

35. Hans-Joachim Kraus argues that it was a commitment to this third sense of "Scripture interpreting Scripture" that provided the primary impetus for the historical development of the discipline of biblical theology. Cf. Kraus, *Die biblische Theologie*, 17, cited in Sailhamer, *Introduction*, 118–20.

was a hermeneutical process in which earlier biblical materials were rewritten in order to make them intelligible and applicable to later situations. . . . This helps to explain an ancient hermeneutical insight. As the rabbis, Augustine, and Luther knew, the Bible, despite its textual heterogeneity, can be read as a self-glossing book. One learns to study it by following the ways in which one portion of the text illuminates another. The generations of scribes who shaped and reshaped the Scriptures appear to have designed them to be studied in just this way.[36]

A similar claim can be found in the justification that Brevard Childs offers for taking a canonical approach to the interpretation of the Old Testament:

> A corpus of religious writings which has been transmitted within a community for over a thousand years cannot properly be compared to inert shreds which have lain in the ground for centuries. This observation is especially in order when one recognizes that Israel's developing religious understanding—the Bible speaks of God's encounter with Israel—left its mark on the literature in a continuing process of reshaping and growth. . . . The canonical method . . . seeks to work within that interpretive structure which the Bible has received from those who formed and used it as sacred scripture.[37]

Attention to this third sense of the maxim is crucial if the claim that Scripture is *sui ipsius interpres* is to carry its full force and validity as a principle of hermeneutics.

The first, passive sense is a legitimate inference from the unity and coherence of Scripture as the product of a single divine author, and this sense functions in obvious and well-recognized ways as a guide to interpretation. But if left to stand on its own, the maxim's passive sense runs the risk of a certain arbitrariness in the way in which it is applied. Who is to say which texts are "obscure" and which are "clear"? What is to prevent the interpreter from using a "clear" (and congenial) text to stifle the voice of an "obscure" (and uncongenial) one? When Luther, for example, appeals to John 6:27 ("on him [i.e., the Son of Man] God the Father has placed his seal of approval" as the one on whom our salvation depends) as a "clear and explicit text" which ought to control our understanding of other texts that seem to make almsgiving a condition of salvation (Dan. 4:27; Luke 6:37–38; Luke 16:9),[38] he leaves himself open to questions of this sort. Have the almsgiving texts really been *interpreted* or merely sidelined? And does the function of the "clear" text within its original context in John 6 really suggest its use as a pronouncement

---

36. Bruns, "Midrash and Allegory," 626–27.
37. Childs, *Introduction to the Old Testament*, 73.
38. Luther, *Sermon on John 6:27*, 16–18, trans. Martin H. Bertram.

against the necessity of almsgiving for salvation, or is it being pressed into service by Luther as a vehicle for his own dogmatic precommitments?[39]

While it can be an entirely legitimate exercise of theological interpretation to seek an understanding of one text that harmonizes with the meaning of another, the decisions made by the interpreter in doing so ought to be informed (as I will argue below) by a prior discipline of attentiveness to the interpretive work that the biblical writers themselves do when they invoke the words of other biblical texts, interpreting them and, in turn, asking to be interpreted in light of them.

The second, active sense is likewise a legitimate inference from the nature of Scripture as divine communication, and Forde makes an important point when he insists that the hearer (and preacher) of Scripture must be concerned not only to discover "what scripture means" but also to experience "what the Word does."[40] But the two tasks of the hearer should never be divorced: experiencing what the Word does goes hand in hand with determining what Scripture means. If we are to understand the scriptural text itself—the very text that illumines our world—without standing over it as if it were an inert object for our examination, then we need to pay attention not only to the way in which Scripture interprets *us* but also to the way in which Scripture interprets *itself*.[41]

If we are to take seriously the form in which Scripture has been given to us, as a canonical collection of the work of multiple human authors across a thousand years or more within a single (albeit, at times, complex) interpretive tradition, there must be more to the doctrine of Scripture's self-interpretation than just the use of clear biblical texts to interpret obscure ones and an openness to the agency of Scripture in interpreting us. Crucial to the claim that "Scripture interprets Scripture" is an awareness of and attention to the significance of the intertextual relationships between the biblical books and the interpretive work of the biblical authors themselves.

Circles, Spirals, and Snowballs

In order for our imaginations to capture the importance of this dynamic for the discipline of hermeneutics, a new metaphor may be required, sitting alongside

39. Cf. the discussions in Mitchell, *Justification of Religious Belief*, 46–47; Starling, "Analogy of Faith."

40. Forde, "*Scriptura Sacra*," 71.

41. As I have argued above, these two dimensions of textual interpretation are inseparably related, particularly in the case of a text that is being read as "a lamp for my feet" and "a light on my path" (Ps. 119:105).

the traditional images that theorists have used to describe the interpretive task. Writers on hermeneutics have for centuries used the metaphor of the hermeneutical circle to speak of the recursive relationship between analyzing the parts and apprehending the whole,[42] or between the preunderstandings of the reader and the disclosures of the text.[43] In recent years, Grant Osborne (among others) has sought to modify the image of the hermeneutical circle, reconfiguring it as something more like a spiral:

> A spiral is a better metaphor because it is not a closed circle but rather an open-ended movement from the horizon of the text to the horizon of the reader. I am not going round and round a closed circle that can never detect the true meaning but am spiraling nearer and nearer to the text's intended meaning as I refine my hypotheses and allow the text to continue to challenge and correct those alternative interpretations, then to guide my delineation of its significance for my situation today. In this sense it is also critical to note that the spiral is a cone, not twirling upward forever with no ending in sight but moving ever narrower to the meaning of the text and its significance for today.[44]

Without wishing to detract from the usefulness of either of those metaphors, I wish to place alongside them a third image, of Scripture as a kind of snowball. Unlike the other metaphors of the circle and the spiral, both of which focus on the relationship between the biblical text and the contemporary reader, the image of Scripture as snowball aims to say something about the interpretive relationships between Scripture's constituent parts. It is not a metaphor for the reader's way into the text but rather a metaphor for (one aspect of) the nature of the text itself, with implications for the way in which we are to read and understand it.

While Christian theology and hermeneutics rightly speak of Scripture as a unity, it is a weighty, complex, multilayered unity. The Bible did not fall from the sky like a single snowflake; it rolled down the hill of salvation history, adding layers as it went. Each new layer of the accumulating collection presupposes what comes before and wraps itself around it; in so doing it offers direction in how to read it and asks, in turn, to be interpreted in light of it.

The meaning we gain when we read the Bible is derived not only from the circular movements between analysis and synthesis, preunderstanding and disclosure, or from our own spiraling approach toward the text, as helpful as those images can be. The text we are approaching is also a text that came

---

42. E.g., Schleiermacher, *Hermeneutics*, 195–96.
43. See especially Gadamer, *Truth and Method*, 268–73.
44. Osborne, *Hermeneutical Spiral*, 22.

into existence through a history in which it was already approaching us, rolling down the hill toward us for hundreds of years, accumulating layers of self-interpretation on its way.

Like all metaphors, the image of Scripture as a "hermeneutical snowball" does not tell the whole story. Among the many limits of the metaphor, two are worth particular notice. First, the image should not be read as implying a simple, one-dimensional "progressive revelation" model for the way in which the internal structures of the canon are configured. While Jesus and the writers of the New Testament do undoubtedly claim a certain finality and conclusiveness for the way in which God's self-revelation in Christ relates to the Scriptures of the Old Testament, they do not wrap their words around the Old Testament in such a way as to make its original message inaccessible or to rob it of a voice of its own that is capable of addressing the Christian reader directly.[45] Nor do they articulate the relationship between what God said "in the past . . . to our ancestors through the prophets" and what God has said "in these last days . . . to us by his Son" (Heb. 1:1–2) simply as a particular instance of a general principle of the superiority of new wine over old.[46]

Second, the image of Scripture as snowball does not readily provide a way of picturing the continuities and discontinuities between inner-biblical and postbiblical interpretation. Should we picture the snowball that rolls down the hill of salvation history continuing in its downward path across the centuries of its reception history within the church, accumulating further layers of interpretation as it goes? Or should we imagine it as reaching the bottom of the hill at the point of the closure of the canon and picture the history of its use in the church through some other metaphor—perhaps, for the sake of the exercise, through the metaphor of the fully formed snowball being picked up, patted down, and thrown around?[47]

Both of these possible extensions of the metaphor have their attractions. It is true that our contemporary interpretations of Scripture are inescapably situated at the end of a twenty-century-long tradition of the completed Bible's reception history and that the church within which we read and interpret the Bible today claims a catholic unity with the church of the

45. See especially Seitz, *Character of Christian Scripture*, 17–25.
46. Cf. the reservations regarding a "progressive revelation" framework expressed in C. Smith, *Bible Made Impossible*, 210; Vanhoozer, "Into the Great 'Beyond'"; Cosgrove, *Appealing to Scripture*, 104–9.
47. Readers familiar with snow and snowballs will know how artificial that sort of extension of the metaphor would be; the kind of snowballs that roll down hills are not, of course, the kind one picks up and throws around.

apostolic era and the intervening centuries. Recent calls for an "evangelical ressourcement"[48] that includes a renewed acquaintance with Protestant-ism's patristic and medieval heritage are a welcome corrective to the various ahistorical, sectarian, and modernist tendencies that have plagued much evangelical exegesis and theology. But the line of ecclesial continuity be-tween the New Testament church and our own is not the only reality that a theological hermeneutic needs to take account of. If the distinctiveness of Scripture as the written word of God is to be honored, our understanding of the hermeneutical task needs also to acknowledge the discontinuity between inner-biblical and postbiblical interpretation and the uniquely authoritative role played by the former.[49]

Rather than side with one of these realities against the other by extending the reach of the metaphor in either of the two ways suggested, a better ap-proach is simply to acknowledge the metaphor's limits and look for a different imaginative language with which to speak of the theological significance of the Bible's reception history in (and outside) the church across the last twenty centuries. Without for a moment wanting to suggest that that history can be dismissed or disregarded as irrelevant, this book will focus on the dynamics of *inner*-biblical hermeneutics and their significance for Scripture's theological interpretation.

The Apprenticed Interpreter

The fact that Scripture is a self-interpreting book (in the reflexive sense I have argued for above, or indeed in either of the other senses of the phrase) does not relieve the contemporary interpreter of any responsibility to work at understanding it. Luther himself—for all his protestations about Scripture's self-interpreting clarity—can still write graphically of the "sweat" and "as-siduous endeavor" that are required of the faithful interpreter:

> There is therefore effort to be expended—not, setting aside the Sacred Scrip-
> tures, that we might crane our necks only toward the human writings of the

---

48. E.g., Williams, *Tradition, Scripture, and Interpretation*, 7–8. The term "ressourcement" is borrowed from the language of the mid-twentieth-century French Roman Catholic theolo-gians who sought to renew the theology of the Catholic Church by returning to its sources in the teachings of Scripture and the interpretive tradition of the church fathers.

49. Henri Blocher speaks of "the neat canonical boundary which sets apart the Word of God among human writings"—a boundary that functions as "a sign of God's real involve-ment in history: his Word comes down to earth without ceasing to be his Word." "Analogy of Faith," 33.

Fathers—but on the contrary, first and foremost, setting aside all the writings of men, all the more steadfastly to soak with our sweat the Holy Scriptures alone, in order that, where the danger is present that one might understand them by one's own spirit, the exercise of this assiduous endeavor, having conquered the danger of whatever kind, might make us certain of the Spirit of Scripture, which is absolutely nowhere to be found except in Scripture.[50]

But good interpretation requires not just sweat but skill, and not just skill but character. Interpretation of the Scriptures is like a craft or a trade that must be learned if we are to draw the right connections, make the right intuitive leaps, and bring to bear on the task the right dispositions, affections, and virtues.[51] Among the various exemplars from which we might learn the habits and practices that are necessary for wise and faithful interpretation, Scripture itself is supreme and uniquely authoritative.

Kevin Vanhoozer's notion of "apprenticeship" is a useful image for the way in which the inner-biblical interpretive practices of the writers of Scripture shape the judgment of the contemporary interpreter:

> The primary conversation that leads to understanding, then, is the Spirit-enabled conversation that takes place within and between the canonical books themselves. . . . Good theological judgment is largely, though not exclusively, a matter of being apprenticed to the canon: of having one's capacity for judging (a capacity that involves imagination, reason, emotion, and volition alike) formed and transformed by the ensemble of canonical practices that constitute Scripture.[52]

Henri Blocher, in a discussion of the closely related principle of the "analogy of faith" to which the Reformers frequently appealed, makes a similar point, arguing that the self-interpreting nature of Scripture should be appealed to not only as a negative criterion of judgment, operating at the end of the interpretive process like a kind of guillotine that trims off the ragged edges. A limited, negative application of the principle, brought to bear case-by-case on individual exegetical judgments, pays insufficient regard to the role played by preunderstanding, disposition, and habit in the work of interpretation. Reaching beyond that more limited application of the principle, Blocher appeals for a more expansive account of the positive, formative role played by Scripture's self-interpretation in shaping the instincts and expectations of the contemporary interpreter:

50. Luther, *Assertio Omnium Articulorum*, WA 7, 97.3–9 (my translation).
51. See especially Zagzebski, *Virtues of the Mind*; Briggs, *Virtuous Reader*.
52. Vanhoozer, *Drama of Doctrine*, 331. On apprenticeship, wisdom, and intellectual tradition more broadly, see MacIntyre, *Three Rival Versions*, 58–81.

We would hesitate to restrict application of the analogy of faith to the end of the process of study; it also yields precious benefits in shaping our expectations, in stimulating our scientific imagination, in balancing our horizons. . . . Our help comes from the general control of scriptural teachings, if we care diligently to enquire about it, and, especially, from hermeneutical lessons and hints offered by the biblical books themselves: "meta-language" in Scripture and preliminary syntheses taught by divine inspiration provide us with invaluable aid. The New Testament writers' use and handling of the Old Testament, if we know how properly to assess it, is part of their authoritative teaching, and best educates our exegetical mind.[53]

In speaking of the contemporary interpreter of Scripture as "apprenticed" to the inner-biblical interpreters, I do not want to reduce the role of the contemporary interpreter to an unthinking, unimaginative mimicry. The distinction between inner-biblical interpretation and our own hermeneutical task is important to acknowledge, even if we put to one side the issues raised by the salvation-historical differences between the situation of the Old Testament writers and our own, and focus exclusively on the interpretive practices of the New Testament. The answer that I would offer to Richard Longenecker's question, "Can we reproduce the exegesis of the New Testament?" lies somewhere between Longenecker's "No" and Richard Hays's "Yes."[54]

On the one hand, Hays is correct to insist that "Scripture interpretation is the theological matrix within which the kerygma took shape" and to warn against the naive assumption that it is possible to "pluck and preserve the flower of apostolic doctrine" while severing it from its "generative hermeneutical roots."[55] But Longenecker, for his part, is correct in pointing to the "revela-

---

53. Blocher, "Analogy of Faith," 37–38.

54. See Longenecker, *Biblical Exegesis in the Apostolic Period* (1st ed.), 214–20; Hays, *Echoes of Scripture*, 178–92; Longenecker, *Biblical Exegesis in the Apostolic Period* (2nd ed.), xxiv–xxix. In fairness to both of these writers, it should be acknowledged that the position argued for by each of them is considerably more nuanced than the one-word summaries in the preceding paragraph might suggest. Hays, for his part, hastens to add that it is "in a sense to be specified carefully" that Paul's readings are normative for contemporary Christian readers (Hays, *Echoes of Scripture*, 183), and the kind of hermeneutical practice that he goes on to advocate could not for a moment be characterized as an "unthinking, unimaginative mimicry" of Pauline interpretation. And Longenecker, in the rejoinder to Hays that he includes in the second edition of *Biblical Exegesis in the Apostolic Period*, takes care to specify the common ground that he and Hays share in how they understand the theologically normative dimensions of Paul's approach to Scripture—"reading it *as a narrative of election and promise*, reading it *ecclesiocentrically*, reading it *in the service of proclamation*, reading it *as participants in the eschatological drama of redemption*, and appreciating *the metaphorical relation between the text and our own reading of it*." Longenecker, *Biblical Exegesis in the Apostolic Period* (2nd ed.), xxxv (emphasis original).

55. Hays, *Echoes of Scripture*, 182.

tory stance" of the New Testament writers and the "circumstantial [and] *ad hominem*" dimensions involved in their contextualization and application of the biblical texts they cite.[56]

The writers of the New Testament (and Jesus himself, for that matter) are interpreters, but what they write and preach is never presented as *just* interpretation, either in the narrower sense of grammatico-historical exegesis or in the broader sense of contextualizing exposition. They have something of their own to say—testimony of their own to bear, arguments of their own to make, exhortations of their own to offer—and their interaction with Old Testament Scripture is embedded in textual genres that serve as vehicles for these other concerns. More than that: in what they have to say, they themselves are speaking as witnesses and mouthpieces of divine revelation in a sense that contemporary preachers and writers are not.[57] In citing Old Testament Scripture they are rarely offering up texts as "proofs" for theological assertions that would otherwise hang suspended in the air without foundation,[58] and the rhetorical effect that they intend the citations to have is directed toward a particular situation into which they are writing, which will never correspond totally with our own. Nor is the interpretive authority that they claim the authority of superior technical expertise in the methods of grammatico-historical exegesis.

Nevertheless (as Hays rightly stresses) the gospel they proclaim is still an irreducibly hermeneutical announcement; they are not simply relaying brute, uninterpreted facts but preaching Jesus as "Christ" and "Lord," "in accordance with the Scriptures," seeking to induct their readers into "the mind of Christ" and (in him) into "all wisdom."[59] To that extent—and it is no small extent indeed, given the breadth and boldness of such claims—their stance and method as interpreters are normative for us; we are their apprentices in the art of reading Scripture, learning from them how to understand Christ (and all things) in the light of Scripture and Scripture (and all things) in the light of Christ.

The apprenticed interpreter is not an infallible interpreter; nor do we ever graduate out of our indenture to the canon into some sort of magisterial

---

56. Longenecker, *Biblical Exegesis in the Apostolic Period* (1st ed.), 219.

57. This claim is sometimes, though not always, explicit within what they speak and write. Whether or not that is the case, the inclusion of the NT writings within the canon of Christian Scripture carries the implication that they are to be read by the church as uniquely authoritative vehicles of divine speech.

58. See, e.g., the instances discussed in Starling, *Not My People*, 44–46, 47–48, 121–22, 213.

59. Observant readers will note that the language of all the quotations within this sentence is uniformly Pauline, but the claims expressed are not unique to Paul; parallel claims (though in a different idiom) could have been harvested from any of the writers of the NT, or indeed from the words of Jesus himself.

interpretive authority of our own. Apprenticeship to the self-interpreting practices of Scripture is not the comprehensive solution to the problem of evangelical Protestantism's "pervasive interpretive pluralism"; a certain amount of plurality in interpretation is (as Jamie Smith argues) a valuable expression of our created, human diversity,[60] and a further measure is an inevitable consequence of our fallibility, our sinful misuse of the text, and the interpretive discords that arise in the absence of an authoritative magisterium. But an increase in our attentiveness to the interpretive practices of the biblical writers and a readiness to educate our interpretive faculties in light of these practices should work as a healthy corrective to the worst excesses of interpretive arbitrariness and foster a healthier and more faithful interpretive conversation.

This Book

What I have in mind for this book, then, is not a system to integrate all the contents of Scripture or a key to unlock all its mysteries, but a few brief exercises of apprenticeship to its interpretive practices. There is a place for theological systems and hermeneutical keys, as long as they are sketched in pencil (in the case of the systems) and provided they are not jammed forcibly into every lock (in the case of keys). But the aim of this book is somewhat less ambitious.

What follows in the remaining chapters is a series of case studies in inner-biblical hermeneutics, focusing in each case on one aspect of the interpretive work done in a particular biblical book and relating it to a theological or ethical issue the church has confronted today or in the intervening centuries. Each chapter will focus on one book of the Bible and on one key interpretive issue that arises in it, tracing the interpretive work of the biblical author, redactor, or compiler against the horizons of the text's first readers,[61] before seeking to draw out the implications of that case study in inner-biblical interpretation for Christian theological hermeneutics. This book will focus principally, then, not on the advancement of exegetical science (worthy as that goal is) but on the getting of hermeneutical wisdom—on what it means to receive the biblical writings as Holy Scripture and how we are to appropriate their words in our own situation. The latter task (i.e., the task of theological hermeneutics)

60. J. K. A. Smith, *Fall of Interpretation*, 167, 196.
61. In general, where the issue arises, I will be focusing primarily on the final, canonical form of the biblical text rather than attempting to dig back into the tradition history that lies behind it (except to the extent that an inquiry along those lines might shed light on the interpretive work done by the redactors or compilers of the text in its final form).

cannot, of course, be undertaken satisfactorily without paying proper attention to the former (i.e., the task of biblical exegesis). But neither can the former task be regarded as sufficient, at least for the purposes of the church, unless it is informed by and contributes to the latter.

The aim is not for comprehensiveness, either in the number of biblical books suggested or in the coverage of the hermeneutical issues raised in each book. But I hope that the range of books examined and the range of issues discussed will be sufficiently broad and representative to at least introduce the possibilities of learning the art of biblical interpretation from the biblical writers themselves and to give us a glimpse into the habits of mind and heart that informed their reading of Scripture and that ought to shape our own.

❧1❧

"Who Meditates on His Law"

The Psalter and the Hermeneutics of Delight

A Pathway into the Holy Scripture

Sometime between 1525 and 1532, William Tyndale published a pamphlet (based on the prologue to his 1525 translation of the New Testament) under the title *A Pathway into the Holy Scripture*. Its content deliberately focused on the controversial issues of the day—"above all, to put you in remembrance of certain points, which are, that ye well understand what these words mean; the Old Testament; the New Testament; the law; the gospel; Moses; Christ; nature; grace; working and believing; deeds and faith."[1] For Tyndale and his intended readers, blazing a pathway into Scripture involved the polemical task of hacking away the tangle of vines and brambles that had previously impaired their access—or, to change the metaphor, ripping away the "veil of false glosses on Moses' face" that had been nailed up by the prelates of the church.[2]

Tyndale's controversy with the church's "false teachers and blind leaders" over the specific issues of grace, faith, and works—along with the very act of translating the New Testament and putting it into the hands of the proverbial plowboy—raised the broader issue of the relationship between the Bible and the church, which became the topic of a heated debate between Tyndale

1. Tyndale, *Pathway*, 4.
2. Ibid., 24. Cf. the reference to "false teachers and blind leaders," p. 4.

and England's Lord Chancellor, Thomas More. For More, Scripture was the
church's book, and the only proper way to "wade" into the Scriptures was
via the authoritative teachings of the church.[3]

Amid the many fierce and noisy disagreements between Tyndale and More,
there was at least one point of implicit agreement: readers of Scripture do not
begin within the text but *approach* the text via a pathway of expectations and
preunderstandings. This much is true for all readers of Scripture, at all times and
in all places. For some, the journey into Scripture begins in infancy, when they are
inducted into the practices of Bible reading by parents and grandparents, within
the fellowship of the church; others are introduced to Scripture as adolescent
or adult converts, or make their first approaches to Scripture along a path of
skeptical or curious inquiry. None of us is born within the pages of the Bible.

The fact that we approach the Scriptures with expectations and preunderstandings of our own does not mean that our reading of Scripture is imprisoned
in the cage of our own subjectivity or trapped incorrigibly in the traditions in
which we were raised. Scripture itself offers "pathways" of its own, inviting
us into the text—pathways that variously confirm and challenge the ways in
which we approach it. Those who come seeking find, but not always exactly
the thing that they thought they would.

The convergence of all such paths is in the person of Christ—he himself
is the "one Instructor" of his people (Matt. 23:10) and the single "way" to
the Father (John 14:6). But the presence of Christ at the junction of all the
scriptural paths does not do away with the necessity of the paths themselves;
there is no true knowledge of Christ that is not "according to the Scriptures,"
just as there is no true knowledge of the Scriptures that does not accord with
Christ. Our approach to the Scriptures—not just our first approach but the
whole set of purposes and expectations with which we return to the Scriptures
each day—needs to be tested and renewed by Scripture itself, so that our feet
walk along the pathways that Scripture opens up to us.

Psalter as Torah

Within the Old Testament, one of the most spacious and well-traveled pathways into Scripture is to be found in the Psalter. The praises of Israel, as they
were offered up in the earliest shrines, in the first and second temples, and
in the synagogues of the exile and diaspora, played a crucial role in teaching
those who worshiped how they were to regard and receive the various words

3. More, *Dialogue concerning Tyndale*, 102.

of law, prophecy, narrative, poetry, and wisdom that came to be collected as the Scriptures of Israel. Among the disciples of Jesus and the members of the early church, too, the psalms continued to be read, sung, and remembered as a means by which believers were encouraged to "teach and admonish one another" when they gathered (Col. 3:16; cf. Eph. 5:19; 1 Cor. 14:26; Heb. 3:7–4:13). Within the psalms they found both a prophetic testimony to Jesus and a liturgy of prayers and praises which Jesus himself had used; when they prayed and sang the psalms, they were teaching one another to trust in Christ, and to join their prayers and praises with his.

This teaching function of the psalms is emphasized by the way in which they are gathered together and given canonical shape within the Psalter. The five-book structure of the Psalter mimics the five-book structure of the Penta- teuch, hinting at its function as a kind of "Torah of David."[4] The songs which are sung by day within the assembly are to be meditated upon alone, in the night (Ps. 77:6, 12; cf. Pss. 16:7; 42:8; 63:2–6); a maskil of Asaph, reciting the ancient story of YHWH's works, is presented as "teaching [tôrâ]" for God's people (Ps. 78:1), suggesting a similar function for the other historical psalms;[5] a string of wisdom psalms, scattered across the Psalter (e.g., Pss. 1; 32; 34; 37; 49; 112; 127; 128; 133), seek to inculcate in those who read them a sense of the blessedness of fearing YHWH and shunning evil. Within the canonical structure of the Psalter, the categories of private and public, liturgical and instructive, overlap and interpenetrate: "One cannot distinguish absolutely the liturgical psalms from the wisdom or didactic poems. . . . Private prayers were adapted for public use; liturgical songs became a personal prayer."[6]

The instructive function of the Psalter does not overwhelm or displace its liturgical form; it is precisely as a collection of prayers and praises that it does its teaching. The worshipers who hear and speak its words are invited to learn not only from its precepts and propositions but also from its practices—when we pray the psalms we are being taught how to sing, how to give thanks, how to lament, how to protest, and how to praise, along with the psalmist and in company with the whole people of God.

Psalter and Torah

While the Psalter's language and structure suggest its use as a book of instruc- tion, it does not present itself as a self-contained curriculum, encapsulating

4. See Braude, *Midrash on Psalms*, 1:5.
5. Mays, *Psalms*, 254.
6. Vesco, *Le psautier de David*, 31, as translated in Wenham, *Psalms as Torah*, 40.

within its 150 psalms all that its readers need to learn; the "Torah of David" directs its readers' attention not away from but toward the "Torah of Moses" and the other various oral and written conduits of the word of YHWH to Israel.

The encouragement in Psalm 1:2 to meditate day and night on the law echoes the charge to Joshua in Joshua 1:8 to meditate on the law of Moses, and is emphatically reinforced in the other two "Torah psalms" that occupy such a prominent place in the collection—Psalm 19, sitting at the center of the first book, and Psalm 119, acting as a kind of hinge between the Egyptian Hallel (Pss. 113–18) and the Songs of Ascent (Pss. 120–34) and dominating the whole fifth book by its sheer size. These three psalms and their placing in the Psalter powerfully express the importance of biblical law for editors of the collection.[7]

But it is not only in the "Torah psalms" that readers' attention is directed beyond the Psalter toward the rest of Scripture and its constituent traditions, or toward the living voice of YHWH encountered in the oracles of the prophets. The commandments and statutes of YHWH are celebrated throughout the psalms as a way for the worshipers to walk in (e.g., Pss. 17:4–5; 18:21–22; 37:30–31; 111:10), in imagery that closely parallels the language in which the psalmists ask for God to guide their steps (e.g., Pss. 5:8; 25:5; 27:11; 86:11) or express their confidence that this is what he does (e.g., Pss. 16:11; 23:3; 25:8–10). The contents of particular, individual commandments are also specifically drawn upon in the Psalter's ethical teaching and in the psalmists' protests of innocence.[8]

The psalmists also appeal frequently to the covenant of YHWH with the nation, with Abraham, and with David the king as the basis for petitions and laments (e.g., Pss. 44:18; 89:19–37; 132:10–12), and they celebrate the covenant as the framework within which the faithfulness of YHWH is experienced (e.g., Pss. 103:7–18; 105:8–11; 111:5, 9). They refer to the saving deeds of YHWH for the individual and the nation over and over again; in some cases they retell the story of YHWH's dealings with Israel at length (e.g., Pss. 78; 105; 106; 107), but in others they make fleeting allusions to the narratives of the Pentateuch (e.g., Ps. 95:8, alluding to Exod. 17:1–7 and Num. 20:1–13; Ps. 103:7–12, alluding to Exod. 32–34) that presuppose a readership familiar with a fuller version to be found elsewhere.

Finally, there is the "voice" of YHWH, which is frequently referred to within the Psalter (e.g., Pss. 18:13; 29:3–9; 46:6; 68:33)—sometimes with echoes of

7. Cf. Wenham, *Psalms as Torah*, 78.
8. See especially the examples cited in ibid., 97–118.

the theophany at Sinai and apparent reference to the rumblings of a thunderstorm, and sometimes in a way that represents YHWH as speaking, or as having spoken, within the sanctuary, in a form that enabled his words to be heard and preserved (e.g., Pss. 60:6–8; 81:5–16; 108:7–9). The prophetic oracle spoken in the name of YHWH in Psalm 95:7 urges its hearers to open their hearts to receive his voice, not only in the words of the psalm itself but also "if [they] . . . hear his voice" through some other vehicle of revelation.[9]

More broadly—behind and beneath all of these explicit references in the Psalter to the voice of YHWH, his laws and covenants, the story of his saving deeds, and the oracles of the prophets—the categories of relationship in which the Psalter frames Israel's dealings with YHWH imply experiences of speech and story, reading and remembering. The praises of YHWH for his faithfulness and steadfast love imply covenant and promise, even where the words "covenant" and "promise" are not used;[10] the categories of "righteous" and "wicked" imply a distinction that is defined, at least in part, by the differing stances that people take toward the laws of YHWH, even where those laws are not mentioned; the appeal to YHWH's name and the decision to hope in him, trust in him, and wait for him imply some knowledge of his ways and some revelation of his intentions.

In a multiplicity of ways, therefore, across all the various categories of psalms and all five books of the collection, the Psalter implies a community of intended readers who have heard God speak, who are familiar with the story of his saving deeds, who possess his laws, and whose ears are (or ought to be) open to his voice.

Rightly Perceiving the Scriptures

How, then, do the prayers and praises of the Psalter train those who use them to perceive the Scriptures (or, in the case of the earliest users of the psalms,

9. The way in which the wording of the oracle echoes the language of Deut. 4–6 suggests the likelihood that the most obvious form in which the worshipers could expect to "hear his voice . . . today" would be in the restatement of the covenant promises and stipulations within the context of the worshiping assembly; alternatively, given the direct divine address embedded within the psalm itself, the experience envisaged as a further possibility for the worshipers may have been a fresh prophetic oracle spoken for the first time "today." Cf. the discussion in Goldingay, *Psalms 90–150*, 94–96, and his argument in favor of reading the "if" of v. 7 as an ordinary condition, not as a pessimistic "if only . . ."

10. The language of *ḥesed* ("steadfast love") within the Psalter and elsewhere in the OT is not limited to contexts where there is already a preexisting covenantal relationship, or to behaviors that merely fulfill covenantal obligations, but it is still in keeping with the character of steadfast, enduring *ḥesed* (including the *ḥesed* of God) to create and keep covenants.

to perceive the various oracles, laws, proverbs, and stories that later came to be written and collected as the Scriptures)? With what expectations and preunderstandings do we approach the Scriptures, if we come trained by the worship of the psalms? Much could be said in answer to that question, but four observations stand out.

Many and One

First, and perhaps most obviously, the psalms present the Scriptures as both a vast diversity and a coherent unity. On the one hand, much of the time, the language that the Psalter uses for Scripture is explicitly and emphatically plural. This is most strikingly the case in Psalm 119, where the massive, acrostic architecture of the psalm implies that something comprehensive and encyclopedic is being said about a vast and multifaceted subject.[11] Within the psalm, eight different words are used for the utterances of YHWH, and the psalmist rings the changes on them in a seemingly endless round of repetitions: *tôrâ* (25x, always in the singular, translated in the English versions as "law" or "instruction"); *dābār* (23x, usually in the singular, translated in the English versions as "word," and referring sometimes to YHWH's commands and sometimes to his promises); *mišpāṭîm* (23x, usually in the plural, referring to the decisions and pronouncements of YHWH as judge); *'ēdōt* (23x, always in the plural, probably referring to the stipulations of the covenant); *ḥuqqîm* (22x, always in the plural, referring to the binding and permanent statutes of YHWH's law); *miṣwōt* (22x, usually in the plural, referring to the commandments of YHWH); *piqqûdîm* (22x, always in the plural, referring to YHWH's authoritative utterances); *'imrâ* (19x, usually singular, translated in the English versions as "word," and referring to YHWH's word of promise).[12] The psalmist repeatedly declares that he is speaking about "all" God's words of one kind or another: "*all* your commands" (vv. 6, 86, 151, 172), "*all* the laws that come from your mouth" (v. 13), "*all* your precepts" (v. 128), "*all* your righteous laws" (v. 160), "*all* my ways" (v. 168).

On the other hand, however, the Torah psalms all speak of the law of YHWH in a way that encourages their readers to see this vast array of promises, statutes, ordinances, and decrees as cohering together in a single "law" or "word." In Psalm 1, it is the one "law" of YHWH that is in view as the object of meditation (in implied contrast with the multitude of "wicked," "sinners," and "mockers" who offer their rival counsels). In Psalm 19, the "statutes," "precepts," "commands," and "decrees" of verses 7b–9 sit under

---

11. Cf. W. Watson, *Classical Hebrew Poetry*, 198.
12. Cf. Wenham, *Psalms as Torah*, 88; Ash, *Bible Delight*, 32–34.

the banner of the single "law" referred to in verse 7a. And in Psalm 119, the psalm's two favorite terms, *tôrâ* and *dābār*, are used almost exclusively in the singular and function broadly as umbrella terms for the whole of YHWH's revelation, given as a promise to trust and a path to walk in.[13] Both the unity and the plurality of Scripture are important to the psalmists:

> That teaching is both one coherent whole (teaching, word) and something made concrete in many specific injunctions and promises (statements, declarations, orders, decisions, laws, commands). I am concerned for both my way and my ways, both to walk in Yhwh's way and to walk in Yhwh's ways. Both the unity and coherence of that teaching and the detailed injunctions and promises are designed to shape my life.[14]

Luminous and Illumining

Among the various images that the Torah psalms use for the word of YHWH, one recurring pattern that stands out is the imagery of light and illumination. It is present, strikingly, in Psalm 19, where the depictions of the stars and the sun in the first half of the psalm echo in the depiction of the law of YHWH in the second half: "The commands of the LORD are radiant," declares the psalmist, "giving light to the eyes" (v. 8). It also occurs repeatedly in Psalm 119 (e.g., vv. 105, 130, 135), in combination with an intersecting pattern of references to eyes, sight, and watching. The two psalms depict the radiance of God's word in terms of both its brilliance as an object to gaze upon and its power to shed light on other things. Thus, in Psalm 19, the law of YHWH is both an object of beauty to be delighted in (vv. 7–10), expressing God's glory like the stars of the sky (cf. vv. 1–4a), and a searchlight on the heart, exposing hidden faults like the hot, glaring rays of the sun (vv. 11–14; cf. vv. 4b–6). In Psalm 119, similarly, the law of YHWH is both a book in which "wonderful things" are to be seen (v. 18) and a lamp by which the psalmist hopes to see his world and find his way (vv. 105, 130). These two functions of the law are closely interconnected; the guidance which the psalmist hopes to find in YHWH's decrees is a function of the gracious shining of YHWH's face (v. 135).

The psalmist does not present these claims about the radiance of YHWH's law as easy or obvious empirical observations; the experiential context which the psalm describes is shot through with tension and perplexity. The psalmist wakes in the earliest hours of the morning to pore over YHWH's word in the

13. Cf. Wenham, *Psalms as Torah*, 86.
14. Goldingay, *Psalms 90–150*, 444.

darkness (v. 148); he has "sought out" (*dārāštî*) YHWH's precepts (v. 94) and prays that the commandment might not be hidden from him (v. 19); his eyes are worn out from looking for YHWH's promise and waiting for its fulfillment (vv. 82, 123); his assertions about the nearness of YHWH and the truth of his commands are made in the face of the threatening and very visible nearness of "those who devise wicked schemes . . . [and] are far from [YHWH's] law" (v. 150). And yet he insists, nonetheless, that the law of YHWH is the light by which he lives, and he prays that his eyes would be opened to see it and to perceive it as "wonderful" (v. 18).[15]

Demanding and Gracious

The fact that the Torah psalms express such longing for and delight in YHWH's law does not mean that the psalmists are blind to its functions of threat and demand, or that these are to be perceived as negatives that are compensated for by the law's more positive functions. All of YHWH's words—the statutes and precepts as much as the promises and assurances—are received by the psalmist as gifts from God and esteemed as precious. The *statutes* teach wisdom (Ps. 19:7); the *precepts* give joy to the heart (Ps. 19:8); the *commands* give light to the eyes (Ps. 19:8); together they warn YHWH's servants away from the paths of destruction and point them toward the paths of blessing and reward (Ps. 19:11). Torah obedience is not the fine print on the back of the salvation contract, the deferred payments on a divine loan scheme. The revelation that the psalmists celebrate is a word of grace from first to last, but it is a converting, transforming grace; it is the kind of grace that seeks out a straying sheep and brings it back to the way of the commandments (Ps. 119:176).

For Israel and the World

The psalmists' emphasis on the law of YHWH as a gracious gift goes hand in hand with their convictions about the particular, electing kindness of God to the people of Israel. It is "to Moses" that YHWH made known his ways, and "to the people of Israel" that he revealed his deeds (Ps. 103:7). "He has revealed his word to Jacob, his laws and decrees to Israel. He has done this for no other nation; they do not know his laws" (Ps. 147:19–20).

When we come to Scripture via the pathway of the psalms, we cannot help but notice that the Bible we are learning to read is a book that belongs to a worshiping community of God's people, a book that was originally given to

15. Cf. Bonhoeffer, *Meditating on the Word*, 136–38.

the particular community that was descended from Abraham and constituted as a nation at the foot of Mount Sinai. The "law" that is celebrated is not, in the first instance at least, a universally accessible "moral law within me"[16] but the particular law that was given to Moses at Sinai. The story of God's mighty deeds (upon which the psalmists urge their readers to meditate) is the story of YHWH's dealings with Israel (e.g., Pss. 78; 105; 106; 111), and the reasons for which it is to be written and read, remembered and retold, have to do—in part, at least—with the purposes of YHWH for the nation: "so the next generation would know them, even the children yet to be born, and they in turn would tell their children. Then they would put their trust in God and would not forget his deeds" (Ps. 78:6–7).

In the psalms that speak in the first person singular—the individual thanksgivings and laments, for example, and many of the wisdom psalms—the "I" of the psalm is still located, implicitly or explicitly, within the "we" of the nation. The poignant, personal testimony of Psalm 116, for example, is still articulated in terms of the creedal traditions of the nation (v. 5, alluding to Exod. 34:6–7) and recounted "in the presence of all his people" (vv. 14, 18). Frequently, though not always, the speaker in the psalms is not only among the people but also a representative of them and a ruler over them. The editorial title that describes Psalm 19, for example, as "a psalm of David" encourages us to read the psalmist's devoted attention to the law of YHWH not only as an expression of the private piety of an individual but also as an articulation of the proper stance to be taken by a ruler of God's people; blessed is the nation whose king ("your servant") is warned by God's decrees, who broods earnestly over his hidden faults, and who longs that he might not be ruled over by his willful sins (Ps. 19:11–13). Even in the untitled Psalm 119, with its pervasive, incessant first person singulars, there are hints that the psalmist is not speaking simply as a private believer but as "your servant" (11x within the psalm)—a ruler of YHWH's people, threatened by the conspiracies of princes, chastened by YHWH for his wanderings, but longing that he might be brought back to the right paths and do justice among YHWH's people.[17]

The fact that the Psalter depicts the Scriptures as belonging to the community of God's people does not mean that it encourages its readers to interpret the Scriptures simply as a projection of the voice and will of the nation.[18] According to the Psalter, the law of Moses is to be received as *YHWH's* word (or, in the second person pronouns of prayer and praise, "your" word), addressing

16. Cf. Kant, *Kant's gesammelte Schriften*, 5:161–62 (my translation).
17. See especially the argument in Soll, *Psalm 119*, 126–54, in favor of reading the "I" of Ps. 119 as a royal figure, perhaps a chastened Jehoiachin in exile in Babylon.
18. See Billings, *Word of God*, 199.

and confronting the nation and (at times) driving a painful wedge between the individual who listens and the "princes" and "teachers" who do not (e.g., Ps. 119:23, 99, 161). The scriptural story of YHWH's mighty works, likewise, is not recounted simply as a piece of triumphalist patriotic propaganda but as a call to national repentance, or as an expression of YHWH's covenantal commitment that is taken up by the community in order to call on YHWH to remember and honor his promises (e.g., Pss. 78; 89; 95; 105; 106).[19]

Nor does the Psalter encourage its readers to regard the Scriptures as if they were intended for Israel's exclusive benefit. The God whose word is celebrated and recounted in the Psalter is the God by whose word the heavens were made (Ps. 33:6); he is not only the God of Israel but also the God of all the earth. The story of his mighty works is to be told not only to the future generations of Israel but also to all the nations of the world (e.g., Pss. 22:27–31; 45:17; 67:2; 96:3–10; 105:1), and his decree concerning his anointed king is to be proclaimed to their kings and rulers (Ps. 2:7–12).[20]

Rightly Receiving the Scriptures

The Psalter teaches its readers not only how to perceive what Scripture is but also how to receive what Scripture does—with what purposes to approach Scripture, and how rightly to anticipate and respond to its various speech-acts. When we approach the Scriptures via the pathway of the Psalter, we are not only learning a theoretical doctrine of Scripture's perfections but also being trained in the sort of practices and dispositions that are to characterize our use of the text.[21]

The opening psalm encourages its readers to approach Scripture not just with attentiveness or acquiescence but with "delight,"[22] and the activity that is depicted as the blessed person's daily and nightly occupation is that of "meditat[ing]" on the law of YHWH. The kind of meditation that is in view in the Psalter, here and elsewhere, is not a dispassionate, wordless contemplation but a heartfelt, vocalized muttering and murmuring that expresses intense and protracted engagement with the text.[23]

19. Cf. Wenham, *Psalms as Torah*, 99, ch. 7.
20. Cf. the account of "Scripture's cosmic mission to Israel" in Work, *Living and Active*, 130–67.
21. See especially O'Donovan, "Reading Church."
22. The context (and the way in which the verb is used elsewhere in the OT) implies a delight that is as much a function of the will as of the emotions—not just the reactive delight that the reader experiences in the encounter with the Scriptures but also the active delight that takes the reader (back) to the Scriptures to read them.
23. Cf. Wenham, *Psalms as Torah*, 81–82; Goldingay, *Psalms 90–150*, 758.

The psalmists depict this meditation as taking place not only in the public light of day but also in the solitary darkness of the night; the law of YHWH is a text that is not only to be studied, discussed, and comprehended but also to be memorized and internalized—in the language of the psalms, it is to be "hidden" in the heart (e.g., Ps. 119:11),[24] among the subterranean springs of character and conduct.

The kind of formative internalization that the psalmists commend is strikingly depicted in Psalms 111 and 112, a pair of acrostic psalms that focus, respectively, on the works of YHWH and the conduct of those who fear him. According to Psalm 111, YHWH has "caused his wonders to be remembered" (v. 4), enabling his works to be "pondered" by those who delight in them (v. 2). The faithfulness of his works is paralleled with the trustworthiness of his precepts (vv. 7–8), suggesting a further connection between pondering God's works and delighting in his words. This implication is picked up in the following psalm, which depicts the blessedness of those who "fear the LORD" and "find great delight in his commands" (v. 1). The righteousness of YHWH, which is celebrated in Psalm 111, is echoed and manifested in the righteousness of those who fear him (Ps. 112:2–9); their works become a lived echo of Israel's creedal affirmation about the graciousness and compassion of YHWH (Pss. 111:4–5; 112:4–5; cf. Exod. 34:6).

The psalmists are under no illusion, however, that this kind of virtuous circle of piety, delight, and prosperity is the normal way in which God's people encounter his word. Again and again, throughout the Psalter, scriptural traditions are evoked in contexts of sin, suffering, and injustice; the law and covenant of YHWH and the story of his mighty works are recalled as a summons to repentance or as a background against which the psalmists lament their situation and cry out for YHWH to act in mercy and justice (e.g., Pss. 78; 89; 95; 105; 106). The depictions of the blessedness of the pious and obedient reader of YHWH's law in Psalm 1 and Psalm 112 sit alongside the testimony of the forgiven and instructed sinner in Psalm 32, the lamenting petitions of the chastened wanderer in Psalm 119, and the anguished recital of YHWH's deeds and commitments in Psalm 89.

But confession and lament are not the last words of the Psalter. All the reading and remembering, pondering and meditating, repenting and petitioning enjoined and depicted within the Psalter are directed toward the crescendo of praise with which the collection concludes. The Psalter's closing sequence commences with Psalm 145, the last Davidic psalm of the collection, in which the psalmist recalls YHWH's mighty works, placing his own praises within the

---

24. Cf. P. Griffiths, *Religious Reading*, 41–47.

joyful narration where one generation tells of those works to the next (vv. 4–6) and the whole creation declares God's praise, "so that all people may know of your mighty acts and the glorious splendor of your kingdom" (vv. 10–12). The remaining five psalms of the Psalter follow this psalmist's lead, drawing together the threads of the story of God's mighty works and summoning his people and the whole creation to sing his praise. And so the Psalter concludes, with a summons to universal praise and an answering doxology that neatly summarize the chief end of all Bible reading: "Let everything that has breath praise the LORD. Praise the LORD."

Traveling the Pathway of the Psalter

The prayers and praises of the Psalter—both as private meditations and as public praises—play an indispensable role in forming the way that God's people approach and receive his word. Christian beliefs about Scripture and dispositions toward it are sustained not only by logical argument and earnest exhortation but also by the practices—like singing and praying the psalms—that train us in how to articulate those beliefs and dispositions. The Psalter is a powerful reminder that a living and active doctrine of Scripture needs to be prayed and sung and practiced, not merely defined and defended. Within the Sunday gatherings of much contemporary evangelicalism, the Psalter has faded almost completely from view, except for the occasional cheerful sentiment plucked from a psalm as a call to worship or a line in a song lyric, hanging in the air like the Cheshire cat's smile. As individuals too, I suspect that—for many of us at least—there is little room in the frenetic and distracting patterns of life that we have constructed for ourselves (or have passively acquiesced to) for the kind of reading, recitation, and meditation on the Psalter in our private and household devotion that might help to remedy that deficiency. But a church that has forgotten the Psalter is a church that has abandoned one of the Bible's chief pathways into the understanding and experience of God's Word. Perhaps it is time for us to rededicate ourselves to the kind of practices and disciplines that apprentice us to the psalmists and join us with the church across the ages—and the people of Israel before them—in order that we might begin traveling that pathway again.

$*2*$

"In Your Mouth and in Your Heart"

Deuteronomy and the Hermeneutics of Law

Moses, Augustine, and Pelagius

In the early years of the fifth century, more than a thousand years before the Tyndale-More dispute (referred to in the previous chapter), an equally fierce debate flared up in Rome, focusing on the commandments of God and how they are to be received and responded to. Pelagius, a British teacher who had been making a name for himself as an ascetic and a moral reformer, was scandalized when he heard a bishop quoting a passage from Augustine's *Confessions*. The offending passage was the one in which Augustine recalled how he had wrestled with God's command of sexual continence before finally casting himself desperately upon the mercy of God: "All my hope is in your great mercy. . . . You command continence; give what you command and command what you will."[1]

Pelagius was enraged by this way of speaking about God's commandment and almost came to blows with the bishop.[2] According to his logic, a commandment given by a wise and righteous God should be received unproblematically,

---

1. Augustine, *Confessions* 10.29, in Augustine, *Selected Writings*, 145, trans. Mary T. Clark.
2. Cf. the account in Augustine, *On the Gift of Perseverance* 20.53.

with glad and immediate obedience, not anguished pleas for grace: "God Himself, that eternal Majesty, . . . has sent us the holy Scriptures, as the crown of his truly adorable precepts; and, so far from [receiving] them at once with joy and veneration, . . . we shout in God's face and say, 'It's hard! It's difficult! We can't! We are but men, encompassed by the frailty of the flesh!' What blind folly! What rash profanity! . . . No one knows better the measure of our strength than he who gave us our strength; and no one has a better understanding of what is within our power than he who endowed us with the very resources of our power. He has not willed to command anything impossible, for he is righteous; and he will not condemn a man for what he could not help."[3]

It would be a mistake to think of Augustine's dispute with Pelagius as if it were merely an episode from the distant past, with no abiding relevance for today. While the austere, ascetic Pelagianism of the fifth century may be distant from the experience of most modern Bible readers, a softer, vaguer semi-Pelagian echo continues to reverberate widely in our own time and functions (as writers as confessionally diverse as Roger Olson, Michael Horton, William Willimon, and Christian Smith all agree) as "the default theology of most American Christians."[4] In our own time, too—as was the case in Augustine's— the battle over how we are to receive and respond to God's commandments (including the commandments about how we are to order our sexual desires and practices) is fought on two fronts: on one side the moralists and managers, mining God's word for "biblical" tips and techniques we can employ in improving ourselves and our world, and on the other, the Manichaeans and Marcionites,[5] disparaging the Old Testament law (and all rules, disciplines, and traditions in general) as oppressive entanglements abolished by Christ in favor of an immediate, inward, intuitive connection of the soul with God.

"To Expound This Law" (1:5): Deuteronomy as Interpretation

If we go searching within the canon for guidance on how the law of Moses is to be received and regarded, then the first voice to listen to is that of Moses

---

3. Pelagius, *Letter to Demetrias* 16, as translated in Stevenson, *Creeds, Councils and Controversies*, 219 (correcting "recovering" to "receiving").

4. Olson, *Arminian Theology*, 30; cf. Horton, *Christless Christianity*, 44; Willimon, *Intrusive Word*, 53; C. Smith and Denton, *Soul Searching*, 118–71. Of course, this contemporary semi-Pelagianism takes a particular form within the culture of North America, influenced by the legacy of Charles Finney's revivalism and the "can-do" ethos of democratic capitalism, but the generic phenomenon can be found far beyond the borders of the United States.

5. Cf. especially Augustine, *Reply to Faustus the Manichaean* and *Against Two Letters of the Pelagians*.

himself, and his most sustained interpretation of the law is presented in the speeches, song, and blessings of the book of Deuteronomy. The character of Deuteronomy as a book of interpretation is obscured by the title given to the book in its Greek, Latin, and English translations, which implies that the book is to be read as a "second law" (Greek: *deuteros nomos*)—an extra helping of the same dish that was served up to Israel at Horeb. But the Moses of Deuteronomy is presented more as an interpreter and a prophet than as a legislator (cf. 1:5; 34:10).[6] Although it contains "decrees and laws" (especially in chs. 12–26), the book as a whole is not so much a collection of legislation as an answer to the question that Moses puts on the lips of "your son" in 6:20: "What is the meaning of the stipulations, decrees and laws the LORD our God has commanded you?"[7]

Three Futures

That this question is presented as one that will need to be answered "in the future, when your son asks you" is one indication that the context into which they are directed by Moses is something broader and longer than the immediate moment of decision facing Israel on the plains of Moab. Again and again, Moses's speeches address the situation of the coming generations of Israel, "when the LORD [their] God brings [them] into the land" (6:10; cf. 4:10; 5:31; 12:1; etc.), and as the book draws to a close, it increasingly emphasizes that this future in the land will be a future without Moses, in which his words will need to be heard and remembered in his absence (cf. 31:1, 2, 24–29; 34:9).

6. The verb *bē'ēr* in 1:5 can mean either "explain" or "articulate clearly." "This law" is probably best read as a reference to what follows in the remainder of the book, described as *tôrâ*, or "instruction," for Israel. But the backward references in v. 3 ("[according to] all that the LORD had commanded him"; cf. 4:5, 10–14) and v. 6 ("the LORD our God said to us at Horeb . . ."), together with the content of what follows, combine to give the impression that Moses is rearticulating, explaining, and applying the commandments given at Horeb, rather than simply adding a few more new bits of legislation to the statute book of Israel. Within 34:10–12, the immediate focus of the depiction of Moses as a prophet is on the way in which "the LORD knew [him] face to face," and on "those signs and wonders the LORD sent him to do," but the future orientation of the immediately preceding chapters (chs. 29–33) and the way in which the activity of a prophet is described in ch. 13 suggest that the role of a prophet is a speaking part, and that a prophet's words include both prediction and exhortation.

7. The word "meaning" in the NIV has no direct equivalent in the Hebrew original. It is an attempt on the part of the translators to convey the intended sense of the question, based on the way it is answered in the following verses. Clearly, what Moses has in mind by the question that he puts in the mouth of "your son" is not merely a request for the content of Israel's laws but an inquiry regarding the purpose and function that they serve within the story of the nation.

But another, more distant, future is also addressed in the book. We are on the threshold of it in 4:25a ("After you have had children and grandchildren and have lived in the land a long time"), and the next step beyond is raised as a hypothetical possibility in verse 25b ("if you then become corrupt . . ."). By verses 27–30 the focus is on the predicament of dispersion and distress which is threatened in verse 26 as the punishment for that apostasy, and that foreshadowed future becomes the new situation addressed: "When you are in distress and all these things have happened to you" (v. 30). A similar movement from contingency toward prediction can be found in chapter 29, where the warnings and threats of verses 18–21 are followed by the depiction in verses 22–28 of a scenario in which it seems that the worst possibilities have happened.[8] This in turn sets the scene for the opening paragraphs of chapter 30: "When all these blessings and curses I have set before you come on you."

Somewhere in these two foreshadowed futures depicted in Moses's speeches is the implied time frame in which the book's narrator addresses its audience (e.g., 34:6, 10–12), and in which the compiler of the book in its final form re-presents Moses's words to a new audience, implicitly urging them to hear and take to heart what was said to their ancestors on the plains of Moab and "writ[ten] in a book" (31:24) for their benefit.

But even this is not the furthest horizon envisaged within the book. Moses's speeches depict a third horizon, and for the book's original intended readers—whether their situation is in the land under the threat of exile, in Babylon in the midst of its reality, or in the Persian period, living with the exile's grim aftermath—this third and most distant horizon remains a future one. In this third, glorious future, Moses says,

> The Lord your God will circumcise your hearts and the hearts of your descendants, so that you may love him with all your heart and with all your soul, and live. . . . The Lord will again delight in you and make you prosperous, just as he delighted in your ancestors, if you obey the Lord your God and keep his commands and decrees that are written in this Book of the Law and turn to the Lord your God with all your heart and with all your soul. (30:6, 9–10)

The Law and the Heart

The emphasis on the "heart" (Hebrew: lēbāb) in these verses (6x in 30:1–10) is characteristic of the book of Deuteronomy as a whole. "All the rhetoric,

8. Cf. Barker, *Triumph of Grace*, 137–38; Driver, *Deuteronomy*, 326. This impression is confirmed unequivocally in the dark predictions of 31:15–29.

the didactic, hortatory style, the urgent appeals, glowing promises, and dire warnings are directed precisely to the heart and mind, the inner world of will and purpose."[9] What is said about the law and the heart in Moses's speeches in Deuteronomy runs like a thread through the whole book, tying together much of the book's narrative, theology, and exhortation; if we can trace this thread, it will take us a long way toward our goal of answering the protests of Pelagius with a steadfast defense of the grace of God, without lapsing into the Marcionism and Manichaeism that lie in the opposite direction.

First Speech: Chapters 1–4

"Do not let them . . . fade from your heart." (4:9)

Moses's first speech, which runs from 1:6 to 4:40, begins by recounting the story of Israel's journey from Horeb (Mt. Sinai) to Moab, emphasizing the people's abortive entrance into the land at Kadesh Barnea (1:20–46) and the divinely enabled victories over Sihon and Og (2:2–3:11). In chapter 4, the mode of address shifts from narration to exhortation ("Now, Israel, hear . . ."), but the narratives of chapters 1–3 (along with the events at Baal Peor, Horeb, and Egypt that are recalled in chapter 4)[10] are not left behind. Undergirding the appeal of 4:1–2—"hear the decrees and laws I am about to teach you," "follow them so that you may live," and "keep the commands of the LORD your God that I give you"—is an appeal to the nation to retain within their hearts a memory of what they have seen with their eyes: "Only be careful, and watch yourselves closely so that you do not forget the things your eyes have seen or let them fade from your heart as long as you live. Teach them to your children and to their children after them" (4:9).

The fact that Moses's hearers on the plains of Moab were not actually among those who saw these things is immaterial in the rhetoric of Moses: the distinction between generations that was emphasized in chapters 1–3 now fades away in favor of an emphasis on the solidarity of Israel as one people (addressed in vv. 9–10 in the first person singular). The nation is to "remember" the things that it has seen by passing down the story from one generation to the next.

"Take to heart this day" (4:39)

The connection between remembering the story and keeping the commands is spelled out in the remainder of the chapter. First, as Moses emphasizes in

9. C. Wright, *Deuteronomy*, 85. Cf. Barker, *Triumph of Grace*, 157–58; Robson, *Honey from the Rock*, 145–46.

10. Cf. 4:3–4 (Baal Peor); 4:10–15, 33, 36 (Horeb); 4:20, 34, 37 (Egypt).

verses 10–31, the story of what Israel saw—"no form of any kind" (v. 15)—
provides a rationale for the commandment against idolatry. But more is to
be remembered than simply the idol that Israel did not see. As the chapter
closes in on its conclusion, in verses 32–40, it emphasizes what Israel did
experience—"the voice of God speaking out of fire" (v. 33) and "[a] god . . .
tak[ing] for himself one nation out of another" (v. 34).

What Israel is to remember and "take to heart this day" is that "the LORD
is God in heaven above and on the earth below. There is no other" (4:39).
That, according to verse 35, is the fundamental lesson to be drawn from
all that they have witnessed, and the logic behind verses 39–40 implies that
taking that reality to heart will be the inward conviction that is to drive
their obedience to all the decrees and stipulations of the covenant that he
has made with them.

Second Speech, Part 1: Chapters 5–11

"Oh, that they had such a heart" (5:29)[11]

Moses's second speech begins where the first speech left off, at Horeb, with
YHWH speaking to Israel out of the fire. An account of the ten "words"
(Hebrew: děbārîm) which he spoke directly to the nation is followed by a
description in 5:23–27 of Israel's response: acknowledging the "glory and
majesty" of what they have seen, astonished that "a person can live even if
God speaks with them" (v. 24), yet fearful of being consumed by fire if they
continue to stand listening, they beg Moses to draw near and listen on their
behalf, then recount God's words to them: "Tell us whatever the LORD our
God tells you. We will listen and obey" (v. 27).

This reaction from the people is warmly and comprehensively endorsed
by God: "I have heard what this people said to you. Everything they said was
good" (v. 28). But he is under no illusions about the likelihood of the people
living up to what they have promised—he immediately follows the warm
endorsement of verse 28 with a poignant statement of "divine wistfulness"[12]
in verse 29: "Oh, that their hearts would be inclined to fear me and keep all
my commands always, so that it might go well with them and their children
forever!"

At one level, the sentiments expressed in 5:29 are grounds for deep pes-
simism. If anyone knows the heart of Israel, it is Israel's God. He is the
one—as we are reminded in 8:2—who has already put Israel to the test in the

11. NASB. The NIV reads, "Oh, that their hearts would be inclined to fear me and keep all
my commands always."
12. C. Wright, Deuteronomy, 91.

wilderness "to know what was in [their] heart, whether or not [they] would keep his commands." The dark predictions that accumulate across the book, as threats and warnings harden into certainties, should not be read as if they were the outworkings of an oppressive, malevolent fatalism, bearing down upon the hearts of an innocent people to turn a good nation bad. Whatever conclusions we may draw from elsewhere about the metaphysics of God's foreknowledge and the relationship between human time and divine eternity, Deuteronomy presents God's bleak and inexorable predictions about the nation's future as informed (in part, at least) by his perfect knowledge of their hearts in the present: "I know what they are disposed to do, even before I bring them into the land I promised them on oath" (31:21).

But at another level, the divine lament in 5:29 is also grounds for optimism: if YHWH himself—the sovereign God who has made known his power in the exodus and has spoken from the fire at Horeb—wishes for Israel to have a different heart from the stubborn and rebellious one that they have at present, then perhaps there is reason to hope that things might not remain forever the way that they are now.

"With all your heart" (6:5)

For now, however, the divine wish of 5:29 is left hanging in the air, and the focus of Moses's rhetoric returns to the decision that Israel must make in the present and to the response that they and their children are to make to what YHWH has commanded them. While there are many "commands, decrees and laws" (6:1) and they are "all" to be obeyed (6:2), in the first part of his speech Moses emphasizes the central demand that underlies all of them: "Hear, O Israel: The LORD our God, the LORD is one. Love the LORD your God with all your heart and with all your soul and with all your strength" (6:4–5).

It would be a mistake to read the commandment in 6:5 through the lens of modern, Western, romantic individualism, as if the "heart" were nothing more than a wellspring of spontaneously erupting emotions, and as if inward, invisible "love" could be disconnected from outward, visible obedience. In Deuteronomy and elsewhere in the Old Testament, the "heart" (Hebrew: *lēbāb* or *lēb*) is not only a place of emotion but also the seat of memory, understanding, and decision, and the love that is commanded in Deuteronomy is inextricably connected with an outward and visible obedience to the statutes and laws of God. But it would equally be a mistake to eliminate altogether the emotional, affective dimension of love (both the love of YHWH for his people and the love that his people are commanded to have for him) as it is depicted within Deuteronomy. The command "Love the LORD your God with all your heart and with all your soul and with all your strength" is not merely language for a political policy of covenant fidelity or for a habit of obedient behavior; it also includes a deep, inward, affective devotion, like the love between a wife and a husband or between a child and a parent.[13] Just as Israel is to love YHWH "with all [their] heart," so too they are to "fear," "walk in obedience," and "serve" him "with all [their] heart and with all [their] soul" (10:12; cf. 11:13); the love and the fear are mutually interpreting,[14] and the wholeheartedness is the common denominator of both.

"These commandments . . . are to be on your hearts." (6:6)

If Israel is to love YHWH in this manner, then the words of the covenant will need to be written not only on tablets of stone but also on their hearts (6:6; cf. 11:18). Here, too, the lens of modern, romantic individualism can distort. What is to be on their hearts is not something vague, sentimental, or contentless; it is "these commandments" (*haddĕbārîm hā'ēlleh*), and the process by which it is to be inscribed there is an emphatically social one, involving recitation, repetition, and ritual: "Impress them on your children. Talk about them when you sit at home and when you walk along the road, when you lie down and when you get up. Tie them as symbols on your hands and bind them on your foreheads. Write them on the doorframes of your houses and on your gates" (6:7–9).[15]

"Do not say in your heart" (9:4)[16]

While the heart can be pictured in 6:6 as a tablet upon which words can be impressed and inscribed, it would be wrong to conclude that the heart is viewed in Deuteronomy simply as a blank slate upon which messages are written by others, or even a set of scales that makes balanced, rational assessments. In this first part of Moses's second speech, he repeatedly pictures the heart as a place in which words are said as well as written, highlighting the importance of what is said in the heart (by an individual or by a nation, collectively) for how one interprets the actions and words of God.

Specifically, the kind of self-talk that is anticipated and prohibited in this first part of Moses's second speech is self-talk that magnifies the power of

13. Cf. Lapsley, "Feeling Our Way."
14. Cf. Arnold, "Love-Fear Antinomy."
15. The NIV's "about" in v. 7 has some warrant in light of the question-and-answer formula in vv. 20–25, but it is not necessarily required by the Hebrew *bām*; and it is likely that the process envisaged in v. 7 included recitation and memorization, not merely chatty, informal conversations "about" the commandments. Cf. Block, *Deuteronomy*, 184–85.
16. NASB. The NIV reads: "Do not say to yourself . . ."

the nations and forgets the power of God (7:17), that interprets wealth and success as a personal accomplishment and not a gift from God (8:17), or that interprets the gift of the land and the destruction of the nations as a reward for Israel's own righteousness (9:4).[17] A heart that rightly receives God's words is a heart whose inward conversation is characterized by gratitude and humble trust.

"Circumcise your hearts." (10:16)

If Israel is to respond to YHWH's commandments with the kind of wholehearted love and fear that is called for in 6:5 and 10:12–13, and (in particular) if they are to imitate his love for the fatherless, the widow, and the foreigner, then they will need to make a radical, inward change from their present, "stiff-necked" arrogance: in the words of 10:16 (echoing Lev. 26:41), they will need to "circumcise" their heart, so that the outward mark of covenant loyalty becomes the image of a humble, inward embrace of the covenant stipulations.

Second Speech, Part 2: Chapters 12–28

If the early chapters of Moses's second speech focus mainly on the central demand of the covenant, its second half extends the scope of the discussion to the covenant's particular and various stipulations (chs. 12–26) and to the blessings and curses attached to it (chs. 27–28). These chapters do not, however, abandon the focus of chapters 5–11 on the heart. Thus, for example, in chapter 15, Moses expresses his exhortations about how to receive the stipulations regarding the year for canceling debts as an explicit challenge to the self-talk of the "hardhearted" creditor (15:7–11); he frames the stipulations regarding kingship in light of the danger that the king's heart would be "led astray" by many wives (17:17) or "lifted up" (17:20)[18] above his fellow Israelites; and the stipulations regarding warfare (20:3–4, 8) challenge the Israelite armies not to be "fainthearted" like their ancestors (cf. 1:28) but take into account the likelihood that many of them will be. The final chapters of the speech, too, which spell out the blessings and curses of the covenant, make it clear that the anticipated root of the various sins on which the covenant curses are pronounced is the fact that the Israelites "did not serve . . . gladly [Hebrew: *bĕṭôb lēbāb*, or "with a glad heart"] in the time of prosperity" (28:47).

17. Cf. also, in later chapters, the warnings in 15:9 and 29:19.
18. NASB. The NIV translates the expression as a warning of the danger that the king would "consider himself better than" his compatriots.

Third Speech: Chapters 29–30

"The Lord has not given you a mind that understands." (29:4)

Moses's third speech, in chapters 29–30, begins by recapitulating the main content of chapters 1–4. Paradoxically, and tragically, although their "eyes have seen" (29:2–3, twice) all the signs and wonders of the exodus, they have not had "eyes that see or ears that hear" (v. 4), because "the Lord has not given [them] a mind [Hebrew: *lēb*] that understands." In asserting that this has been the case "to this day," Moses's statement (like the divine lament in 5:29) is both a tragic summary of what has not been learned in forty years of wilderness wanderings and a whispered half-hope that such a heart might one day be given.

Neither the tragedy nor the half-hope, however, is viewed as abolishing the responsibility of the nation, or of the individuals in it, for their response in the present to the promises and warnings of YHWH—this much is made clear in the solemn warnings in 29:18–19 about the individual whose heart "turns away" to other gods, while inwardly invoking a complacent, hypocritical self-blessing.

"The Lord your God will circumcise your hearts." (30:6a)

Finally, in chapter 30, comes the full-blooded expression of the hope that has been half-whispered in 5:29 and 29:4 and foreshadowed briefly in 4:29–31:

> When all these blessings and curses I have set before you come on you and you take them to heart wherever the Lord your God disperses you among the nations, and when you and your children return to the Lord your God and obey him with all your heart and with all your soul according to everything I command you today, then the Lord your God will restore your fortunes and have compassion on you and gather you again from all the nations where he scattered you. (30:1–3)

The process described is painful—only after "all these blessings and curses [have] come" on them will Israel finally "take them to heart." It involves a wholehearted repentance ("when you and your children return to the Lord your God and obey him with all your heart and with all your soul") that amounts to the very "circumcis[ion]" that was commanded in chapter 10, now performed within Israel's heart by God himself. The effect of this circumcised heart will be (1) a wholehearted love (30:6b), corresponding to the love that was commanded in 6:5, and (2) the placement of the word of YHWH's commandment in Israel's mouth and in their heart (30:14) for them to obey.[19]

19. Many commentators (and most English translations) supply present-tense verbs in 30:11–14, reading the paragraph as if Moses has already shifted his focus back from the future

How to Read a Broken Law

For the original hearers of Moses's speeches on the plains of Moab, however, and for the original readers of Deuteronomy, the day for the fulfillment of that ultimate hope was still a future one. Their task was to read God's law from their own vantage point, in the middle of history—neither at the beginning of the story, when the nation was brand-new and the law was freshly given, nor at its ending, when every promise had been fulfilled and every hope satisfied. The law they were to read was a law they had repeatedly broken (from the very first day it was given to them, as they are reminded in ch. 9), not an easy ten-step formula for success, given to a pristine people.

So how are you to read a broken law?

With Repentance...

The first part of the answer is obvious: with repentance. The command "Take to heart all the words I have solemnly declared to you this day" (as Moses puts it in 32:46) means taking to heart a word that speaks "as a witness . . . against them" (31:19, 26, 28). Moses's own lamentation and prayer in 9:18–29 provide a model for what it might look like to take that sort of testimony to heart.

...And Faith

But the word that is to be taken to heart is not only a word of condemnation that passes sentence on the past, but also a word of hope that offers guidance for the future; the commands of the covenant come attached to a promise that they will one day be written on Israel's heart, and God's people will be enabled to love him. In this sense, the commandment, read in the light of the promise, is to be received as a "message concerning faith" (cf. Rom. 10:8); it is to be received with trust that God will one day bring about the fulfillment of the commandment's "righteous requirement" (cf. Rom. 8:4) and with prayer for that enabling—or even just a foretaste of it—to be experienced in the present.

---

day of Israel's restoration to their present situation on the plains of Moab. There are good reasons, however, to translate the *ki* at the start of verse 11 as "for," rather than "now," and read the whole paragraph as describing the future day when Israel will be enabled to obey the commandment given at Horeb and reiterated at Moab (cf. 30:8; or perhaps, the implied commandment to repentance in 30:2, 10). Cf. the arguments in Barker, *Triumph of Grace*, 182–98; Coxhead, "Deuteronomy 30:11–14."

Reading the Commandments Today

Our own situation, of course, is not identical with that of the first hearers of Moses and the original readers of Deuteronomy. On this side of the re-constitution of God's people in Christ, the law's righteous requirement to be "fulfilled in us" looks very different from what it would have looked like if we were members of the nation that YHWH made his covenant with at Horeb,[20] and Paul's description of us as those who "live . . . according to the Spirit" (Rom. 8:4) reminds us that we live in days when the Spirit of God has already been poured out upon his people.

But even for us, the experience of the Spirit is only an experience of "first fruits"; we are not yet in the age when hope has become sight. If we understand our own hearts even a little, we will know that there is something profoundly deficient in Pelagius's unproblematic, self-confident moralism; when we read God's commandments, there is good reason for us, along with Augustine, to cast ourselves upon his mercy and pray urgently (though not despairingly) for his enabling grace. "All my hope is in your great mercy. . . . Give what you command and command what you will."[21]

The grace to which our hopes are directed in Deuteronomy is certainly not a cheap grace, bereft of moral demands or transformative power. This is a book that cuts to the heart and magnifies the seriousness of our encounter with God's commandments. But it is at the same time a book that situates those commandments, and the whole of our lives, within a story that is, from beginning to end, a story of divine grace. If we are to receive the command-ments of Moses with the kind of gratitude and earnestness that they merit, rightly relating them to the history and promise of God's grace—if we are to fend off the moralists on one side and the Marcionites on the other—then we will need to begin by spending time first with Moses himself, attentively listening to his own interpretation of the commandments and apprenticing our interpretation to his.

---

20. See especially the insightful discussions of how the law of Moses informs the Christian life in Robson, *Honey from the Rock*, 148–201; Rosner, *Paul and the Law*.

21. Augustine, *Confessions* 10.29, in Augustine, *Selected Writings*, 145, trans. Mary T. Clark.

✤3✤

"This Kindness"

Ruth and the Hermeneutics of Virtue

Virtue and Interpretation

What sort of readers make the best interpreters (of Scripture or, for that matter, of any text)? In recent decades a growing number of writers have said that good interpretation requires not just skill but character—that, all else being equal, virtuous people, whose interactions with the world are characterized by habits of attentiveness, charity, honesty, courage, and humility, are most likely to understand the texts they read and do justice to them in the way in which they respond.[1]

Stephen Fowl makes the claim succinctly: "Given that Christians are called to interpret Scripture as part of their ongoing journey into ever-deepening communion with God, it is not surprising that those who have grown and advanced in virtue will tend to be masterful interpreters of Scripture."[2]

Questioning Virtue

While much in the claims made by proponents of virtue hermeneutics seems both obvious and important, the approach has not been without its critics.

---

1. On virtue and interpretation generally, see Zagzebski, *Virtues of the Mind*; Vanhoozer, *Is There a Meaning?*; Jacobs, *Theology of Reading*. On virtue and biblical interpretation, see Fowl and Jones, *Reading in Communion*; Jones, "Formed and Transformed"; Briggs, *Virtuous Reader*.
2. Fowl, "Virtue," 838.

To begin with, questions might be asked about the notion of "virtue" itself, and its origins within ancient pagan cultures in which wealthy, freeborn men competed with one another to demonstrate their prowess, display their magnanimity, and accumulate titles of honor: "If the language and logic of virtue tips in any direction, it is away from Christianity and toward the Greek context in which it originated. For Christians, it can be used with great reward, but it must be purified as used or else bear bad fruit."[3]

In addition to these general questions about the concept of virtue itself are the particular questions we might ask about its applicability to our interaction with the text of Scripture. Fowl's picture of the "masterful" interpreter who brings to the text a full complement of virtuous dispositions raises some obvious theological questions. Is faithful reading of Scripture really a matter of "mastery"? And if there is a place for "virtue" in the way we describe the interaction between Scripture and its readers, is it in the description we offer of the character which the reader *brings* to the Scriptures or the character which the Scriptures *form* in the reader?[4]

Calvin's comments in the "Prefatory Address" to the *Institutes* provide a memorable example of Protestant unease about the notion of virtue as a description of something that we bring to God and to his word:

> For what is more consonant with faith than to recognize that we are naked of all virtue, in order to be clothed by God? That we are empty of all good, to be filled by him? That we are slaves of sin, to be freed by him? Blind, to be illumined by him? Lame, to be made straight by him? Weak, to be sustained by him? To take away from us all occasion for glorying, that he alone might stand forth gloriously and we glory in him?[5]

Ruth and Hermeneutics

What light does the Bible shed on the role of virtuous character in faithful and wise interpretation? One corner of the canon to which we might be wise to turn in contemplating a question of this sort is the book of Ruth, which functions within the Old Testament as a kind of case study in virtuous interpretation.[6] In

---

3. Hauerwas and Pinches, *Christians among the Virtues*, 57.

4. In fairness to Fowl, it should be noted that his account of "virtue in interpretation" sits alongside a complementary account of "virtue through interpretation," in which he describes the role played by Scripture in forming the same virtuous dispositions that the reader, in turn, brings to the text as an interpreter.

5. Calvin, *Institutes*, "Prefatory Address," 13, trans. Ford Lewis Battles.

6. B. Webb (*Five Festal Garments*, 54) describes the book of Ruth as "a study in the application of the Mosaic Torah to the daily life of the people of God"; similarly, Lacocque, *Ruth*, 1,

form, the book of Ruth presents as a heartwarming, gently comic short story or novella.[7] Just beneath the surface of the story, however, lurks a string of interpretive questions about how to understand and apply the commandments of the law of Moses—in particular, the law on redemption of land in Leviticus 25, the levirate marriage provisions in Deuteronomy 25, the stipulations regarding gleaning in Leviticus 19 and 23, and the ban on Moabites in Deuteronomy 23. Underneath these, in turn, are questions of fundamental importance about the character of YHWH, as it is described in the core confessions of the nation of Israel, and how it is to shape the conduct of his people.

The Virtuous Interpreter

Much in the story told by the book of Ruth can be read as supporting the role of virtue in interpretation. From one angle at least, Boaz could be seen as the paradigmatic virtuous interpreter, the "blessed . . . one" celebrated in texts like Psalms 1; 41; 112 as the ideal reader of Torah. Barry Webb highlights the way in which Boaz's conduct, as narrated in chapter 2, encourages us to view him as "a pious Israelite, with a fine sense of his obligations and a readiness to accept them."[8] The narrative hints that the same cannot safely be assumed of all Israelite men: Boaz orders his men not to "lay a hand on" Ruth (2:9), and Naomi warns her that "in someone else's field you might be harmed" (2:22). Boaz's obedience to the Mosaic laws regarding gleaning is generous and ungrudging (2:15–16), and in chapter 4 his enthusiastic readiness to fulfill the purpose of the Leviticus 25 law for the redemption of land—and, at the same time, to step into the breach and be a *levir* ("husband's brother," fulfilling the responsibility described in Deut. 25:5–6) to Ruth—contrasts strikingly with the self-interested timidity of his rival next-of-kin.

If we move beyond the conceptual world of the Old Testament, Boaz's character has obvious affinities with that of the "magnanimous man" who is the exemplar of virtue in Aristotle's *Nicomachean Ethics*.[9] Boaz's very name—Hebrew for "in him is strength" (the name later given to one of the

---

70–71; E. Campbell, *Ruth*, 31. John Wilch (*Ruth*, 99) suggests that "the story of Ruth complements the Law of Moses by providing an excellent example of how faithful believers fulfilled the intent and spirit of the Law of God in practice."

7. Cf. E. Campbell, *Ruth*, 3–10; B. Webb, *Five Festal Garments*, 37; Wilch, *Ruth*, 1–2.

8. B. Webb, *Five Festal Garments*, 44.

9. See especially the discussions of generosity, magnanimity, and honor in Aristotle, *Nicomachean Ethics* 4.1–4. Note the frequent use of the language of "magnanimity" to describe the actions and motivations of Boaz, by commentators including Matthews, *Judges and Ruth*, 240; Fischer, "Ruth," 798; Bush, *Ruth, Esther*, 155; Wilch, *Ruth*, 3.

physical pillars of Solomon's temple)—indicates his social position.[10] As an
'îš gibbôr ḥayil—a "man of standing" (2:1)—he reads the law of Moses from
a position of wealth and social prestige, and uses these resources liberally for
the good of others.[11] He has a proper sense of honor and shame, prudently
averting the potential scandal that could have arisen from Ruth's nocturnal
visit to the threshing floor (3:14) and expertly navigating the public transac-
tions at the city gate the following day (4:1–12). All in all, it seems, in his
motivations, his capacities, and his social position, Boaz is the very model
of a virtuous interpreter. Given his prominence in the narrative and his involvement in all the actions that require the interpretation and application of
Torah, the book of Ruth is a good case study in the importance of readerly
virtue in biblical interpretation.

Two Empty Readers

But Boaz is not the only reader of God and his purposes presented to us in the
book. Among the other characters the most prominent are Naomi and Ruth,
who interpret God's words and actions from a very different angle;[12] their
function within the narrative poses a significant challenge to the sufficiency
of "virtue" as a category for theological hermeneutics.

In contrast with Boaz's virtuous fullness as an *'îš gibbôr ḥayil*, Ruth and
Naomi arrive in Bethlehem "empty" (1:21), at least according to Naomi's
self-estimation. Unlike Boaz, whose place in the world of the story is secure
and stable as a blessed and prosperous occupant of the land, they enter from
stage left, returning (in Naomi's case) or arriving (in Ruth's) after a tersely
narrated episode of marriages and bereavements in Moab.

It is tempting to characterize the Naomi of chapter 1 as a paradigmatic
*mis*reader of God and his purposes, projecting the "bitter[ness]" of her own
situation onto her reading of God's motives in his dealings with her (1:20)
and tacitly passing over the loyal love of her daughter-in-law as not worth
counting compared to the husband and sons she has lost in Moab (1:21).[13]
It is hard to deny that, to some extent at least, "her repentance is flawed,
and her perception of her condition distorted."[14] But repentance it still is,
nonetheless, as emphasized in the repeated use of the language of "return"

10. Cf. Pressler, *Joshua, Judges, and Ruth*, 276; Linafelt and Beal, *Ruth and Esther*, 25.
11. Cf. Lacocque, *Ruth*, 71.
12. Cf. the discussion in Bauckham, "Book of Ruth," 39–40.
13. Contrast the assessment of her neighbors in 4:15: "your daughter-in-law, who loves you
and who is better to you than seven sons."
14. B. Webb, *Five Festal Garments*, 42–43.

(Hebrew: *šûb*),[15] a repentance occasioned and motivated by news of the end of the famine in Judah, interpreted as the work of "the LORD . . . com[ing] to the aid of his people by providing food for them" (1:6).

Viewed from the perspective of Ruth and Naomi, the action of God in ending the famine, the Mosaic provisions for gleaners to find grain at the margins of the field, and the generous hospitality of Boaz are all to be understood as expressions of the "kindness" (*ḥesed*) of YHWH (2:20). The actions that they take in returning to Judah and gleaning in Boaz's field reflect—as Boaz rightly perceives—their decision to "take refuge" under the wings of YHWH (2:12). As "empty" readers, they resort to the word of God not primarily to clarify the extent of its demands on them but to take refuge in its promises and in the God whom it makes known.

Intersecting Readings

Boaz's virtuous reading of the requirements of the Mosaic law and Naomi and Ruth's bold ventures of trust, in which they cast themselves upon the kindness of YHWH, do not take place as disconnected, independent events. In treating Ruth honorably and generously, Boaz is motivated, at least in part, by what he has heard of her kindness and fidelity to Naomi and of her decision to throw in her lot with the people of Israel and take refuge under the wings of their God (2:11–12). And the rising hopes of Naomi, culminating in the potentially scandalous scheme of chapter 3, are encouraged in turn by what Ruth reports back to her about the extravagant generosity of Boaz (2:18–23).

Underlying both developments—the swelling tide of Boaz's generosity and the rising boldness of Naomi and Ruth—are intuitive, imaginative connections that each of them draws between the actions of the other and the kindness of YHWH. In the two widows' situation of need, and in Ruth's status as a foreigner in the land (highlighted in her first words to him, in 2:10), Boaz receives—if he has eyes to see it—a mirror of his whole nation's story and a reminder of the identity of "the LORD, the God of Israel" (2:12), as a refuge for the widow and the foreigner (cf. Deut. 10:18–19) and as the original giver of all the abundance Boaz enjoys (1:6; cf. Deut. 8:6–18).[16] In that context, Boaz

15. Twelve times within ch. 1, in vv. 6, 7, 8, 10, 11, 12, 15 (twice), 16, 21, 22 (twice). Cf. ibid., 41.

16. The words for "foreigner" are not the same in the two passages—Ruth 2:10 uses *nokrîyâ*, and Deut. 10:18–19 uses *gēr*—but there is nothing in Ruth's situation that would exclude her from being described as a *gēr* in the sense in which the term is used in Deut. 10. Cf. Lacocque, *Ruth*, 70–71.

interprets Ruth's fidelity to Naomi (as Naomi herself interpreted it in 1:8) as an act of *ḥesed* analogous to the kindness of YHWH with which Boaz hopes she will be rewarded (2:11–12; 3:10); depending on how his words in 3:10 are interpreted, he may also see himself as included among those to whom she has extended her *ḥesed*.[17] Naomi and Ruth, in turn, are emboldened by the words of his blessing in 2:12 ("May you be richly rewarded by the LORD, the God of Israel, under whose wings you have come to take refuge") to risk everything on a nocturnal appeal to Boaz: "Spread the corner of your garment [literally 'your wing'] over me" (3:9), she asks, daring him to act in line with his words.[18]

Connected with all of these convergent assessments of character and circumstance is a bold and striking reading of the law of Moses, which informs both Ruth's proposal in 3:9 and its acceptance by Boaz. In linking her appeal to Boaz to extend his garment over her in marriage with his status as *gō'ēl* to Naomi and her family, Ruth implies a connection between the rationale of the law of levirate marriage and that of the provisions for redemption of property, appealing for an action by Boaz that goes far beyond the letter of the law of Moses and anything (to the best of our knowledge) that was strictly required by Israelite custom.[19] Her appeal to Boaz is deeply and explicitly informed by the laws and customs of Israel, but it is not simply a request that he do his legal and customary duty; her appeal reads Israel's laws and customs not merely as prescriptions of duty but also as expressions of the *ḥesed* of YHWH, which is to be imitated and manifested in the actions of his people.

17. On one reading of 3:10 (cf. E. Campbell, *Ruth*, 137; Wilch, *Ruth*, 291), the "kindness" that Boaz sees in Ruth's proposal is her continuing fidelity to Naomi; in proposing marriage to Boaz, she is seeking to secure the welfare of her mother-in-law rather than operating solely on the basis of self-interest and marrying a younger man with no likelihood of acting as *gō'ēl*. Alternatively, given the uncertainties about his own prowess and fertility that would have been associated with his predicament as an older man, 3:10 can be taken as an indication that Boaz sees *himself* as included among the objects of Ruth's kindness (cf. B. Webb, *Five Festal Garments*, 47; Linafelt and Beal, *Ruth and Esther*, 57–58; Lacocque, *Ruth*, 98). The latter reading would suggest a sharp contrast between Boaz and Aristotle's magnanimous man, who prefers to remember his own acts of generosity rather than the benefits he has received from others, and who would be loath to admit to any debt owed to those below him on the social ladder. Cf. the discussion in Milbank, *Theology and Social Theory*, 352.

18. Cf. Trible, *God and the Rhetoric of Sexuality*, 184.

19. Depending on how 4:1–12 is translated—including the question of whether the verb in 4:5 is read as *qānîtâ* ("you must acquire") or *qānîtî* ("I acquire")—it is reasonable to surmise that there may have been some customary basis for the moral obligation that Boaz appears (on one reading, at least) to be urging on the closer relative not to purchase the land without marrying Ruth, and for the way in which the elders and the people (and the closer relative himself) accede to the force of Boaz's assertion. Cf. the discussion in Bush, *Ruth, Esther*, 211–33.

Ruth's proposal in 3:9 and its acceptance by Boaz in verses 10–11 are remarkable not only for the way in which they reach beyond the strict legal requirements of the levirate law and the law for redemption of land; they are also (and much more) remarkable for the fact that the marriage which Ruth proposes and Boaz welcomes is one between an Israelite man and a Moabite woman, despite the ban on Moabites entering the assembly of YHWH in Deuteronomy 23:3–6, the terrifying precedent of Numbers 25, and the explicit ban on intermarriage with the seven nations in the land in Deuteronomy 7:1–6.[20]

While the Deuteronomic bans on Moabites and on intermarriage with the original inhabitants of the land are never explicitly cited in the book of Ruth, the repeated description of Ruth as "the Moabite"[21] makes it clear that this dimension of the story can hardly be ignored. Why, then, are Ruth and Boaz so confident that the bans on Moabites and intermarriage do not apply to them? The implication of the narrative is that Ruth and Boaz's bold assurance regarding the purpose of the Deuteronomic bans and the limitations on their applicability derives from their knowledge of the ḥesed of YHWH—the ḥesed that has been echoed in the kindnesses of Ruth, appealed to by Ruth and Naomi, and experienced and imitated by Boaz. A law designed to safeguard the loyal love of Israel to YHWH and enact judgment on the cruelties of Moab is hardly to be invoked against a marriage to a woman who has abandoned the gods of Moab and made Israel's God her own, who has demonstrated a gracious fidelity that unmistakably reflects the covenant-making and covenant-keeping kindness of YHWH, and who—together with her widowed mother-in-law—has cast herself, in desperate need, upon the mercy of YHWH and his people.[22]

The final chapter of the book publicly confirms the rightness of this judgment (in keeping with Boaz's forecast in 3:11). The mutual understanding of Ruth and Boaz, grounded in and informed by the core Israelite confession of YHWH as "abounding in ḥesed" (Exod. 34:6), is endorsed by the people and the elders of

20. As a Moabite, of course, Ruth was not a member of one of the seven nations, but Ezra 9:1–2, 11–12 demonstrates the possibility of a reading that applies the Deut. 7:3 commandment more broadly.

21. Six times in all, in 1:22; 2:2, 6, 21; 4:5, 10.

22. The moral of the story is not that we should consider ourselves at liberty to improve on the morality of the biblical authors in light of the more sophisticated attitudes of our own times; it is, rather, that we should interpret and apply the various commandments given by God to Israel in light of the particular contexts and situations that they envisage, their place within the larger story of God's dealings with the nation, and the revelation of God's character and purposes that that story and its climax in Christ make known. Cf. the comments and cautions offered by Daniel Doriani and Kevin Vanhoozer in response to the "redemptive-movement" hermeneutic of William Webb, in Meadors, *Moving beyond the Bible*, 255–70.

the city. Their blessing in 4:11–12 further confirms the fittingness of the marriage by locating it in the larger story of YHWH's dealings with his people, invoking the typological correspondence between the childless Moabite widow Ruth and the childless Canaanite widow Tamar (and perhaps, also, hinting at the correspondence between the righteous desperation of Tamar's schemes that led to the conception of Perez, and the schemes of Naomi that led to the conception of Obed). In verse 13, YHWH answers the prayers for blessing by permitting Ruth to conceive (after a ten-year-long childless marriage in Moab). The women of the town offer up praises to God, in verses 14–15, in language that gently but emphatically reverses the way Naomi had earlier interpreted her own story in 1:20–21.[23] Finally, in verses 17–22, the narrator adds his own voice to this chorus of confirmation, reminding his readers of what he and they—blessed with a retrospective view—already know: that this precarious narrative of exile and return, emptiness and filling, is to be read as a chapter in the story of how the family line of Perez continued all the way down to "Jesse, the father of David."

Virtue, Love, and Hermeneutics

What the book of Ruth suggests, one might conclude, is that the proper interpretation of Torah is not simply a matter of the skillful application of objective principles of scientific jurisprudence. Rightly reading the law and knowing how to interpret its implications for the shaping of one's conduct requires love, courage, generosity, and humility—to this extent, the book strongly confirms the claims made by the proponents of virtue hermeneutics.

But the moral universe in which those readerly virtues flourish—and in which they can be understood as the equal possession of a destitute, widowed, Moabite *'ēšet ḥayil* ("woman of noble character") and a wealthy, landowning, Israelite *'îš gibbôr ḥayil*—is far more expansive than the universe presupposed in Aristotle's *Nicomachean Ethics*. The love, courage, generosity, and humility that contribute to right interpretation in the book of Ruth depend on a larger vision of the kindness of YHWH, manifested in the story of his dealings with his people. The generous reader is not merely a person who understands the public honor accorded to the virtue of generosity, but a person who understands himself or herself as a recipient of the generosity of God; the courageous reader does not simply navigate the channel between rashness and timidity, but interprets and acts with a boldness that is invited and sustained by God's favor and faithfulness.

23. Cf. Trible, *God and the Rhetoric of Sexuality*, 193–94.

And the social matrix in which the story of God's kindness is remembered and reechoed is one that requires something much more complicated and beautiful than the small circle of wealthy, freeborn, virtuous men which Aristotle imagines as necessary to safeguard the flourishing of good character.[24] The "radical and controversial . . . kindness"[25] that is enacted in the book of Ruth comes about as the commandments of YHWH and the story of his ways are read together by rich and poor, men and women, outsiders and insiders, full and empty, as their lives intersect within the community of God's people and under his sovereign hand. Good Bible reading, in our own time no less than in the time of the book of Ruth's original readers, flourishes in communities shaped by the remembrance and extension of the saving kindness of God; and good Bible reading, in turn, generates and grows such communities. That is a virtuous circle indeed!

---

24. See especially Aristotle, *Nicomachean Ethics* 8.3; the discussion of friendship and character in Hauerwas and Pinches, *Christians among the Virtues*, 31–51; and the comments on openness to outsiders in Fowl and Jones, *Reading in Communion*, 110.

25. B. Webb, *Five Festal Garments*, 37.

4

"To Fulfill the Word
of the LORD"

1–2 Chronicles and the Hermeneutics of History

After History

History is precious. We can gain some sense of just how precious it is by trying
to imagine a world without it. Perhaps the most memorable attempt in modern
literature to perform that feat is George Orwell's novel *1984*: in the dystopic
world that Orwell imagines, history (as a series of events) has not stopped hap-
pening, but the *writing* of history, as a careful, critical discipline aimed at creating
a true, durable, and meaningful account of the past, has been systematically
extinguished. The novel's hero, Winston Smith, spends his days at the ironically
named Ministry of Truth, working in tandem with the Records Department to
adjust and improve the past, consigning all its inconvenient facts to the furnace
and rewriting it to suit the needs of the Party: "Day by day and almost minute
by minute the past was brought up to date. . . . All history was a palimpsest,
scraped clean and re-inscribed exactly as often as was necessary."[1]

Of course, systematic incineration and rewriting is not the only way in
which historical consciousness can be extinguished. Aldous Huxley's *Brave
New World* imagines a future in which history has been obliterated no less

---

1. Orwell, *Nineteen Eighty-Four*, 47.

effectively—"whisked away" like so much dust—but by very different means. In
Huxley's version of the future, history has been not so much burned and rewritten as rendered redundant and withdrawn from circulation—locked away in the
studies of the elite and driven out of the minds of the majority by an intoxicat-
ing fog of pleasures and distractions.[2] Either way, the imagined consequence is
frightening. A civilization that has burned or locked away its history is a thin,
shallow, foolish civilization, pathetically vulnerable to deceit and propaganda.

While all history is important, biblical history has (or ought to have) a
unique importance for Christian faith and understanding. The importance of
biblical history in the Christian understanding of God and the world can be
gauged, albeit crudely, by the proportion of Scripture given over to the "historical books," as they have traditionally been categorized; added together, and
not counting the narrative sections of the Pentateuch, the prophets, and the
New Testament letters, they make up nearly one-third of the Old Testament
and more than one-half of the New. Learning how to read biblical history
is no small part of learning how to read the Bible, and the quiet neglect that
biblical history suffers in much contemporary Christianity—crowded out by
the triple tyranny of the relevant, the efficient, and the eudaemonic—only
makes the task more difficult and more urgent.

Chronicles as History and Interpretation

If we are to look in the canon for a place to begin our apprenticeship as interpreters of biblical history, the two books of the Chronicler—which present
themselves as both history and interpretation—are an obvious candidate.[3]

The books of the Chronicler are themselves a history: after an extended
genealogical introduction, they narrate the story of the Davidic dynasty and the
temple of Jerusalem, from the death of Saul to the edict of Cyrus decreeing the
return of the exiles and the rebuilding of the temple. Along the way these books
frequently refer to the sources of information on which they draw ("records
. . . from ancient times," as the author puts it in 1 Chron. 4:22), implying both
a claim that their author is transmitting testimony and tradition rather than
fabricating pious fictions, and an admission that he is selecting from a larger
pool of information the material that is relevant to his themes and purposes.[4]

2. Huxley, *Brave New World*, 29.
3. In speaking of the "Chronicler" as the "author" of these books, I am not intending to
rule out the possibility that the books of 1–2 Chronicles, in their final form, were the work of
multiple authors, editors, and compilers.
4. For arguments in favor of reading Chronicles as history, see Japhet, "Chronicles: A History"; Rainey, "Chronicler and His Sources."

It is possible, as some have argued, that the close correspondences in content and wording between 1–2 Chronicles and the books of 1–2 Samuel and 1–2 Kings (Samuel-Kings) derive solely from the fact that both histories depend on a common source.[5] Most commentators, however, opt for the simpler explanation and argue that the Chronicler is most likely using Samuel-Kings as one of his sources[6] and writing a new account of the history of the Jerusalem temple and monarchy to address the needs of his own time, after the return from exile and the rebuilding of the temple. His purpose in doing so does not appear to be to displace the earlier history of Samuel-Kings and consign it to the incinerator. Despite the wide scope of his work, stretching all the way from Adam to Cyrus, much of what he writes (in both the genealogies of 1 Chron. 1–9 and the narratives that make up the remainder of 1–2 Chronicles) makes sense only if his readers are already familiar with the larger, messier account in the Pentateuch and the books of the Former Prophets.[7] His own account, it seems, is designed to sit alongside them, interpreting and extending them, not to render them redundant.

If so, then 1–2 Chronicles are not only biblical history but *interpreted* biblical history and therefore of particular relevance to the topic of this chapter. Like all histories, they interpret events and sources, telling a story of their own about the past. But at the same time, through the way in which they retell the story told in the earlier, biblical history of Samuel-Kings, they interpret a written text that (for us, at least, whatever its status may have been at the time of the Chronicler) belongs among the canonical Scriptures. In drawing on sources outside Samuel-Kings and extending, editing, and supplementing the story that those books tell, 1–2 Chronicles go beyond the boundaries of mere "interpretation" (on any definition of that word) and far beyond the narrower boundaries of pure "exegesis."[8] But there is still an irreducible interpretive dimension to their work, and one that is carried out with creativity, care, and manifest, deliberate intention; 1–2 Chronicles offer a reading

5. E.g., Auld, "What Was the Main Source?"

6. The discovery of the Qumran versions of the text of the books of Samuel (4QSam[a, b, c]), which are in some cases closer to 1–2 Chronicles and LXX 1–2 Samuel than to the MT, has lent strong support to the argument that the version of Samuel-Kings used by the Chronicler was not necessarily the same as the MT version of those books.

7. E.g., the fragmentary references to Saul's reign in 1 Chron. 5, 9, 10 (without any introduction, any account of his accession to the throne or any summation of his reign, beyond the brief mention of his disobedience in 10:13), the reference to "Michal daughter of Saul" in 1 Chron. 15:29 (which makes sense only if readers know that she is David's wife), and the references to Ahab in 2 Chron. 18, 21, 22 (which imply the assumption that the reader is aware of the stories about Ahab in 1–2 Kings).

8. This last point is rightly stressed in Williamson, "History," 32–33. See also Ackroyd, "Chronicler as Exegete," 23.

of Samuel-Kings that places the story told in those books within the larger
story of God's dealings with Israel and the world (going all the way back to
Adam and reaching forward to the time of the Chronicler and his readers),
and interprets it in the light of the law and the prophets—the Chronicler's
work adds up to nothing less than "[an] attempt to interpret the Old Testament from beginning to end."[9] For our purposes, three brief case studies will
illustrate the Chronicler's interpretive approach to the biblical history that
he read in Samuel-Kings.

David (1 Chron. 11–29)

The account of David's reign in 1 Chronicles 11–29 differs markedly from the
version in 1–2 Samuel. On the one hand, the Chronicler omits almost entirely
1–2 Samuel's lengthy and absorbing account of David's rise from obscurity, his
apprenticeship under Saul, the years of banishment from Saul's court, and the
protracted process by which he consolidated power after Saul's death, along
with the affair with Bathsheba, the murder of Uriah, and most of the other
dark and scandalous events of David's reign.[10] On the other hand (principally
in 1 Chron. 22–29), the Chronicler adds to the story an enormous quantity of
material about David's preparing for Solomon his son to build the temple and
assembling the various divisions of priests and Levites to oversee its liturgy.

In the middle, in chapter 21, the Chronicler places his account of the event
he presents as David's great sin—his arrogant project (incited, according to
the Chronicler, by Satan)[11] of commanding a census of all Israel to determine
the number of his fighting men. By omitting the reference in 2 Samuel 24:1 to
YHWH as the one who "incited" David to take the census, by strengthening
the references to Joab's opposition to the project (1 Chron. 21:3, 6; cf. 2 Sam.
24:3, 8), and by making it clear that David repented only after YHWH had
punished the nation (1 Chron. 21:7; cf. 2 Sam. 24:10), the Chronicler sharpens
the emphasis on David's culpability. This tendency can also be seen in David's
own words to YHWH in 2 Chronicles 1:17, which (even more emphatically
than the corresponding speech in 2 Sam. 24:17) lay the blame for the events
on the shoulders of David and David alone.[12] Having confessed his sin and
pleaded on behalf of the nation and having seen YHWH relent and stay the

---

9. Selman, 1 Chronicles, 42.

10. The Chronicler's occasional, passing references to these events (e.g., in 1 Chron. 3:5;
11:2; 12:1, 19, 29; 14:3–4) suggest that he is not seeking to obliterate their memory but that
they are peripheral to his own interests.

11. Or perhaps by a human śāṭān, i.e., adversary; cf. Japhet, I & II Chronicles, 373–75.

12. Cf. Knoppers, "Images of David," 455–61.

hand of the destroying angel, David is commanded in the closing verses of the chapter to secure the threshing floor of Araunah the Jebusite as a site on which to build an altar and offer up prayers and sacrifices; at the start of the following chapter he announces that this is to become the new location for the house of YHWH.

Throughout the Chronicler's account of David and his kingdom, the language used highlights the parallels and connections between these events and the earlier events narrated in the Pentateuch: the "destroying angel" of 1 Chronicles 21:15, for example, is described in language taken from Exodus 12:23, and the "fire from heaven" in 1 Chronicles 21:26 recalls the fire that fell upon Aaron's sacrifice at the commencement of his priestly ministry (Lev. 9:24).[13] Second, the words of the narrator are echoes of the language of the psalms (e.g., Ps. 136:1 in 1 Chron. 16:41), and the Chronicler's accounts of David's prayers and praises include large slabs of material common to the Psalter (e.g., the praises that David commands for Asaph and his associates to sing in 1 Chron. 16:8–36; cf. Pss. 96; 105; 106) and include brief phrases paralleled in the psalms (e.g., 1 Chron. 29:15; cf. Pss. 39:12; 102:11). Third, and crucially, the Chronicler's account highlights the role of the words of the prophets in the history of David and its aftermath, particularly emphasizing the significance of the covenant promises given to David through Nathan (1 Chron. 17:1–15). The promises and conditions of the Davidic covenant are recalled not only as a template for obedience in the initial context of Solomon's commissioning and temple building (cf. 1 Chron. 22:6–13; 28:2–10; 2 Chron. 6:4–11, 14–17) but also as a call to repentance and hope in the later context of the fallen fortunes of his successors (e.g., 2 Chron. 13:5, 8; 21:7; 23:3; 36:23).

The story of David's reign, as told in 1–2 Samuel, is thus not simply duplicated in 1–2 Chronicles, or supplemented with a few miscellaneous *paraleipomena* ("things left on the side," as the books' title in the LXX implies); it is, instead, taken up as the subject of a careful, purposeful, interpretive retelling, in the light of the subsequent history of Israel and the broader context of the Law, the Prophets, and the Psalms. The overall effect is a portrayal of David that is (as Steven Tuell has argued) "not so much idealized as *focused*, narrowly and precisely."[14] The Chronicler's David is an example not of perfection but of penitence, and his penitence is directly tied to the role that he plays in establishing Jerusalem as the center point of all Israel's future worship; his story functions for its readers in the Chronicler's day as a call to repentance, worship, and hope, and as a lens through which

13. Cf. Selman, *1 Chronicles*, 40.
14. Tuell, *First and Second Chronicles*, 43 (emphasis original).

the whole message of the Law, the Prophets, and the Psalms can be refracted into the readers' situation.

Manasseh (2 Chron. 33)

Another striking variation on the content and emphases of Samuel-Kings can be found in the account of Manasseh's reign that the Chronicler presents in 2 Chronicles 33. Samuel-Kings portrays Manasseh with an unremitting negativity: he did evil in the eyes of YHWH, imitating the worst practices of the Amorites and of Ahab the king of Israel. He was the one who led the people of Judah astray, so that they outdid the evil of the nations whom YHWH had driven out before them, and it was in response to the idolatry and bloodshed of his reign that YHWH pronounced his terrible sentence of destruction in 2 Kings 21:10–14.

In 2 Chronicles 33, the depiction of Manasseh commences in much the same manner as the account in 2 Kings 21; the description of his sins in 2 Chronicles 33:1–9 reproduces almost verbatim the description in 2 Kings 21:1–9, and where the description departs from the wording of the original—for example, in referring to "Baals and Asherah poles" (plural), and "children" (plural) sacrificed in the fire—the changes have the effect of painting an already black picture even blacker. In verses 10–17, however, the account takes a dramatically different turn. While 2 Kings 21 emphasizes the divine sentence of future destruction, the Chronicler's account refers only briefly to that divine message (v. 10, where it is presented, by implication, more as a warning than as a fixed decree) and then immediately speaks of a judgment that fell on Manasseh and the people in his own lifetime, which involved his being bound in shackles and led by the nose to Babylon. In response to that judgment, the Chronicler tells us, Manasseh humbled himself.[15] He entreated the favor of YHWH and was brought back to Jerusalem, where he rebuilt the walls of the city, purged it of foreign gods, and restored the worship of the temple (vv. 11–17).

The closing verses of the account claim that the whole story of Manasseh—not only the account of his sins but also "his prayer . . . and the words the seers spoke to him in the name of the LORD . . . and how God was moved by his entreaty"—is derived not from the theological imagination of the Chronicler but from ancient sources: "the annals of the kings of Israel" and "the records of the seers."[16] Nevertheless, it is not difficult to see how the details that the

15. The narrator's language recalls the promise given in 2 Chron. 7:14–16, which was also quoted earlier in the chapter, in v. 4.
16. The former of these sources, while speaking of "the kings of Israel," is presumably referring to the same document as the one named in 2 Kings 21:17 as "the annals of the kings

Chronicler has retained from 2 Kings and added from his other sources fit with the overall emphases of the larger story he is telling.

Like David, the Chronicler's Manasseh becomes an example of repentance and restoration, and the Babylonian location of his captivity (a surprising detail, given that it was the Assyrians, not the Babylonians, who were the imperial overlords in his time) suggests an obvious connection with the later story of the exile and restoration of the whole nation. Like David, too, he modeled a *worshiping* repentance, which involved giving energetic attention to the temple cult in Jerusalem, offering up sacrifices (in his case, fellowship offerings and thank offerings, after his restoration), and attempting to call the nation back to exclusive devotion to YHWH.

Josiah (2 Chron. 34–35)

If the Chronicler's account of the reign of Manasseh introduces a note of repentance and restoration into a story that was, in its earlier telling in 2 Kings, relentlessly focused on sin and judgment, his account of the reign of Josiah pulls in the other direction, adding into the original story a crucial episode recounting Josiah's failure to heed a word from YHWH and connecting it with the tragic events that led to his death.

The Chronicler's Josiah, like the Josiah of 2 Kings, is certainly not without repentance. When the book of the law is discovered and read to him, he tears his robes and sends his servants to inquire of YHWH. The message that comes back to him is one of mercy: the nation will indeed be judged, in keeping with the covenant curses, but YHWH also assures him: "Because your heart was responsive and you humbled yourself before God when you heard what he spoke against this place and its people, and because you humbled yourself before me and tore your robes and wept in my presence, I have heard you. . . . Your eyes will not see all the disaster I am going to bring on this place and on those who live here" (2 Chron. 34:27–28). And as with David and Manasseh before him, Josiah's repentance and restoration are expressed in the cultic life of the nation: having renewed the covenant and purged the land of idols, Josiah goes on in 2 Chronicles 35:1–19 to preside over an enormous and lavish Passover celebration, the like of which has never been seen in Israel.

The lengthy and loving detail with which the Chronicler recounts Josiah's Passover celebrations significantly expands on the minimalist account in

of Judah"; for the Chronicler, it seems, it was important to emphasize that "Judah was still an integral part of Israel in its full sense" and that—after the fall of Samaria—it carried sole responsibility for bearing the mantle of "Israel." Cf. Williamson, *Israel in the Books of Chronicles*, 106, 128.

2 Kings 23:21–23, but his version of the disaster that ensues in the remainder of the chapter differs even more strikingly from the way in which it is presented in 2 Kings. On the one hand, the account in 2 Chronicles 35 does not include the glowing summation of Josiah's reign that 2 Kings 23:25 offers, or the reminder in the following verse that not even Josiah's reforms could avert the inexorable sentence of destruction hanging over the nation because of Manasseh's sins. On the other hand, it adds to the story a series of lengthy expansions on the account of Josiah's death, which the original version in 2 Kings 23 presents as a terse, tragic, two-verse postscript after the concluding formula in 2 Kings 23:28. The Chronicler, unlike the author of 2 Kings, tells us that Josiah decides to go into battle against Pharaoh Necho despite a message from Pharaoh assuring Josiah that he had no quarrel with him and warning him of divine destruction if he opposed God by engaging in battle; according to the Chronicler's version, Josiah died because "he would not listen to what Necho had said at God's command but went out to fight him on the plain of Megiddo" (2 Chron. 35:22).

The Chronicler clearly did not intend by this addition to blacken Josiah's name or to evacuate the pathos from the story of his death—the Chronicler's version goes on to recount the laments of "all Judah and Jerusalem," including the prophet Jeremiah, for Josiah, and to emphasize "his acts of devotion in accordance with what is written in the law of the LORD" in the concluding summary of his reign. The account does, however, tragically emphasize the importance of heeding the word of YHWH—even when it comes on the lips of Pharaoh—and underline the fact that YHWH's dealings with the nation for its collective response to his word do not obliterate the significance of the various responses that individuals make to what they hear from him. Here, as elsewhere in 1–2 Chronicles (most obviously in 2 Chron. 24–32), the words of Ezekiel 18 about individual response and accountability echo loudly in the subtext of the story.[17]

How to Read Biblical History

The interpretive task that the Chronicler was performing is by no means identical to the task we perform when we are interpreting Old Testament history. He read the story of the temple and the kings of Judah from a different vantage point in salvation history and with access to sources and traditions that we have no access to, and the account that he wrote under the inspiration of the

17. Cf. Selman, *1 Chronicles*, 41–42.

Spirit functions with a kind of authority among the people of God that our books and sermons can never have. Nevertheless, even when those differences have been taken into account, we can learn much from the Chronicler about how to read a biblical history.

Historically

First—and at the risk of stating the obvious—the Chronicler's use of Samuel-Kings offers precedent and support for the validity of reading biblical history *historically*, that is, for making use of the texts of biblical history as a source, alongside others, to attempt to reconstruct the events of the past and their relationship to one another. The kind of questions that a historian asks are not the only questions to ask in reading a biblical history, but they are legitimate ones; and if we fail to ask them, we fail to take seriously the claims of the text about the action of God in the real lives of men and women, families and nations.

Intertextually

But the historian's questions are not the only questions to ask in interpreting a biblical history, and the parallel sources of extrabiblical evidence, to which the historian looks for comparison and contextualization, are not the only texts to which the biblical histories are to be related. The multitude of echoes and citations from the Law, the Prophets, and the Writings that the Chronicler evokes in retelling the story in Samuel-Kings remind us of the importance of reading biblical history intertextually and (ultimately) canonically; biblical history is to be read by God's people not only for its function as testimony about events in the history of the world but also for the way in which it functions in the canonical economy of divine, covenantal communication.

Read in that context, the various and particular stories of God's saving and judging involvement in the life of his people need to be interpreted in relation to the prior and subsequent speech and action of God. The actions of the story's human characters are to be evaluated in relation to the law of God, the patterns of divine and human action that are held out in Scripture as exemplary (for good or for bad), and the expressions of divine purpose that the human characters' actions serve or oppose. Thus, the Chronicler (like the author[s] of Samuel-Kings before him) constantly assesses the actions of the kings in his story by the way in which they conform, or fail to conform, to the pattern established by "the decrees and laws that the LORD gave to Moses for Israel" (1 Chron. 22:13; cf. 1 Chron. 29:19; 2 Chron. 7:17, 19; 33:8; 34:31) and by the positive and negative examples of their forebears (e.g., 2 Chron. 33:2–3, 22–23; 34:2). The consequences of their actions, likewise, are understood not in terms of a set of impersonal, mechanistic laws of causation but in terms of the purposes and promises of God (e.g., 2 Chron. 33:7–8, 12–13; cf. 2 Chron. 7:12–18, 36–39).

Similarly, the various possible functions of the historical narratives are to be discerned not solely by examining the events themselves, to which they testify, but also by pondering the warnings, commandments, proverbs, or promises that those narratives might be read as dramatizing, reinforcing, qualifying, or problematizing. The Chronicler's account of the reigns of Jotham, Ahaz, and Hezekiah, for example, in 2 Chronicles 27–32, functions (by the selectivity with which he includes or omits events and the language with which he narrates them) as a kind of historical illustration of the scenarios depicted in Ezekiel 18:1–20, suggesting that the accounts of Manasseh, Amon, and Josiah in the following chapters be read in relation to the same prophetic schema.[18]

Typologically

One key dimension of this intertextual reading of biblical history is the discernment of typological correspondences between the various events and characters in the story.[19] Because of the genealogical connection between past and present, brought to the foreground in 1 Chronicles 1–9, and the unity and consistency of God's ways and plans, as they are made known throughout 1–2 Chronicles in the recollections of the books of the law and the words of the prophets, particular events and characters can be understood in relation to one another, in patterns of recurrence and correspondence; within the Chronicler's account of Israel's history, typology "serves as a cross-reference from one incident to another, inviting the reader to draw parallels and conclusions that go beyond the immediate statement of the text."[20]

This sort of typological reading necessarily involves a certain amount of selectivity and stylization. The Chronicler omits almost all of the details of the story of Saul, for example, to allow a clear and narrow focus on the fact that he was "unfaithful . . . and did not keep the word of the LORD" (1 Chron. 10:13), anticipating the later unfaithfulness and rebellion of the whole nation and its various kings (e.g., 1 Chron. 5:25; 9:1; 2 Chron. 28:19; 29:19; 33:19). The account of David's reign, too, is told in such a way as to highlight his function as a type

18. Cf. ibid., 41.
19. Cf. Hahn, *Kingdom of God*, 6–9.
20. Williamson, "Eschatology in Chronicles," 21.

of the repentant king and the sponsor of faithful worship,[21] omitting much of the material that might obscure or distract from this focus. The Chronicler's recasting of the story of Manasseh shows how the model of David's repentance shapes the telling of the repentance and restoration of his descendant; it also, incidentally, highlights the selectivity of the earlier narration in 2 Kings, in which (by omitting the material on Manasseh's repentance that the Chronicler later includes) the writer chooses to present Manasseh as a type-figure of impiety.[22]

Eschatologically

The interpretation of Samuel-Kings in 1–2 Chronicles is not only one that discerns a coherent unity and patterns of typological correspondence within the story; it is also one that reads the events of David's reign and its aftermath eschatologically, as part of a story that is open to the future and to be read with hope in the coming fulfillment of YHWH's promises to his people.

The subject of eschatology in 1–2 Chronicles has often been debated. According to many interpreters, the view of history in 1–2 Chronicles is profoundly non-eschatological, and the history of Israel is presented as having reached a satisfactory (if somewhat underwhelming) conclusion in the postexilic restoration of Jerusalem as a province of the Persian Empire and a hierocratic cult-center.[23] There are, however, good reasons to reject this interpretation of 1–2 Chronicles. The contexts in which the Chronicler recalls the Davidic covenant (e.g., 2 Chron. 21:7; 23:3) do not suggest that he understands its fulfillment as having been completed in the reign of Solomon or obliterated by the faithlessness of Israel's kings, or that he interprets the "house" the covenant speaks of as referring one-dimensionally to the Jerusalem temple and not (also) to the dynasty of David's descendants.[24] And the Jerusalem cult that is celebrated within the Chronicler's account does not simply endorse the hierocratic status quo but anticipates the glorious future in which Israel will be fully delivered and the praises of God will be joined by all the nations (cf. 1 Chron. 16:23–36).[25] For the Chronicler, the history of

21. The multiple echoes of Exodus and Leviticus in the account of David's preparations for the temple and its worship point back to Moses and Aaron as earlier type-figures to whom David himself is being compared.
22. Abadie, "From the Impious Manasseh," 90.
23. See especially the survey of non-eschatological interpretations of 1–2 Chronicles in Kelly, *Retribution and Eschatology*, 137–47.
24. Note also the genealogy of 1 Chron. 3:17–24, which traces the line of Davidides down from "Jehoiachin the captive" to the present (or recent past) of the Chronicler's readers.
25. Cf. the arguments for an eschatological reading of 1–2 Chronicles in Kelly, *Retribution and Eschatology*, 156–85.

Israel is an unfinished history, and there is reason in the promises of God and in his steadfast love to hope for a coming salvation that gloriously eclipses the measure of fulfillment to be found in the edict of Cyrus with which the final chapter closes.

Repentantly

The strong notes of hope that are sounded in 1–2 Chronicles do not drown out the urgency of the book's call to repentance. The Chronicler tells the history of David's house in a way that highlights its function as a solemn reminder that God restores the penitent and destroys the impenitent. The writer conveys this message partly through the programmatic prayers and oracles of prophets and kings (e.g., 2 Chron. 6:14–42; 30:6–9; 34:23–28), along with the words of YHWH spoken directly to Solomon in a vision (2 Chron. 7:13–16), and partly through the positive and negative examples of David and his successors. There is still a place in the theology of the Chronicler for deferred judgment and collective accumulation of guilt (e.g., 2 Chron. 34:28; 36:15–19),[26] and for unconditional divine purposes of blessing and salvation (e.g., 1 Chron. 16:13–14, 25–27; 2 Chron. 21:7), but this larger, longer-term perspective is complemented by a closer, more immediate perspective on the dealings of YHWH with individual kings and generations, who repent (or fail to repent) in response to his word.

Doxologically

Finally, the form and content of the Chronicler's retelling of the story of David and his successors model the importance of interpreting biblical history (and, for that matter, all history and all created reality) doxologically. The focus of 1–2 Chronicles on the temple and the cult reminds readers that Israel was created for the praises of YHWH and that his judgments and deliverances are to be responded to with prayer and thanksgiving. The psalms that are sung and cited and echoed again and again throughout the Chronicler's history connect the past events which the books narrate with the present worship of the psalms' readers—the familiar words of the Psalter reecho in the narrative, so that the history's readers, like the psalms' original address-ees, find themselves summoned to "remember the wonders he has done, his miracles, and the judgments he pronounced" (1 Chron. 16:12).[27] The refrain of Chronicles (recurring in 1 Chron. 16:41; 2 Chron. 5:13; 7:3, 6; 20:21) itself

26. Contra Japhet, *I & II Chronicles*, 44.
27. Cf. Nielsen, "Whose Song of Praise?," 334–35.

echoes Psalm 136:1: "Give thanks to the Lord, for he is good. His love endures forever." And the closing words of the Chronicler's David (coming hard on the heels of his sober echoes of Pss. 39:12; 102:11 in 1 Chron. 29:15) summon the people to praise: "Then David said to the whole assembly, 'Praise the Lord your God.' So they all praised the Lord, the God of their fathers; they bowed down, prostrating themselves before the Lord and the king" (1 Chron. 29:20). Here, as elsewhere in the work of the Chronicler, past and present, history and liturgy, converge and summon the reader to respond to God in prostrate humility and joyful praise.

❈5❈

"More Than for Hidden Treasure"

Proverbs, Job, and the Hermeneutics of Wisdom

Not an Easy Book

Reading the Bible is not easy. Hard work can be involved in reading any book well, but the Bible poses some particular difficulties for Christian interpreters. First, as a book about the God whom it presents in its opening pages as the creator of all things, it has implications for how we are to understand the whole shape and purpose of created existence; all its small and messy particulars are connected, one way or another, with the great universal questions of life. Second, hand in hand with that, the Bible is given to us not only to inform our understanding but to guide our steps. For both of these reasons, the task of understanding the Bible is, for us, inextricably connected with the task of understanding the whole world, including the immediate circumstances in which we must choose our paths and make sense of our experiences. Third and finally, we read the Bible as a book that is not just *about* God but *from* God, as the chief vehicle for the authoritative self-communication of the God with whom we are in covenant relationship; if we struggle to understand or to believe what it says, then our difficulties are not only intellectual but emotional, existential, and spiritual. To interpret the Bible is to interpret the universe, and to wrestle with the Bible is to wrestle with God.

"As for Hidden Treasure" (Prov. 2:4): Proverbs and the Getting of Wisdom

The interconnections between interpreting Scripture and interpreting all of life (and the challenges involved in both tasks) are hinted at in the opening chapters of Proverbs and return as a theme later in the book (particularly ch. 28).

The prologue of Proverbs (chs. 1–9) functions hermeneutically, inviting the reader to pursue wisdom and providing a depiction of wisdom's purposes and benefits that prepares the way for the sayings and admonitions of chapters 10–29 and the poetry and instruction in chapters 30–31.[1] More than that, the book's opening verses claim that wisdom itself, as taught in the collection that follows, functions hermeneutically:

> The proverbs of Solomon son of David, king of Israel:
>
>> for gaining wisdom and instruction;
>>> for understanding words of insight;
>> for receiving instruction in prudent behavior,
>>> doing what is right and just and fair;
>> for giving prudence to those who are simple,
>>> knowledge and discretion to the young—
>> let the wise listen and add to their learning,
>>> and let the discerning get guidance—
>> for understanding proverbs and parables,
>>> the sayings and riddles of the wise. (1:1–6)

That is, a kind of interpretive circle is involved in getting wisdom. Wisdom is required for "understanding words of insight . . . proverbs and parables, the sayings and riddles of the wise," and wisdom is, in turn, provided by "the proverbs of Solomon son of David, king of Israel," as collected within the book. But traveling the circle is not a matter of a single, quick, and easy loop of enlightenment: the same wisdom that offers "prudence to those who are simple, knowledge and discretion to the young," also invites the wise to "listen and add to their learning," and the discerning to "get guidance." The journey toward wisdom is, it seems, a long, slow spiral.

---

1. Cf. Van Leeuwen, "Proverbs," 173; Longman, *Proverbs*, 61.

Within that slow, spiraling advance toward wisdom and understanding, wisdom is gained by (and required for) not only the interpretation of texts but also the interpretation of experiences and observations. The student of wisdom is encouraged not only to sit in the study, poring over collections of the sayings of the wise, but also to look out the lattice window at the doings on the street (Prov. 7:6–27), or to spend some time outdoors watching ants (6:6–8). Without this sort of comprehensive education in wisdom, the sayings and exhortations collected in wisdom's textbooks are liable to be misread and misapplied; those who are "discerning" and have "found knowledge" are able to see how the words of wisdom's mouth are "right" and "upright" (8:8–9), but in the mouth of a fool, a proverb is like "the useless legs of one who is lame" or (worse) "a thornbush in a drunkard's hand" (26:7, 9).

This interconnection between the wise interpretation of proverbial wisdom and the wise interpretation of persons and circumstances derives, in part, from the nature of proverbs as generalizations from experience—an aspect of the nature of proverbs that is frankly admitted in the collection (e.g., 26:4–5). The ability to decide, or instinctively to recognize, whether a given situation is one in which a fool must be answered according to his folly (so that he does not become wise in his own eyes) or one in which a fool must *not* be answered according to his folly (so that one does not become a fool like him) requires something more than just verbal recall and comprehension of the relevant proverbs: "One must not only know the proverbs but also be able to read the people and the circumstance to know which applies. Proverbs otherwise are useless or even dangerous."[2]

For this reason, among others, the prologue of Proverbs depicts the path toward wisdom as an arduous and costly one:

> If you call out for insight
>   and cry aloud for understanding,
> and if you look for it as for silver
>   and search for it as for hidden treasure,
> then you will understand the fear of the LORD
>   and find the knowledge of God. (2:3–5)

> The beginning of wisdom is this: Get wisdom.
>   Though it cost all you have, get understanding. (4:7)

Those who think that wisdom can be bought cheaply and mastered quickly, like a textbook purchased and crammed the night before an examination,

---

2. Longman, *Proverbs*, 31. Cf. Van Leeuwen, "Proverbs," 173.

have only themselves to blame if it malfunctions spectacularly when their mastery of it is put to the test.

"Proverbs of Ashes": Job and the Limits of Wisdom

One such example of the malfunctioning of proverbial wisdom can be found in the counsel that Job's friends offer him in the three long cycles of debate that make up the core of the book. We cannot for certain say whether the book of Job is an interpretation of the final form of the canonical book of Proverbs, but the debate which it contains is certainly constructed as one in which Job's friends present themselves as mouthpieces of proverbial wisdom. The lacerations they inflict as they circle around him in their wearisome iterations of debate and accusation vividly demonstrate the damage that can be done by "a thornbush in a drunkard's hand."

Job's "Friends" Explain

The function of Job's friends as self-appointed wisdom-teachers is most obvious in Eliphaz, the first to reply to Job's complaint.[3] From the start, his speech is permeated with allusions to the language of the proverbs. He begins politely: Job's piety (*yir'ātĕkā*; more literally, his "fear") should be his confidence (Job 4:6; cf. Prov. 3:26; 14:26), and he should take comfort from the fact that—as Eliphaz's own observations have confirmed—"those who plow evil and those who sow trouble reap it" (Job 4:8; cf. Prov. 22:8). As his tone toward Job darkens and becomes more hostile, Eliphaz's ideas and language continue to draw upon proverbial sources, implicitly depicting Job as among the common herd of fools who "die without wisdom" (Job 4:21; cf. Prov. 5:23; 10:21) and urging him not to "despise the discipline of the Almighty" (Job 5:17; cf. Prov. 3:11–12); only if he submits to the discipline of his sufferings will he "come to the grave in full vigor, like sheaves gathered in season" (Job 5:26; cf. Prov. 10:27). When Job continues in obdurate resistance to his wise counsel, Eliphaz vents his frustration. "Are you the first man ever born?" he asks Job, exasperated. "Were you brought forth before the hills? Do you listen in on God's council? Do you have a monopoly on wisdom?" (Job 15:7–8; cf. Prov. 8:25). Job must "submit to God" by submitting to Eliphaz, since the torrent of proverbial wisdom proceeding from Eliphaz's mouth is really coming from the mouth of God (Job 22:21–22; cf. Prov. 2:6).

3. Cf. Clines, *Job 21–37*, 563–64; Alter, *Art of Biblical Poetry*, 89.

While Eliphaz takes the lead in appropriating the wisdom tradition and applying it to Job's predicament, Job's other friends are not far behind. Thus, Bildad commences by appealing to "the former generation" and "their ancestors" (Job 8:8) in support of his warning to Job about the perishing hopes of the godless (Job 8:13; cf. Prov. 10:28; 11:7) and his assurance, "If you are pure and upright, even now he will . . . restore you to your prosperous state" (Job 8:6). The note of warning returns as the dominant theme of his second speech, where the theme is once again cast in the language of the proverbs: exasperated, he reminds Job forcibly and at length of the way in which "the lamp of a wicked man is snuffed out" (Job 18:5–6; cf. Prov. 13:9; 20:20; 24:20) so that his "memory . . . perishes," and "he has no name in the land" (Job 18:17; cf. Prov. 10:7). Zophar, similarly, draws on the language of the proverbs to express his frustration at Job's recalcitrance: the very first line of his opening speech is a rhetorical question about whether "all these words" (*rōb děbārîm*) can be allowed to go unanswered (Job 11:2; cf. Prov. 10:19). When Elihu's turn finally comes around, he is quick to point out that "it is not only the old who are wise, not only the aged who understand what is right" (Job 32:9), but the content of his speeches draws as heavily as the other friends' did on the language and ideas of the proverbs, including a reminder of the retributive workings of providence (Job 34:11; cf. Prov. 24:12) and the self-destructive nature of human wickedness (Job 35:6–8; cf. Prov. 8:36; 9:12).

Job Replies

Job's speeches in reply to his friends make it clear that they are not the only ones who are familiar with the language and ideas of the proverbs. At times he is happy to paint with the palette of colors that the proverbs provide him with, using the language of the proverbs to lament the way in which his own situation has come to resemble proverbial wisdom's frightening depictions of the fate of the wicked (e.g., Job 3:25; cf. Prov. 10:24), or to express his nostalgic remembrance of the days when his own life reflected the proverbs' depiction of the blessed life of the righteous (Job 29:4; cf. Prov. 3:32), or of the esteem and influence of a king among his people (Job 29:23–25; cf. Prov. 16:15). At other times, though, the extremity of his experiences and the rawness of his emotions demand that he paint with much darker shades and more violent brushstrokes, throwing the relative mildness of the proverbs that he echoes and parodies into sharp relief. If Lemuel's mother prescribes beer and wine as opiates for the anguished (Prov. 31:6), Job insists on pushing the issue further, asking why "those in misery" and "the bitter of soul" are given life and light at all (Job 3:20). If the prologue to Proverbs urges the reader to "look

for [wisdom] as for silver and search for it as for hidden treasure" (Prov. 2:4),
Job asks about the predicament of those whose misery is such that they long
simply for oblivion—"who long for death that does not come, who search
for it more than for hidden treasure" (Job 3:21).

Throughout his speeches, Job rails against the assumption of his friends
that his situation is a sign of divine displeasure and evidence of a secret sin,
and he sharply questions the way in which his friends have taken the generalizations of the proverbs as if they were easily verified universal laws. If
Bildad is happy to echo the sentiments of the proverbs about the snuffing out
of the lamp of the wicked, wielding them against Job as menacing warnings
(Job 18:5–6; cf. Prov. 13:9; 20:20; 24:20), Job insists in return that Bildad take
an honest look at all the situations around him in which the wicked are *not*
snuffed out but "spend their years in prosperity and go down to the grave in
peace" (Job 21:13):

> How often is the lamp of the wicked snuffed out?
> How often does calamity come upon them,
> the fate God allots in his anger? (21:17)

Goaded by the intensity of his sufferings and the smug assumptions of his
friends, Job asks sharply worded questions about the frequency with which
the generalizations of Proverbs come true and their adequacy as an answer to
the phenomena of (unpunished) evil and (undeserved) suffering. But this does
not mean that he rejects the message of the proverbs outright.[4] If his friends
wield proverbs as weapons against him, Job himself is capable of wielding
proverbs as weapons against his friends (e.g., Job 13:5; cf. Prov. 17:28), and
in the defense that he mounts against his friends' accusations, he frequently
appeals to the ethical and theological axioms that the proverbs teach: he is as
happy as they are to affirm that God sees all (Job 31:4; cf. Prov. 5:21; 15:3),
that God is the one who drew the boundaries of the universe (Job 26:10; cf.
Prov. 8:29), that rich and poor are formed in the womb by the same hands
(Job 31:15; cf. Prov. 22:2), that the concealment of sin is pernicious and futile
(Job 31:33, 40; cf. Prov. 28:13), and that sin itself is a culpable crime and a
destructive fire (Job 31:9–12; cf. Prov. 6:27–29). His screams of protest against

4. Thus, Lindsay Wilson argues that "the book of Job protests not against Proverbs, but
against a fossilized misunderstanding of retribution that had misrepresented the mainstream
wisdom tradition of Proverbs. . . . Job's friends are examples of those who have ignored the
flexibility of Proverbs . . . and simply read off a person's spiritual state from their circumstances."
Wilson, "Job," 153, citing Holmgren, "Barking Dogs Never Bite." Similarly, McCann, "Wisdom's
Dilemma," 19–20; Van Leeuwen, "Wealth and Poverty"; Longman, *Proverbs*, 62.

the contradictions that he sees between the phenomena he has witnessed and experienced and the ordered world depicted in the proverbs affirm, in their own way, the rightness of that order in his eyes.

While the proverbial sayings echoed by Job and his friends are a prominent and important focus of the interpretive tug-of-war between them, they are not the only biblical traditions that are echoed and interpreted in the book. Job's anguished wrestling with the proverbs and the way in which his friends have interpreted and applied them is accompanied by a string of additional intertextual references to the Torah (e.g., the echoes of the Decalogue in Job 31) and—even more prominently—to the Psalms and the Prophets.[5]

The echoes of the proverbs in Job's speeches (and in those of his friends) are generally in the context of speech *about* God, but Job's echoes of the Psalms and Prophets are frequently in the context of speech *directed to* God,[6] or of complaints and imprecations that seem to be intended for God to hear. The pattern is set in the searing complaint with which Job breaks the silence in chapter 3, which opens with an extended echo of Jeremiah's laments (cf. Jer. 10:18; 15:10; 20:14–18) and closes with a string of echoes from the Psalms (e.g., Pss. 6:6; 22:1, 14; 38:8; 42:3–4; 80:5). In chapter 7, Job addresses God more directly, culminating in the bitter psalm-parody that closes the chapter:

> What is mankind that you make so much of them,
>   that you give them so much attention,
> that you examine them every morning
>   and test them every moment?
> Will you never look away from me,
>   or let me alone even for an instant?
> . . . .
> Why do you not pardon my offenses
>   and forgive my sins?
> For I will soon lie down in the dust;
>   you will search for me, but I will be no more. (Job 7:17–19, 21)

In parodying the Psalms, Job is not rejecting them but using them as a vehicle for his protests against the arguments of his friends and against the sufferings that God has permitted or inflicted. Will Kynes makes the point well in relation to Job's parody of Psalm 8 in verses 17–19:

5. For brief summaries of the main arguments in favor of taking the intertextual parallels as instances of Job alluding to and parodying the relevant texts in Psalms, Isaiah, and Jeremiah (and not vice versa), see Kynes, "Job and Isaiah 40–55"; Kynes, *My Psalm Has Turned into Weeping*, 49–54; Greenstein, "Jeremiah as an Inspiration."

6. Cf. Janzen, "'He Makes Peace in His High Heaven,'" 257.

If Job were to reject the psalm, he would agree with Eliphaz [in 15:14–16; cf. also Bildad in 25:5–6] that humanity is unworthy of God's loving care, and would thereby undercut his case against God by removing the basis for arguing that God should treat him differently. It is more reasonable to argue that, though Job parodies the psalm, he does so not to ridicule or reject it but to appeal more powerfully to the paradigm of divine-human relationship it presents in order to strengthen his appeal against God. If his parody creates a "rivalry" between the view of God he depicts and the one given in the psalm, it is a contest he hopes the psalm will win.[7]

A similar point can be made in relation to Job's echoes of the language of the Prophets (e.g., the multiple echoes of Isa. 40–55 in Job 9:2–12; 12:7–25).[8] Kynes comments:

> Though each of the affirmations from Isaiah 40–55 [echoed in Job's parodies] may carry comfort when placed in the soteriological context of that text, all carry a threatening aspect, which Job experiences and complains of and his friends use to silence his complaints. And yet, if Job does indeed use his parodies to try and convince God to change God's ways, then the positive side of that imagery must inform his interpretations as well. He feels the threat but longs for the comfort Isaiah 40–55 offers, and so this text is an ideal resource to express his frustration.[9]

Job's anguished parodies and echoes of the Psalms and Prophets underline the high expectations of God that deepen and intensify his interaction with biblical wisdom and its interpreters. He expects of God not merely the distant supervision of a neat system of retributive equilibrium, but a personal concern expressed in visiting, redeeming, and comforting his people. The God he believes in (and against whom he protests so vehemently) is an interventionist God, however much the logic and timing of his interventions may remain shrouded in mystery.

YHWH Judges

In the end—and it is a long time coming—Job gets his wish. YHWH himself speaks to Job from out of the storm and (after Job's reply and repentance in 42:1–6 and his intercession for his friends in 42:7–9) acts to restore his

7. Kynes, "Job and Isaiah 40–55," 100. In a sense, of course, human "unworth[iness] of God's loving care" is also implied by the rhetorical questions of Ps. 8:3–4, but the view of humanity implied by the way in which the question is posed and answered in the psalm is still strikingly different from the contemptuous perspective that Job's friends articulate in Job 15:14–16; 25:5–6.
8. Cf. Isa. 40:26, 28; 43:13; 44:24; 45:9 (echoed in Job 9:2–12); Isa. 40:23; 41:20 (echoed in Job 12:7–25).
9. Kynes, "Job and Isaiah 40–55," 105.

fortunes and return comfort and blessing to his house. While YHWH's words to Job include an element of stern rebuke (e.g., 38:2; 40:2), they certainly do not endorse his friends' approach (cf. 42:7). Neither should Job's "repentance" in 42:6 be taken as a concession to their accusations; read against the background of YHWH's speeches in chapters 38–41 and Job's responses in 40:4–5 and 42:1–5, Job's words of repentance in 42:6 (however they are to be translated)[10] function not as a vindication of the wisdom of his friends but as an admission of the limits of his own—a concession: "I spoke of things I did not understand" (42:3; cf. 38:2).

The divine verdict on the "wisdom" of Job's friends is searingly negative: "I am angry with you and your two friends," YHWH says to Eliphaz, "because you have not spoken the truth about me, as my servant Job has" (42:7). However accurately Job's friends may have reiterated the content of proverbial wisdom, the way in which they have related it to Job's circumstances makes it clear that they have understood neither it nor him. Their failure results in part from their unwillingness to listen to Job (6:26), to weigh his sufferings (cf. 6:1–3), and to deal honestly with the evidence before their eyes (13:7–8); it is compounded by their inability to see the gap between the total knowledge and perfect wisdom possessed by God and the true but partial insights granted to humans.

It is this gap that is the principal theme of YHWH's speeches in chapters 38–41, with their vertigo-inducing tour of the majestic, mysterious, uncontrollable, and inexplicable corners of the creation:

> God's poetry enables Job to glimpse beyond his human plight an immense world of power and beauty and awesome warring forces. This world is permeated with God's ordering concern, but as the vividness of the verse makes clear, it presents to the human eye a welter of contradictions, dizzying variety, energies and entities that [humans] cannot take in. . . . If Job in his first response to the Lord (40:2, 4–5) merely confessed that he could not hope to contend with God and would henceforth hold his peace, in his second response (42:2–6), after the conclusion of the second divine speech, he humbly admits that he has been presumptuous, has in fact "obscured counsel" about things he did not understand.[11]

This perspective, implied so powerfully by the vivid imagery and the barrage of rhetorical questions in chapters 38–41, is anticipated explicitly in the wisdom poem of chapter 28. For all the brilliance and daring of human

---

10. Cf. the discussion of the various options in Clines, *Job 38–42*, 1218–23.

11. Alter, *Art of Biblical Poetry*, 110. Clines comments similarly: "It was the theology of wild animals that convinced him, the inexplicability of whole tracts of the natural order, the apparent meaninglessness of creatures useless to humankind but unquestionably created by God nevertheless. Now he knows that was a paradigm for all knowledge of God." Clines, *Job 1–20*, xlvii.

exploration and discovery, wisdom (of the kind possessed by God) remains inaccessible to human enquiry—"hidden from the eyes of every living thing, concealed even from the birds in the sky" (28:21). God alone, whose eyes see everything, knows the way to it. True human wisdom is not a God's-eye view of the universe but an engagement with the mysteries of the world from a stance of humility and integrity: "The fear of the Lord—that is wisdom, and to shun evil is understanding" (28:28).

Getting Wisdom

The book of Job is not, in the end, a negation of wisdom but a reaffirmation of it. The quest for wisdom is a worthy quest; wisdom is, indeed, worth more than gold and silver, precious beyond rubies (Job 28:15–19; cf. Prov. 3:14–15; 8:10–11, 19; 16:16; 20:15; 31:10). But the wisdom that is affirmed by the book of Job as accessible to humans is a humble, limited wisdom that fears God and shuns evil.

The crucial formulation at the end of Job 28 (v. 28, above) must not be read in isolation from the concentric circles of debate and narrative that surround it. "The fear of the LORD" is, after all, a traditional motif in the language of Israelite wisdom, and even in the book of Job it can hardly be said to emerge at the end of chapter 28 as a brand-new idea. From the very first paragraphs of the opening speech of Eliphaz, Job's friends have had no trouble in speaking of "fear of God" (ESV 4:6; 15:4; 22:4; NIV "piety") as the basic stance which they are commending to Job, echoing the language and sentiments of the proverbs. But it is Job, not they, who perceives how much more that "the fear of the LORD" involves than the sententious recitation of biblical texts (cf. 6:14–15), and it is Job who is described from the start as living a life that practices that kind of fear (1:1, 8–9).

While the Job of the story's epilogue (42:7–17) can be appealed to as an encouragement to Christian hope (cf. James 5:11b), it is the Job of the previous forty-one chapters who must serve as an example of Christian wisdom. The fear of the Lord that is at the heart of the interpretive wisdom taught by the book of Job is not a magic key that unlocks the meaning of difficult texts or resolves the tensions between Scripture and experience. It does not transform the task of Bible reading into an easy or painless exercise; nor does it amount to an unquestioning willingness to swallow all the traditional nostrums of conventional piety. What it amounts to, this side of the resurrection, is a way of living with unanswered questions that still bears true witness, keeps faith with friends, maintains integrity, and hopes in God. On wisdom of that sort the book of Job pronounces a solemn and sincere blessing.

❧6❧

"The Word of the LORD Came"

Zechariah and the Hermeneutics of Prophecy

Prophecy and Posterity

Predictive prophecy is a precarious genre to write in for anyone who hopes to attain some sort of literary posterity. On the one hand, if a prophecy is fulfilled, a question arises about its continuing usefulness: once the prediction has come true, what reason is there to preserve it, any more than one would think of preserving yesterday's weather forecast or last week's horoscope? On the other hand, if a prediction continues to hang in the air, unfulfilled, a question begins to arise about its plausibility: how long should we persevere in hope (or fear), holding onto the prophecy and giving it the benefit of the doubt?

In the cultures of the ancient Near East, prophecy of various types was not uncommon, and written versions of the prophets' words could sometimes be produced, either to convey those words to their immediately intended recipient or to preserve them for posterity in the royal archives.[1] Nothing, however, exactly parallels the kind of collection of prophetic scrolls that emerged among the people of Israel and Judah and came to make up such a substantial

---

1. See especially van der Toorn, "From the Oral"; Nissinen, "Spoken, Written, Quoted, and Invented."

proportion of the Hebrew Bible.[2] Something about the nature of Hebrew prophecy and the role that prophecy played in the economy of God's dealings with his people generated the impetus for retaining and collecting prophetic oracles in written form on a large scale and including them in the canon of Scripture. If we are to learn how to read the Bible, no small part of that task will be learning what to do with the vast collections of prophecies that it contains.

Not all prophecy is prediction, of course: there is good sense in the frequently quoted maxim about biblical prophecy being as much a matter of "forthtelling" as it is a matter of "foretelling."[3] But the foretelling dimension of prophecy is still unmistakably present and prominent in all of the books of the Old Testament prophets and poses particular hermeneutical challenges for Christian readers of the Bible. What are we to make of all its various predictions—fulfilled, partially fulfilled, and as-yet-unfulfilled? How are we to relate them to the history of ancient Israel, the story of Jesus, our own circumstances (local and global, personal and political), and the coming future of the world?[4] What does it mean for prophecy to be *Scripture*—written down, preserved, collected, and authoritative in the life of the people of God?

A full and final answer to these questions cannot, of course, be given without taking into account the New Testament's testimony to Jesus as Scripture's fulfillment; it is there that we are taught what it means for prophecy to be *Christian* Scripture. But the beginnings of an answer can be sketched from what we find within the prophetic books themselves, in the ways that they appropriate the spoken words of the prophets and relate them to the world of their readers. In this chapter I will focus on how the book of Zechariah appropriates prophecy as Scripture.[5]

"Do Not Be like Your Ancestors" (Zech. 1:4): Zechariah and the Earlier Prophets

The book of Zechariah opens with an introductory paragraph that immediately directs our attention toward the longevity of prophecy and its

2. Cf. Edelman, "From Prophets to Prophetic Books," 29; Ben Zvi, "Concept of Prophetic Books," 73.

3. E.g., the comments in Boda, *Haggai, Zechariah*, 49–50.

4. Cf. Mark Boda's comments on debates over the meaning and fulfillment of biblical prophecies about Israel as symptomatic of "major hermeneutical conflict in the church's interpretation of the Old Testament in general and prophecy in particular." Ibid., 51.

5. In speaking of the "appropriation" of prophecy as Scripture I have in mind not the *divine* appropriation of human discourse, helpful as that concept is—cf. Wolterstorff, *Divine Discourse*, 51–53—but rather the closely related *human* processes involved in the collection, redaction, and canonical reception of the prophets' words within the books that bear their names.

continuing function as Scripture beyond the time of its fulfillment.[6] The
opening verses represent Zechariah as delivering to the people of his day
a word from YHWH about their ancestors and about the words that the
prophets spoke to them:

> In the eighth month of the second year of Darius, the word of the LORD came
> to the prophet Zechariah son of Berekiah, the son of Iddo: "The LORD was very
> angry with your ancestors. Therefore tell the people: This is what the LORD
> Almighty says: 'Return to me,' declares the LORD Almighty, 'and I will return
> to you,' says the LORD Almighty. Do not be like your ancestors, to whom the
> earlier prophets proclaimed: This is what the LORD Almighty says: 'Turn from
> your evil ways and your evil practices.' But they would not listen or pay attention
> to me, declares the LORD. Where are your ancestors now? And the prophets, do
> they live forever? But did not my words and my decrees, which I commanded
> my servants the prophets, overtake your ancestors?" (1:1–6a)

The punctuation of the English translations struggles to accommodate
the extent to which the opening paragraph nests quotations within quotations. In verse 4, for example, at the center of the paragraph, the narrator is
telling the book's readers about what YHWH said to Zechariah about what
Zechariah was to say to the people about what YHWH had to say about what
the earlier prophets had said about what YHWH had to say to the ancestors
of the people of Zechariah's time. The ancestors to whom those words were
originally spoken have long since died, as verse 5 reminds us, and the same is
true of the prophets who were their contemporaries.[7] But the words that were
spoken to them live on, reverberating solemnly as a quotation of a quotation
of a quotation of a quotation of a quotation, embedded at the center of the
introduction to the book.

The particular prophetic words quoted in verse 4 are not presented as
the exact words of one particular prophet on one particular occasion; they
are a synopsis of the message of "the earlier prophets" to "your ancestors."
If we go looking for an original oracle that might have served as a kind of
template for the wording of the summary, the closest candidate that emerges
is Jeremiah 25:5—a verse in which Jeremiah himself is, in turn, summarizing
the message that was spoken by YHWH to the people of Judah through "all

---

6. See especially Seitz, *Prophecy and Hermeneutics*, 342–43; Wenzel, *Reading Zechariah*,
55–86.

7. The force of the contrast in v. 5 is much the same, regardless of whether "the prophets"
refers to the same true prophets referred to in v. 4 (as most commentators assume), or (as Michael
Stead argues) refers to the false prophets who encouraged the people in their rejection of the
true prophets' message; cf. Stead, *Intertextuality of Zechariah 1–8*, 82–83.

his servants the prophets," "again and again" (v. 4).[8] For the readers of the book of Zechariah, the prophets are to be remembered not for a patchwork of disparate predictions and occasional exhortations but for a single message, consistently and repeatedly proclaimed to their ancestors.

That message, as Zechariah 1:4 summarizes it, is not, strictly speaking, a prediction but an exhortation: "Turn from your evil ways and your evil practices." The context, however, with its reminder of how that word overtook their ancestors (v. 6a), requires us to read the exhortations of the earlier prophets in close connection with their warnings and predictions, particularly their predictions of the exile that would come upon Judah if they did not "turn" as they were being urged to.[9] The book of Zechariah recalls the dreadful events of the exile for its readers in order to underline the weightiness of YHWH's word and to support the exhortation of verse 4a: "Do not be like your ancestors."

In this respect, the reminder of the prophetic message given in Zechariah 1:4 functions somewhat differently from the reminder in Jeremiah 25:5. In the latter, an oracle spoken before the exile recalls the long history of Judah's failure to heed the prophets (including within that history the twenty-three years of Jeremiah's own unheeded prophecies) as a prelude to the apparently inexorable sentence of Jeremiah 25:8–11.[10] In the former, in the exile's aftermath, Zechariah urges his listeners not to replicate the impenitence of their ancestors, and the book reminds readers in verse 6b of the repentance that resulted: "Then they repented and said, 'The LORD Almighty has done to us what our ways and practices deserve, just as he determined to do.'"

The prophetic message, unheeded in its day, lives on in the life of God's people as an abiding manifestation of the word of YHWH. Its warnings, now fully realized in the events of the exile, are to be remembered as evidence of the justice of YHWH and his steadfastness of purpose; its exhortations retain their currency and are to be received with added seriousness in the light of the

8. See especially the discussions in ibid., 30–32; Wenzel, *Reading Zechariah*, 61–85.

9. Similarly, in Jer. 25, the summary of the prophets' message in vv. 5–6 links their exhortation, "Turn . . . from your evil ways and your evil practices," to a promise that if the nation did turn they would be allowed to remain in the land; the fact that this exhortation went unheeded then forms the basis for Jeremiah's prediction of a seventy-year exile that will come upon the people as an outpouring of YHWH's wrath.

10. On the apparent inexorability of the sentence of exile Jeremiah was given to pronounce, see Jer. 4:28; 7:16, 27 (though note also the implicit warning of Jer. 18:5–10 against universalizing such texts into a hermeneutic of prophetic fatalism). Of course, for readers of the *book* of Jeremiah, upon whom the threatened sentence of exile has already descended, the reminder of the unheeded exhortations in 25:5–7 and the now-fulfilled judgment oracle in 25:8–11 implicitly encourages them to heed the book's exhortations and trust its promises as they bear upon the readers' new situation.

fulfillment of the warnings that accompanied them. In the covenant history of the nation, the response of Zechariah's hearers simultaneously expresses their solidarity with their ancestors (remembering the judgment of the exile as an event that fell upon "us," in accordance with "what our ways and practices deserve") and radically reverses it. Unlike the ancestors, they take the word to heart and respond to it with repentance.

For all its seriousness, therefore, the brief narrative in the opening paragraph of Zechariah commences the book on a note of hope and possibility. The message of the prophets lives on, and the story of its rejection in previous generations is not forgotten; but the repentance of Zechariah's hearers models a response to the message that is a genuinely new development in the nation's story.

The chapters that follow are full of echoes from the earlier prophets' promises of restoration after exile—promises now brought tantalizingly close by the completion of the "seventy years" of Babylonian exile (1:12; cf. Jer. 25:12–14) and the contrition and repentance offered by the people in 1:6. In the account of Zechariah's first night vision, for example, the climactic oracle in 1:14–17 is saturated with allusions to Isaiah 54:1–12; the third night vision (narrated in 2:1–13 [MT 2:5–17]) and the fourth night vision (narrated in 3:1–10) draw heavily on the language and imagery of Ezekiel 40–48; and the sign-act narrated in 6:9–15 echoes the promises of a "righteous branch" and a restored priesthood in Jeremiah 23:1–8; 33:14–26.[11]

By chapter 7, however, when the message of the earlier prophets is recalled a second time (in a passage that narrates an incident in Zechariah's ministry which is described as having occurred just two years after the incident narrated in the opening chapter), the authenticity and durability of the communal repentance described in 1:6 have begun to look somewhat less secure. A delegation from Bethel asks the priests in Jerusalem whether the fast of the fifth month is to be continued, now that "so many years" have passed since Jerusalem's fall and the city has begun to be rebuilt. The oracle that Zechariah is given as a reply to the question asks rhetorically, "When you fasted and mourned in the fifth and seventh months for the past seventy years, was it really for me that you fasted?" (7:5), and goes on to remind the people of the

---

11. See especially Stead, "Sustained Allusion," 156–63; Stead, *Intertextuality of Zechariah 1–8*, 130–31, 248. Examples from chs. 1–3 include (1) the way in which the language of "angry," "mercy," "overflow" (literally, "spread out"), and "rebuilt" in Zech. 1:14–17 draws on similar language in Isa. 54:1–12, (2) the way in which the vision of the man with the measuring line in Zech. 2 echoes the language and imagery of Ezek. 40, and (3) the way in which the promises to Joshua in Zech. 3:7 ("you will . . . have charge of my courts, and I will give you a place among these standing there") echo the language of Ezek. 40–46 regarding the courts of the rebuilt temple and the priests who have charge of them (e.g., Ezek. 40:44–46; 44:16–19).

words spoken by the earlier prophets "when Jerusalem and its surrounding towns were at rest and prosperous, and the Negev and the western foothills were settled" (v. 7). The summary of the earlier prophets' message that follows in verses 8–10, describing the sort of repentance that would have been required for the exile to have been averted, focuses on the ethical demands of the covenant, drawing heavily on the temple sermon of Jeremiah 7: "This is what the LORD Almighty said: 'Administer true justice; show mercy and compassion to one another. Do not oppress the widow or the fatherless, the foreigner or the poor. Do not plot evil against each other.'"

The allusion to Jeremiah's temple sermon (and a string of other similar preexilic prophecies) in Zechariah 7 makes a powerful and important point about how the restoration promises, refracted through the night visions of chapters 1–6, are to be interpreted: if the restoration after exile that was promised by the prophets was conditional on the nation's repentance, then the community of Zechariah's day needs to know that the repentance required of them involves more than an expression of contrition and a commitment to rebuild the temple.[12] The glorious promises of chapter 8, likewise, are accompanied by a string of imperatives that stress the ethical transformation required if the people of Judah and Jerusalem are to experience the fullness of the promised restoration: "'These are the things you are to do: Speak the truth to each other, and render true and sound judgment in your courts; do not plot evil against each other, and do not love to swear falsely. I hate all this,' declares the LORD" (8:16–17).

The discussion in chapter 7 is also recalled by the promise in 8:19 of a reversal of the exilic fasts—not just the fast of the fifth month (cf. 7:3) or the fasts of the fifth and seventh months (7:5) but the fasts of the "fourth, fifth, seventh, and tenth months," and not just a cessation of fasting but a transformation of fasts into joyful festivals. With the promise comes an imperative that also recalls the commands of chapter 7: "Therefore love truth and peace" (cf. 7:9–10). The promised restoration, in other words, is far greater than anything experienced by the remnant of Zechariah's day, but it is conditional on a repentance that goes far deeper than mere temple construction and cultic observance.[13] Mark Boda summarizes the point neatly:

> Zechariah 1:1–6 and 7:1–8:23 draw attention to the message of the earlier prophets in order to emphasize that repentance is essential for the realization of restoration. Zechariah 1:1–6 presents a model of the appropriate response of the community to the ancient message of the prophets as the prophet summarizes

12. Cf. Stead, *Intertextuality of Zechariah 1–8*, 251.
13. Cf. ibid., 235; Childs, *Introduction to the Old Testament*, 484–85.

their message (1:2–6a) and the people respond through repentance and confession of guilt (1:6b). This short pericope shapes our reading of 1:7–6:15, reminding the reader that the comforting message of restoration that follows is given to a penitent community. After this comforting message with its broader agenda of restoration, 7:1–8:23 returns the reader to the initial message and tone of 1:1–6 and reveals that restoration will not be realized unless the entire community renounces the patterns of the past and lives in faithfulness to the covenant. The final picture is one of glorious hope, but this will not be realized until there is a transformation in the behavioral patterns of the community.[14]

The composite picture that emerges from Zechariah 1–8 is a powerful reminder of the continuity and durability of prophecy as Scripture in the life of God's people: the book of Zechariah reminds its readers of the message of Zechariah the prophet, which was in turn an echo and reminder of the preaching of Jeremiah (itself a reminder of the message of "all the prophets"), saying to the nation: "Turn now, each of you, from your evil ways and your evil practices" (Jer. 25:5). The book says to its readers, as Zechariah had said to his hearers: "Do not be like your ancestors."

"Then You Will Know" (Zech. 2:9): Prophecy and Vindication

The appropriation of prophecy as Scripture—as the previous section of this chapter has argued—enables its continuing work of exhortation in the life of the covenant people: the call to repentance that the prophets issued to the people of their own day echoes and reechoes to subsequent generations, with a force amplified by the divine judgments that fulfilled their threats and warnings.

But the commencement of the processes involved in the writing, retention, and collection of prophecy does not wait until all its predictions have been fulfilled. The fleeting glimpses that the prophetic books give us into the earliest stages of this process suggest a willingness of the prophets and their disciples to take risks—both epistemological and political—as a continuation and extension of the risks involved in the prophecies' original proclamation. In Isaiah 8, for example, the "testimony of warning" is to be written down by the prophet himself and "seal[ed] up" among his disciples (8:16, 20); the disciples, like the prophet, will be required to "wait for the LORD, who is hiding his face from the descendants of Jacob" (8:17). Similarly, in the episode narrated in Jeremiah 36, the writing, and rewriting, of the words on the scroll predicting the destruction of the land and the overthrow of Jehoiakim's kingdom take

---

14. Boda, *Haggai, Zechariah*, 41.

place while Jehoiakim is still very much on the throne, ready and waiting to
cut the prophecy into pieces and burn it in the fire.

In Zechariah's case, the epistemological risk involved in appropriating
prophecy as Scripture is captured in the formula the prophet is quoted as at-
taching to his oracles four times in the first eight chapters of the book: "then
you will know that the LORD Almighty has sent me" (2:9, 11; 4:9; 6:15). The
formula is traditional, expressing "the thought of Deuteronomy 21:18 . . .
in the vocabulary of Ezekiel and Jeremiah,"[15] but it performs an important
function, both in the rhetoric of the prophet and in the rhetoric of the book.
When the prophet first proclaims the prophecies, he asks his hearers to take
his claims on trust; they are to receive him on the assumption that he is, as he
has claimed, a messenger of YHWH. Only when his predictions are fulfilled
will that trust (and the prophet himself) be vindicated; it is *"then"* that they
will know that he was sent, as he claimed to be, by YHWH.

By the time the book has been redacted into its final form (and, in all likelihood, by the time the oracles and visions contained in the first half of the book
have been collected and promulgated),[16] at least some of these predictions
have already come to be fulfilled. The hands of Zerubbabel, which laid the
foundation of the temple, have indeed (in fulfillment of the prophecy in 4:9)
completed it. But the full extent of what is promised in the four oracles still
reaches far beyond anything experienced in the early Persian period: however
we interpret the words in 2:8–9 about the punishment of "the nations that
have plundered [them],"[17] and whatever we make of the mysterious sign-act
in 6:9–15,[18] the promised future depicted in 2:10–11 clearly outshines even

15. Stead, *Intertextuality of Zechariah 1–8*, 121. See also the similar expression in Num.
16:28–30.

16. Most commentators argue that Zech. 1–8 was first compiled and promulgated not long
after the date of the superscription in 7:1—"in the fourth year of King Darius" (i.e., 518 BC)—
probably at the time of or very soon after the dedication of the temple in 515 BC. Cf. Boda,
Haggai, Zechariah, 29–30.

17. Mason (*Haggai, Zechariah and Malachi*, 37–39, 43, 61) argues that this prophecy should
be read as a recycled oracle from late in the Babylonian period, foretelling the overthrow of
Babylon by Cyrus. Boda ("Terrifying the Horns," 39–40) argues that the prophecy originates
from the early Persian period and foretells the harsh treatment inflicted on the Babylonian elite
during the early years of Darius. Tollington (*Haggai and Zechariah 1–8*, 219–20) likewise dates
the oracle to the early Persian period, but reads "Babylon" in 2:7 as a reference to any nation
(present or future) that mistreats and plunders Israel.

18. Boda (*Haggai, Zechariah*, 334–43) argues that the "shoot" (*ṣemaḥ*) named in the vision
should be understood as a reference to Zerubbabel and that the events in view in v. 15 are those
of the early Persian period; similarly, Stead, *Intertextuality of Zechariah 1–8*, 143. Curtis (*Up the
Steep and Stony Road*, 145–47), contrastingly, reads *ṣemaḥ* as a reference to a future messianic
figure and sees the events depicted in v. 15 as pointing forward to a future time beyond the era
of Persian domination; similarly, Petterson, *Behold Your King*, 100–120.

the most optimistic account that could be given of the realities of postexilic Jerusalem. Readers of the book can bolster their confidence in the prophet's credentials by recalling the events that have already taken place in fulfillment of his word, but the message of the book as a whole amounts to more than just a call to repentance and a record of prophecy fulfilled; in the as-yet-unfulfilled dimensions of the book's predictive prophecies, its readers are being summoned not only to obedience but to hope—a hope that includes the final vindication of their own decision to put their trust in the prophet and his word.[19]

"I Will Return" (Zech. 8:3): Prophecy and Hope

The function of the book of Zechariah as a call to hope takes on a heightened urgency against the backdrop of the events that stand behind the oracles and sign-acts of chapters 9–14 and the composition of the final form of the book. If the first half of the book reflects a time of restoration and rebuilding, under a leadership whose integrity and legitimacy the prophet vigorously endorses, the book's second half addresses a generation given over to corrupt and worthless shepherds, and anticipates still worse times to come (10:3; 11:4–17).[20] Byron Curtis offers the following summary:

> In Zech 1–8 the author writes in order to bolster a nascent leader and to anticipate a messianic leadership. In Zech 9–11 the author writes to condemn a tyrannical leadership and to anticipate a messianic leadership. In Zech 12–14 the author writes to rebuke the house of David and to anticipate a divine leadership. Thus, in respect to the leadership theme, chs. 9–14 stand partly in continuity with chs. 1–8, and partly in discontinuity.[21]

Within that context, the book preserves the words of Zechariah as a call to patient, enduring hope. The joyful summons of 2:10 ("Shout and be glad, Daughter Zion. For I am coming, and I will live among you") is not only retained in the book's first half but recycled in 9:9, with renewed emphasis and redoubled force:

> Rejoice greatly, Daughter Zion!
> Shout, Daughter Jerusalem!

19. Cf. B. Webb, *Message of Zechariah*, 84.
20. Cf. Stead, *Intertextuality of Zechariah 1–8*, 262–64; Curtis, *Up the Steep and Stony Road*, 3–4; Mason, "Second Zechariah," 26.
21. Curtis, *Up the Steep and Stony Road*, 264.

> See, your king comes to you,
>   righteous and victorious,
> lowly and riding on a donkey,
>   on a colt, the foal of a donkey.
> I will take away the chariots from Ephraim
>   and the warhorses from Jerusalem,
>   and the battle bow will be broken.
> He will proclaim peace to the nations.
>   His rule will extend from sea to sea
>   and from the River to the ends of the earth.
> As for you, because of the blood of my covenant with you,
>   I will free your prisoners from the waterless pit.
> Return to your fortress, you prisoners of hope;
>   even now I announce that I will restore twice as much to you.
>   (9:9–12)

While the language of 9:9 unmistakably echoes 2:10, the scene depicted is not identical; the divine return announced and anticipated in 2:10 is presented in 9:9 as being manifested in the arrival of a (human) "king," one who is "righteous and victorious, lowly and riding on a donkey." The message is still a word of hope—if anything, that note is accentuated—but it is a message of hope being proclaimed to "prisoners" (vv. 11–12), for whom the coming of YHWH means deliverance from the "waterless pit" (v. 11), through a king who is himself the lowly object of divine deliverance.[22]

Like the call to repentance issued by the earlier prophets, Zechariah's promise of divine deliverance is a durable word, resonating in the changed circumstances of the book's final form with a continuing force, a sharpened and expanded reference, and a sober anticipation of the dark and dreadful days between the giving of the promise and its eventual fulfillment.[23] The book as a whole is thus not only a call to return to YHWH but a promise of YHWH's return. The promise of return that is proclaimed by the book as a whole reaches forward far beyond the proximate return in blessing and protection that is promised in 1:3 to the generation of Zechariah's original hearers and conditioned on their communal repentance, to speak of a day of YHWH that is catastrophic, glorious, and certain—a day that will not wait for Israel's repentance but will bring it about (cf. 12:10–13:9), and a day on which YHWH will be not only king in Jerusalem but king over all the earth (cf. 12:1–9; 14:1–21).

22. The expression "righteous and victorious" in v. 9, rendered more literally, is "righteous and delivered [*nôšāʿ*]," implying that the king himself has been delivered by YHWH; cf. Petterson, *Behold Your King*, 139.

23. Cf. Childs, *Introduction to the Old Testament*, 483.

Reading Prophecy as Scripture

What, then, can we learn from the book of Zechariah about what it means to receive prophecy not only as a word from YHWH spoken to a particular people in a particular time but also as *Scripture*, to be written and retained and collected and read as authoritative divine address within the people of God? Three things stand out from what we have seen in this chapter about how Zechariah's preaching appropriates the message of the earlier prophets and how his own prophecies are collected and repromulgated in the book.

First, the book makes an implicit claim about the unity and coherence of the message of the prophets: while it is true that the word of God through the prophets came (in the words of Heb. 1:1) "at many times and in various ways," the book of Zechariah reminds us of how the prophets and their re-dactors understood their many and varied words not as a disparate collection of oracles but as a single tradition echoing and reechoing in the life of the covenant people—the words of "all the prophets," epitomized by Jeremiah, reechoed in the preaching of Zechariah, and repromulgated in the final form of the book.

Second, the book reminds us of the tight integration between "foretelling" and "forthtelling" in the continuing function of prophecy as Scripture; even when the predictive words of the prophet have been fulfilled, they continue to warrant the authenticity of the prophet and amplify the urgency of the message as a perpetual exhortation for the people of God. Prophecy as Scripture does not become law, but it does (like law) serve to instruct and exhort God's people, guiding their steps and forming their character.

Third, and finally, the as-yet-unfulfilled dimensions of prophecy as Scripture (even after the return to the land and the rebuilding of the temple) remind us of the forward-looking nature of the whole Old Testament, as a revelation that points beyond itself to a day when YHWH himself will come and Jeru-salem's king will proclaim peace to the nations. At the same time, the fact that these grand, universal promises remain unconsummated (even this side of the coming of Christ) continues to require of the reader a willingness to embrace risk in receiving the prophets as what they claim to be—messengers of YHWH—looking forward to the day when prophecy will be vindicated completely.

"Everything I Have Commanded You"

Matthew and the Hermeneutics of Obedience

Red Letter Christians

In the spring of 2005, as part of a promotional tour for his new book, *God's Politics*, Jim Wallis sat down for an interview with a Nashville radio presenter:

> "I'm a secular Jewish country-music songwriter and disk jockey," my interviewer on a Nashville radio station said. "But I love your stuff and have been following your book tour." Then he told me he believed we were starting a new movement, but he noticed we hadn't come up with a name for it yet. "I've got an idea for you," he said. "I think you should call yourselves 'The Red Letter Christians.' You know those Bibles that highlight the words of Jesus in red letters? I love the red-letter stuff. The rest I could do without."[1]

And so the embryonic movement of preachers, activists, writers, and theologians received its name. From the beginning, more conservative critics were dubious about the legitimacy of the approach to Scripture implied by the movement's name, arguing that privileging the red letters necessarily takes away

1. Campolo, *Red Letter Christians*, 9.

some of the authority of the black. Stan Guthrie's comments in a *Christianity Today* article published not long after the official launch of the movement are a representative example of such criticisms:

> Though I own several Bibles with the words of Christ printed in red, I've always found the concept a bit iffy. After all, we evangelicals believe in the plenary, or full, inspiration of Scripture, don't we? Setting off Jesus' sayings this way seems to imply that they are more holy than what is printed in ordinary black ink. Sure, Christians understand that Jesus the incarnate Word fulfills the written Word. But if all Scripture is God-breathed, then in principle Jesus' inscripturated statements are no more God's Word to us than are those from Peter, Paul, and Mary—or Ezekiel.[2]

When Tony Campolo published a short book the following year as a manifesto for the movement, he was careful to make it clear that—unlike the enthusiastic Nashville disk jockey—he and his fellow red letter Christians had no desire to "do without" the rest of the Bible: "We affirm the authority of the whole Bible, not just the explicit sayings of Jesus, often found highlighted in red. . . . We are Christians with a very high view of Scripture. The writers of Scripture, we believe, were invaded by the Holy Spirit and were uniquely guided by God as they wrote, providing us with an infallible guide for faith and practice."[3] Nevertheless, he insisted, to be a red letter Christian meant particularly emphasizing Jesus's words and granting them an interpretive priority of some sort in the task of understanding and applying the rest of Scripture: "We emphasize the 'red letters' because we believe that you can only understand the rest of the Bible when you read it from the perspective provided by Christ."[4]

The exact nature of that interpretive priority is not made clear, however, in the rest of the book. In some chapters there are no red letters at all: the chapter on the environment, for example, in which Campolo makes his first foray into the list of specific issues which the book addresses, begins with Genesis 1:26–28 (with an appeal to John Calvin and Ron Sider as interpreters who have seen the implications of those verses for environmental ethics), then launches into the writings of Paul without even alluding to a word from Jesus. "Whenever I preach on the calling of Red Letter Christians to environmentalism," Campolo writes, "I quote from Romans 8:19–22."[5] In other

2. Guthrie, "When Red Is Blue."
3. Campolo, *Red Letter Christians*, 10–11, 23.
4. Ibid., 23.
5. Ibid., 55.

chapters, the words of Jesus are present (e.g., the blessing pronounced on peacemakers in Matt. 5:9 is quoted in the chapter on the Israeli-Palestinian conflict, and Jesus's sharp words in Luke 17:2 [NKJV] about "offend[ing] one of these little ones" are appealed to as the basis for a Christian interest in the economics of education policy[6]), but it is difficult to say how they are functioning as an interpretive lens through which the rest of Scripture is being read. Within the book, the closest Campolo comes to explaining how the red letters guide us in interpreting the black is his claim in the opening chapter that "what differentiates Red Letter Christians from other Christians is our passionate commitment to social justice."[7] Beyond that, the book sheds surprisingly little light on how the hermeneutical stance implied by its title is to be interpreted. If the point is so important as to be the watershed between two different kinds of Christians, then closer and more careful attention is surely warranted.

Matthew and the Hermeneutics of Obedience

The first and most obvious place to turn in our quest to understand how the red letters of Jesus's teaching relate to the black letters of the rest of Scripture is the Gospel of Matthew. The focus of Matthew's Gospel is not, of course, on the political debates that arise within a modern democracy about how the power of a secular state ought to be exercised. But on the broader (and related) questions of the righteousness that Christians ought to seek and the obedience that Christians are called to, the Gospel of Matthew has much to say, with an explicit interest in how Christian obedience and the Christian vision of righteousness ought to be shaped by Scripture and the words of Jesus.

"Everything I Have Commanded You" (Matt. 28:20)

A useful starting point for our inquiry is the closing verses of Matthew, which quote Jesus giving his final commission to the gathered community of his disciples:

> Then Jesus came to them and said, "All authority in heaven and on earth has been given to me. Therefore go and make disciples of all nations, baptizing them in the name of the Father and of the Son and of the Holy Spirit, and teaching them to obey everything I have commanded you. And surely I am with you always, to the very end of the age." (Matt. 28:18–20)

6. Ibid., 71.
7. Ibid., 23.

One of the most striking features of the commission is how it focuses the obedience of Jesus's disciples (present and future) on the commandments that he himself has given to them. Language that the Old Testament uses for the law of Moses ("teaching . . . obey . . . commanded") is applied here to the words of Jesus,[8] in line with the sweeping claim about his authority with which the paragraph commences. A similar authority-claim is implied in Jesus's words elsewhere in the Gospel. In the six famous "antitheses" of Matthew 5, for example, Jesus boldly contrasts "you have heard that it was said . . ." with "but I tell you . . .," and the parable of the two builders with which the Sermon on the Mount concludes dramatically portrays for Jesus's hearers the contrasting outcomes of two different responses to "these words of [his]" (7:24, 26). No wonder, then, that we are told in the following paragraph that "the crowds were amazed at his teaching, because he taught as one who had authority, and not as their teachers of the law" (7:28–29).

Jesus's own authority-claim at the end of Matthew's Gospel is anticipated by the words of God himself in an earlier mountaintop scene, at the center of the Gospel. In this story, like Mark and Luke, Matthew begins by placing Jesus—gloriously transfigured—in company with Moses and Elijah, before singling him out for a special divine endorsement: "This is my Son, whom I love" (17:5b). By the end of the episode, we are told, the disciples "saw no one except Jesus" (17:8). Modern commentators are probably correct to reject as an oversimplification the traditional reading in which Moses and Elijah are taken as representatives of the Law and the Prophets, respectively; Elijah, after all, was not a writing prophet, and the echo of Deuteronomy 18:15b in verse 5c suggests that it is Moses the prophet as much as Moses the lawgiver whose memory is being invoked here.[9] Nevertheless, the narrative clearly implies that Moses, Elijah, and Jesus cannot simply be accommodated alongside each other in "three shelters," as Peter proposes; there is an unparalleled uniqueness to Jesus's identity as the beloved Son, and it is that identity, not merely his function as a "prophet like [Moses]" (Deut. 18:15), that stands behind the command to "listen to him!" (17:5c). The assertion in verse 5b is the Father's confirmation of the confession Peter just made in the preceding episode: "You are the Messiah, the Son of the living God" (16:16); the command in verse 5c is its practical implication: "Listen to him!"

8. See, e.g., Deut. 5–6, especially Deut. 6:1–2, where two of the three terms (and two other terms expressing concepts closely related to the third) all occur within two verses (LXX: *eneteilato* [commanded] . . . *didaxai* [to teach] . . . *poiein* [to do] . . . *phylassesthai* [to keep]).

9. Cf. the discussions in Keener, *Gospel of Matthew*, 438; France, *Gospel of Matthew*, 649. For examples of the traditional interpretation, see Origen, *Commentary on Matthew* 12.38; Augustine, *Sermons on Selected Lessons of the New Testament* 28.2.

The assertion and command uttered by the voice from heaven in Matthew 17:5 (and echoed in Jesus's own assertion and command in Matt. 28:18–20a) are the twin foci around which Matthew arranges the material of his Gospel. At one level, his Gospel is organized as a narrative testimony to the identity and authority of Jesus as the Son of God.[10] But at another level, equally important, the structure of Matthew's Gospel reflects the divine (and dominical) imperative that that authority implies: built into the overarching narrative stand five big blocks of red-letter content (chs. 5–7; 10; 13:1–52; 18; 24–25),[11] each of which is composed (with the partial exceptions of chs. 5–7 and ch. 13) of teaching delivered to the disciples,[12] and followed by a formula along the lines of "when Jesus had finished saying these things" (7:28; 11:1; 13:53; 19:1; 26:1). The bulk and prominence of these five blocks of teaching suggest that Matthew intended not only to narrate Jesus's story but also to preserve and propagate his teachings, so that his disciples might learn and obey them. Evidently, according to the shape and content of Matthew's testimony, the redness of the red letters in his Gospel is of no small significance to Jesus, to Matthew, and to God himself, and ought to be of no small significance to the Gospel's readers.

"Not . . . to Abolish . . . but to Fulfill" (Matt. 5:17)

But what exactly is the nature of that significance? How does Matthew want us to understand the relationship between Jesus's words and the words of Old Testament Scripture (and, for that matter, Matthew's own words as the writer of the Gospel)?

The first part of our answer is that the red letters of Matthew's Gospel can hardly be interpreted as an attempt to wrest authority away from the black. Any notion we might have that Jesus's words could replace or supersede the words of Old Testament Scripture is dispelled as soon as Jesus starts speaking. The very first saying of Jesus recorded in the Gospel (his response in 3:15 when John tries to deter him from undergoing baptism) implicitly appeals

10. See especially the classic account of this dimension of Matthew's editorial arrangement in Kingsbury, *Matthew*, 1–39.

11. Ch. 23 is best read as a speech distinct from chs. 24–25, delivered to a different audience and in a different location; it culminates a two-day cycle of public controversies narrated in 21:12–23:39 and follows neatly after Matthew's reference to the silencing of the Pharisees and Sadducees in 22:46.

12. Chs. 5–7 and ch. 13 are only partial exceptions. In the former, the sermon explicitly commences with a reference to Jesus going up on a mountain and sitting down to teach his disciples (5:1–2), and only at the very end, in 7:28–29, are we told of the presence of the listening crowds; in the latter, the parables are first preached to the crowds and then (in vv. 13–23, 36–52) explained in private to the disciples.

to Scripture. As Jesus embarks on his public ministry as Son and Servant, he justifies the surprising content of what is "proper" for him to do by appealing to the criterion of what is necessary to "fulfill all righteousness"—language that makes best sense, when read within the context of Matthew's Gospel, as referring to the salvation-historical vision of the prophets.[13] The second saying of Jesus recorded in the Gospel directs our attention to Scripture even more explicitly and emphatically: confronted by the tempter in the wilderness, Jesus responds with words from Deuteronomy that place him in dependent solidarity with Israel (and, indeed, with all of humanity) as one who feeds on the words of God. Both in form and in content, Jesus's response to the tempter affirms Scripture's authority and indispensability: "It is written," Jesus declares: "'Man shall not live on bread alone, but on every word that comes from the mouth of God'" (4:4).

The pattern continues across the following chapters. The Beatitudes, for example, with which Jesus's Sermon on the Mount commences (5:1–12), are soaked in recollections of the Scriptures, particularly Isaiah and the Psalms;[14] the implication is that Jesus's hearers should receive the eschatological wisdom of the Sermon not as a brand-new invention but as an extension and completion of the message of the Psalms and the Prophets. This implication becomes explicit in verses 17–19:

> Do not think that I have come to abolish the Law or the Prophets; I have not come to abolish them but to fulfill them. For truly I tell you, until heaven and earth disappear, not the smallest letter, not the least stroke of a pen, will by any means disappear from the Law until everything is accomplished. Therefore anyone who sets aside one of the least of these commands and teaches others accordingly will be called least in the kingdom of heaven, but whoever practices and teaches these commands will be called great in the kingdom of heaven.

It is hard to imagine a stronger claim for the enduring importance of the Law than the language that Jesus uses in verse 18. Interpretations that seek to put a time limit on the assertion by taking "until heaven and earth disappear" and "until everything is accomplished" as references to the death and resurrection of Jesus are strained and unconvincing[15] and fail to offer an adequate account of what is said in the following verse about the continuing role that

---

13. See especially Meier, *Law and History*, 79–80; Hagner, *Matthew 1–13*, 56; France, *Gospel of Matthew*, 120–21.

14. Note especially the echoes of Isa. 61:1–3 in vv. 3–4, Ps. 37:11 in v. 5, and Ps. 24:3–6 in v. 8. Cf. France's comments in *Gospel of Matthew*, 163–64.

15. See, e.g., the attempts to make a case for this reading in Moloney, *Living Voice of the Gospels*, 105; Meier, *Matthew*, 142–48.

"these commands" will play in shaping teaching and practice in the kingdom
of heaven; the same can be said of interpretations that limit Jesus's "fulfillment" of the Law to his own vicarious obedience, offered up to God on our
behalf. But it would also be a mistake to read these verses as simply a static
endorsement of the Law, as if its function and effect continued unchanged by
the coming of Jesus. Given the explicit inclusion of "the Prophets" alongside
"the Law" in verse 17, and the description in 11:13 of "the Prophets and the
Law" as having "prophesied until John," a strong argument can be made that
Jesus's statement about having come to "fulfill" the Law and the Prophets
should be read within the larger pattern of fulfillment language in Matthew's
Gospel, as an eschatological, salvation-historical claim:

> We might then paraphrase Jesus' words here as follows: "Far from wanting to
> set aside the law and the prophets, it is my role to bring into being that to which
> they have pointed forward, to carry them into a new era of fulfillment." On
> this understanding the authority of the law and the prophets is not abolished.
> They remain the authoritative word of God. But their role will no longer be
> the same, now that what they pointed forward to has come, and it will be for
> Jesus' followers to discern in the light of his teaching and practice what is now
> the right way to apply these texts in the new situation which his coming has
> created. From now on it will be the authoritative teaching of Jesus which must
> govern his disciples' understanding and practical application of the law.[16]

"Go and Learn What This Means" (Matt. 9:13)

The immediately following context in the Sermon on the Mount offers six
worked examples of how the authoritative interpretation of Jesus applies the
teachings of the Law to the new situation of his disciples, calling for a new
righteousness that "surpasses that of the Pharisees and teachers of the law"
(5:20). Within the six antitheses of 5:21–48, the authoritative pronouncements
of Jesus ("But I tell you . . .") are not contrasted with the Law of Moses per
se, but with the Law of Moses as cited, interpreted, and expanded by the
Pharisees and the teachers of the law: the counterpart to "but I tell you" is
not "it is written," but rather "you have heard that it was said."

Across the remainder of Matthew's Gospel, Jesus continues to endorse
the enduring currency of the Law and the Prophets, and to speak as their
authoritative interpreter. While the radicalization of the Law's demands that
is evident in the antitheses of chapter 5 is one key dimension of Jesus's teaching on how the Law is to be obeyed in the age of fulfillment, it is not the sum

16. France, *Gospel of Matthew*, 183.

total of his hermeneutic. His interpretation of the Law also insists that it has a focus in the exhortations to love God and neighbor (on which "all the Law and the Prophets" depend; 22:34–40); that some matters in it—such as its calls for justice, mercy, and faith—are "weightier" than others (23:18–24); that its commandments and permissions, given because the people's "hearts were hard," should be read as steps along the path toward the larger purposes that God the lawgiver had in mind "from the beginning," as the creator (19:1–9); and that those who want to interpret it rightly must read it in light of his word, given through Hosea (6:6): "I desire mercy, not sacrifice" (Matt. 9:13; 12:7):

> Jesus' teaching provides a dramatic new hermeneutical filter that necessitates a rereading of everything in the Law in light of the dominant imperative of mercy. In contrast to the scribes and Pharisees, who are said to "tie up heavy burdens, hard to bear, and lay them on the shoulders of others" (23:4), the wisdom taught by Jesus yields a very different reading of Torah.[17]

When Jesus sends his hearers back to the Scriptures, saying, "Go and learn what this means . . ." (9:13), he is both endorsing the continuing authority of Scripture and calling for a new way of reading and applying it—a way that is established and modeled by his own mission "not . . . to call the righteous, but sinners" (9:13b).

The autobiographical reference in 9:13b reminds us that the place occupied by Jesus in the hermeneutics of Matthew's Gospel cannot be confined to his role as the authoritative interpreter of Scripture or to the red letters of his teaching. It is the whole story of his life, not just the content of his teachings, that is to shape the moral vision of his disciples and direct their reading of Scripture:

> Perhaps the most important difference [between the Gospel of Matthew and the Qumran literature] is precisely in the characteristic form of the litera- ture produced by each group. Both produce rulebooks, reinterpretations of scripture, exhortations, apocalypses. From Qumran, however, we have no biography, no "gospel." We do not even know the name of the Righteous Teacher. . . . The person vanishes behind the organization he founded and the interpretations of prophecy and Torah that his followers continued. Not so the Jesus of Matthew. Mark had made his story the "gospel" itself, the proclamation of the eschatological good news. Matthew makes that story part of the grammar of Christian ethics. The commandments are not sepa- rable from the commander, the teachings from the teacher. Discipleship is

17. Hays, *Moral Vision*, 100.

"following" the person identified in the story, who, raised from the dead, goes on leading the community.[18]

For the readers of Matthew's Gospel, the calling of the disciple is not only to live by the teacher's teachings but "to be like the teacher" (10:25)—to ready themselves to endure a fate like the teacher's fate and to find a way (within the changed circumstances of the post-Easter community) to imitate the teacher's conduct.[19] And because the teachings of Jesus, as Matthew preserves them for the readers of his Gospel, come embedded in a message that announces the coming of the kingdom of heaven and in a ministry that enacts its drawing near, obedience to Jesus's teachings and imitation of his example require a life that participates in the kingdom he proclaimed and a heart that seeks that kingdom's consummation above all things.

"New Treasures as Well as Old" (Matt. 13:52)

The obedience that Matthew's Gospel aims to teach its readers is, therefore, an obedience that requires a particular kind of hermeneutical competence. The vision of righteousness that Jesus's disciples are to seek and the obedience they are to enact require interpretive wisdom—the kind of wisdom that is taught by a "teacher of the law who has become a disciple in the kingdom of heaven . . . like the owner of a house who brings out of his storeroom new treasures as well as old" (13:52).[20]

From the very first pages of the Gospel of Matthew, with their constant interleaving of biographical narrative, typological allusions, and scriptural citations, Matthew is teaching a way of reading that enables a wisdom of this sort. The conception of Jesus must be understood in relation to Isaiah's word to Ahaz; Jesus's birth in Bethlehem in light of the prophecy of Micah; his flight to Egypt in light of Hosea's remembrance of the exodus; the murderous rage of Herod in light of the weeping of Rachel, appropriated by Jeremiah as a lament for the exiles of Judah. The pattern, as Craig Keener observes, is both striking and instructive: "Matthew has constructed almost every paragraph following the genealogy and until the Sermon on the Mount around at least one text of Scripture. He thus invites his ideal audience to read Jesus

18. Meeks, *Moral World*, 143.
19. For a long list of instances in which the teaching of Jesus in Matthew's Gospel is echoed or exemplified in his conduct, see Hood, *Imitating God in Christ*, 77–79. For a brief discussion of the hermeneutical implications of the location of 10:24–25 in the unique circumstances of the first disciples' commissioning for their pre-Easter mission to Israel, see Meeks, *Moral World*, 141–42.
20. See especially Witherington, *Matthew*, 6–10, 273–74.

in light of Scripture and Scripture in light of Jesus—to recognize that the person and work of Jesus are central to Scripture's character."[21] Over and over again, from the infancy narrative to the account of Christ's passion and death, Matthew wants us to know that "all this took place to fulfill what the Lord had said through the prophet" (1:22; cf. 2:15, 17, 23; 4:14; 8:17; 12:17; 13:35; 21:4; 26:56; 27:9), so that we might learn to read Scripture, and to understand Christ, accordingly.

The lesson that Matthew is intent on teaching his readers is vital for the kind of project in which we are engaged in this book: apprenticeship to Scripture's self-interpretation may function as a useful *formal* principle for the getting of hermeneutical wisdom, but the *material* principle that ought to determine the quest is not merely intertextual but christological. At the heart of the Bible's self-interpretation is the message of the Scripture-echoing heavenly voice conveyed to us by Matthew at the center of his Gospel: "This is my Son, whom I love; with him I am well pleased."

One key implication of that message is the imperative that immediately follows: "Listen to him!" The red letters of Jesus's teaching do indeed have a special significance for disciples of the Lord Jesus and fulfill a particular function in the economy of Scripture. Christians who think that they can be believers in Jesus without building their lives on his words, or who attempt to read the Scriptures as a timeless, undifferentiated compendium of divine commands, may revere Scripture but can hardly be said to have understood its message: those who faithfully trace the lines of Scripture's black letters must inevitably be led to the place where they become hearers (and doers) of the red.

But the relationship between the black letters and the red is not a one-way street; it is a recursive, reciprocal relationship. The black letters of Old Testament prophecy and apostolic testimony lead us to Jesus and urge us to listen to him; the red letters of Jesus's teaching, in turn, commission and authorize his apostles as heralds of the gospel and send us back to the Old Testament to learn its meaning and its implications afresh in light of his coming. The red letters of Matthew's Gospel are joined to the black in an indispensable, mutually authorizing, and mutually interpretive relationship; what God has joined together no interpreter should attempt to separate.

For evangelicals in our own time, confronted with the claim that we must choose between two different kinds of Christianity—one defined by the red letters of Scripture and the other defined by the black—the Gospel of Matthew provides a timely warning against false dichotomies and needless schisms. It

21. Keener, *Gospel of Matthew*, 81.

reminds "red letter Christians" of the indispensability of the black letters and reminds "black letter Christians" of the centrality of the red (or, more precisely, of the one who speaks them). If we are to learn how to read the Bible rightly and live out a Christian obedience that is full-orbed and authentic, Matthew's Gospel is essential reading.

❦ 8 ❦

"Fulfilled in Your Hearing"

Luke and the Hermeneutics of the Gospel

Which Gospel?

Sooner or later, in a book that aims to offer an explicitly and deliberately evangelical contribution to our understanding of biblical hermeneutics, the time must come to discuss the gospel—both the gospel's role in our interpretation of Scripture and Scripture's role in our comprehension of the gospel. So far in this book the road we have taken toward that discussion has been long and winding—we have deliberately charted a path through Scripture on the assumption that the hermeneutical wisdom we need for life and salvation is to be found not only in the New Testament but also in the Old. But our path has still led toward the gospel, and now the time has come to bring the gospel into center-screen and deliberate focus. (The previous chapter, of course, took us close to that theme, exploring how Matthew's Gospel encourages us to understand the relationship between Jesus's authority and the authority of the Old Testament, and observing his narrative strategy for teaching us to interpret Scripture in light of Christ and Christ in light of Scripture. In this chapter, however, we focus not only on Christ, as the figure at the center of the gospel announcement, but on the gospel itself, as the message announced by and announcing Christ; what is implicit in the previous chapter becomes explicit in this one.)

While evangelicals in our day generally agree that the gospel ought to play a central role in our reading and interpretation of Scripture, there is also an ironic consensus that the meaning of "the gospel"—even (and perhaps especially) among evangelicals—is vigorously contested. Is it a formula for individual salvation? A program for social renewal? An announcement of Jesus's resurrection? An explanation of the meaning of his death? According to one recent writer, "The energy generated by discussions about the gospel points to a general fog of confusion that swirls around it these days. . . . Christians just don't agree on what the gospel is—even Christians who call themselves evangelical."[1] Another writer, Scot McKnight, disagrees energetically with the former writer about the gospel's meaning but agrees nonetheless about the "fog of confusion" that swirls around the term in contemporary evangelical understanding:

> You may think the word gospel . . . is the one thing we do understand. You may think that's the one thing around which there is no fog at all. You may think the gospel is the simple thing, whereas everything else—like politics and eschatology and atonement theory and poverty—cries out for debate. Those issues need to be debated, but we really cannot debate them in a Christian manner until we get the gospel question resolved. I think we've got the gospel wrong, or at least our current understanding is only a pale reflection of the gospel of Jesus and the apostles. We need to go back to the Bible to find the original gospel.[2]

For McKnight, the quest for "the original gospel" includes an exploration of two key relationships: (1) the relationship between the gospel that the apostles preached about Jesus and the gospel that Jesus himself preached; and (2) the relationship between both of these and the story of Israel, which (McKnight insists) stands behind them as the essential interpretive frame within which the gospel of Jesus and the apostles is to be understood. A full and thorough exploration of those two relationships would require a survey of the whole New Testament, but a good place—perhaps the best place—to commence the quest is in the two-volume project of Luke-Acts. Here, within two closely interrelated books by the same biblical writer, we find a sustained, narrative-shaped account of exactly those two relationships. In the remainder of this chapter, we will survey the hermeneutical bridge that Luke built between the story of Israel told in the Scriptures of the Old Testament, the gospel of the kingdom proclaimed by Jesus, and the gospel that the apostles preached to Israel and the nations in Jesus's name.

1. Gilbert, *What Is the Gospel?*, 17.
2. McKnight, *King Jesus Gospel*, 23–24.

The Gospel and Israel's Story

We will begin our survey with the story in Luke 4 of Jesus's visit to Nazareth and the synagogue sermon that he preaches there—an episode with which Luke commences his account of Jesus's public ministry and which serves (as most commentators agree) as a kind of programmatic statement of Jesus's gospel, "of central importance to the Gospel as a whole, and thus also to Luke-Acts."[3] Beginning with that episode and tracing the lines that develop and extend its themes across the two volumes of Luke-Acts, I will propose eight theses about the hermeneutics of the gospel, and then offer concluding reflections about their implications for our gospel proclamation and our interpretation of Scripture.

1. The Gospel Announces an Event in the Story of Israel

The first observation is perhaps the most obvious: by commencing his account of Jesus's gospel proclamation with a synagogue sermon on a passage from Isaiah 61, Luke highlights the fact that the gospel Jesus proclaimed announced an event in the story of Israel. Luke's narrative frame for Jesus's words in 4:18–19 is as explicit and emphatic as it could possibly be about their textual origins in Israel's Scriptures. On three occasions Luke refers to "the scroll" (to biblion) from which the words are taken; it is "the scroll of the prophet Isaiah" (v. 17), and the narrator recounts for us frame by frame the whole sequence in which Jesus receives the scroll, unrolls it, finds the place where his text is written, reads out the words, rolls up the scroll again, and returns it to the attendant.

In their original Isaianic context, the words Jesus reads out address the returned exiles of Israel—"those who grieve in Zion" (Isa. 61:3)—announcing to them a day of restoration and release that the prophet describes as "the year of the LORD's favor" (61:2). The listed descriptions of the beneficiaries of this announcement—"the poor . . . the brokenhearted . . . the captives . . . the prisoners" (Isa. 61:1)—do not, in the first instance at least, refer to multiple, discrete categories of people but to a series of parallel images for the same group: the brokenhearted remnant of postexilic Israel.

The preceding chapters of Luke's Gospel further confirm that Luke intends us to interpret Jesus's words in relation to their original Isaianic function as a promise of restoration to Israel. Again and again in the opening chapter of his Gospel, this gentile writer makes sure that his readers (many of whom,

3. Green, *Gospel of Luke*, 207; similarly Bovon, *Gospel of Luke 1:1–9:50*, 157; Bock, *Luke*, 1:394.

one assumes—including the dedicatee, Theophilus—are gentiles like himself)
are aware that the story being told is one that has unfolded in fulfillment of
ancient promises to Israel: "The God of Israel . . . has come to his people and
redeemed them. He has raised up a horn of salvation for us in the house of
his servant David (as he said through his holy prophets of long ago) . . . to
show mercy to our ancestors and to remember his holy covenant, the oath that
he swore to our father Abraham" (1:68–73; cf. 1:16–17, 54–55; 2:10, 29–32,
38). The "good news" that Jesus refers to in 4:18 as the message he has been
given to proclaim is not just any good news: it is the Old Testament, Isaianic
good news of an end to Israel's exile, the restoration of Israel's brokenhearted
remnant, and the glorious return of Israel's God.[4]

A similar vision is evoked by Jesus's references to "the kingdom of God,"
the characteristic term that he uses in Luke's Gospel to specify the content of
the good news that he preaches (e.g., 4:43; 8:10; 9:2; 16:16); the language in
this case is drawn not from Isaiah but from the apocalyptic visions of Daniel,
depicting the overthrow of pagan empire and the final vindication of "the holy
people of the Most High" (cf. Dan. 2:44–45; 7:27). But whether the idiom is
Isaianic or Danielic, the implication is that the content of the announcement
is an event that involves a dramatic divine intervention to fulfill Israel's hopes
and God's promises for the nation.

2. The Gospel Announcement Is Itself an Event in the Story of Israel

But Jesus's gospel announcement, as the narrator presents it in Luke 4,
is not merely an announcement *about* an event in the story of Israel; it is
an announcement that is *itself* an event in the story of Israel. The narrative
frame in verses 16–17, 20–21 that surrounds the quotation from Isaiah that
Jesus reads from the scroll emphasizes not just the scriptural source of Jesus's
words but also the dramatic nature of the performance in which he quotes
and comments on those words: the Jesus of this pericope is described like an
actor on a stage, and the first words that he speaks after rolling up the scroll
are not an interpretation of the words that he has just read but a declaration
about the significance of the event that has just taken place in his reading them:
"The eyes of everyone in the synagogue were fastened on him. He began by
saying to them, 'Today this scripture is fulfilled in your hearing'" (4:20–21).

The character of the gospel announcement as an event in Israel's history is
not restricted to the single "today" of the Nazareth sermon: the whole mission
of Jesus and his disciples, with its kingdom announcement and accompanying

---

4. Cf. the earlier uses of the same verb, *euangelizō*, in Isa. 40:9; 52:7; 60:6.

signs, anticipates within history the final fall of Satan (10:18),[5] and the sights
they have seen on their mission are sights that "many prophets and kings
wanted to see . . . but did not" (10:24). The kingdom-proclaiming mission of
Jesus and his disciples initiates a whole new era in salvation history and in
the history of the reception of Israel's Scriptures: "The Law and the Prophets
were proclaimed until John. Since that time, the good news of the kingdom
of God is being preached, and everyone is forcing their way into it" (16:16).

3. The Gospel Announces Jesus as the Climax of Israel's Story

The reason this is so has to do with Jesus himself as the one in whom the
kingdom is manifest (cf. 11:20; 17:21). Jesus's sermon in Nazareth is not only
an announcement about the "today" in which the Scripture is fulfilled but
also an implicit claim about the identity of the "me" to whom the Scripture
refers: Jesus's words in 4:21 are unmistakably self-referential—a fact of which
the listening crowds described in verse 22 are acutely aware.[6]

The self-referential character of Jesus's gospel announcement that is everywhere implicit in the Gospel of Luke becomes explicit in the preaching of Acts.
Again and again the apostles use christological terms to sum up the content
of the gospel they are preaching: "Jesus . . . the Messiah" (5:42); "the word of
the Lord . . . about Jesus" (8:25); "Jesus" (8:35); "the Lord Jesus" (11:20). On
other occasions, in the one-line summaries of the good news they preached,
the name of Jesus is joined to a claim about his resurrection from the dead, his
fulfillment of Israel's Scriptures, or his inauguration of the kingdom of God
(e.g., 8:12; 10:36; 13:32–33; 17:18). If the preaching of Jesus in Luke's Gospel
announces the kingdom of God (and Jesus as the one in whom the kingdom
has become manifest), the preaching of the apostles in Acts proclaims Jesus
(and the kingdom of God as having become manifest in him).

The claims about Jesus's identity that are asserted (implicitly or explicitly)
in the preaching of Luke and Acts are grand and audacious. In the Nazareth
sermon of Luke 4, the Isaianic figure whose words Jesus appropriates and
claims to fulfill is simultaneously prophetic and messianic, announcing and
accomplishing the fulfillment of the missions of both the Servant of Isaiah
40–55 and the Branch of Isaiah 11. Read in the wider context of Luke's Gospel, the claim about Jesus's identity implied by the gospel he announced is
even larger. The "good news" of Isaiah 61:1 recalls the "good news" of Isaiah
40:9, which announces to the towns of Judah not only the restoration of their
fortunes but the return in glory of their God. Jesus's appropriation of Isaiah's

5. Cf. Green, *Gospel of Luke*, 419; I. H. Marshall, *Gospel of Luke*, 428–29.
6. Cf. McKnight, *King Jesus Gospel*, 99–100.

gospel in Luke 4 is preceded by the account of John's gospel proclamation in
Luke 3, which identifies John as the one "calling in the wilderness, 'Prepare
the way for the Lord'" (3:4). Here, as in the earlier words of John's father,
Zechariah (1:76), the context carries the strong implication that an Old Testament text about the coming of YHWH is to be interpreted as fulfilled in the
coming of Jesus, in such a way as to suggest "the fundamental correlation and
continuity between the God of Israel and Jesus."[7] It is therefore no surprise
that the gospel preaching of Acts announces Jesus not only as "Christ" but
also as "Lord of all" (10:36; cf. 2:36; 28:31).

The gospel's claim that Jesus's coming fulfills the Old Testament's promises about the return of YHWH is not only a claim about the identity of
Jesus; it is also a vindication of the Old Testament's claims about the existence, uniqueness, sovereignty, and covenant faithfulness of Israel's God.
To Jewish hearers weary of waiting for YHWH's coming, the gospel announcement includes the glorious reassurance that "what God promised our
ancestors he has fulfilled for us, their children, by raising up Jesus" (Acts
13:32–33); to pagan hearers whose heritage has been the worship of many
gods, the gospel announcement entails a command "to turn from these
worthless things to the living God, who made the heavens and the earth and
the sea and everything in them" (Acts 14:15). In preaching Jesus, the gospel
preaches God.

4. The Gospel Announces as the Climax of Israel's Story the Jesus Who Was Rejected by Israel

But in proclaiming Jesus as the climax of Israel's story, the gospel does
not simply endorse the preexisting versions of that story already being told
in Jesus's time and in the time of the apostles. The gospel that Luke recounts
necessitates a retelling of Israel's story that subverts all other first-century
tellings of it.[8] This subversive dimension of the gospel announcement is vividly
dramatized in Luke's account of Jesus's Nazareth sermon. Already, within
the reading that Jesus offers from Isaiah, a question about the anticipated
shape of Israel's story is raised by the omission of Isaiah's reference to "the
day of vengeance of our God" (61:2b).[9] The question is sharpened in the
following verses, as Jesus asserts, "Today this Scripture is fulfilled in your
hearing" (v. 21), before provocatively reminding the crowds that "no prophet

---

7. Rowe, *Early Narrative Christology*, 77; cf. Hays, *Reading Backwards*, 65.
8. Cf. N. T. Wright, *New Testament*, 382–83.
9. See especially the comparison between Jesus's synagogue sermon and the interpretation of Isa. 61 in 11QMelch, in Sanders, "From Isaiah 61 to Luke 4."

is accepted in his hometown" (v. 24). By the end of the pericope, the people of Jesus's own hometown are so furious that they drive him out of the town and attempt to throw him off a cliff (vv. 28–29).

In this respect, as in others, the episode is a kind of microcosm of the larger story that Luke tells in his Gospel. When the episode is read in the context of that larger story, its subversive effect is confirmed and redoubled. Jesus's rejection at Nazareth is not just an unfortunate misunderstanding or a temporary setback; it contributes to and anticipates the decisive rejection of him by the whole nation of Israel and its official leadership—a rejection that Jesus solemnly foretells as the necessary outworking of "everything that is written by the prophets about the Son of Man" (18:31; cf. 9:22, 44). The Jesus proclaimed as Lord and Christ in the gospel announcements of Luke-Acts is "this Jesus, whom you crucified" (Acts 2:36); it is in his sufferings and death that the arm of YHWH is revealed (cf. Isa. 53:1; Acts 8:32–35, quoting Isa. 53:7–8), and the divinely ordained necessity of his sufferings is the lesson at the heart of his postresurrection explanation to his disciples of "what was said in all the Scriptures concerning himself" (Luke 24:27).

5. The Gospel Is an Announcement for Israel and All the World

While the gospel announces Jesus as Israel's Messiah and the climax of Israel's story, the gospel is not presented in Luke-Acts as an announcement for Israel's ears alone: it is, rather, an announcement to be made to "all people everywhere" (Acts 17:30). Already in the story of Jesus's visit to Nazareth in Luke 4, he provocatively anticipates the inclusion of the gentiles as addressees and beneficiaries of the gospel announcement: he reminds the people of his hometown that, as the eschatological prophet foreshadowed in Isaiah 61, he follows in the footsteps of a long line of prophets who were rejected by their own people but brought salvation and blessing to others beyond the boundaries of Israel. But the extension of the gospel to the gentiles is not merely an outworking of Israel's rejection of the message: it is also, and more basically, an implication of the fact that Israel's Messiah is "Lord of all" (Acts 10:36) and that Israel's God is "Creator of the ends of the earth" (Isa. 40:28).

The Jesus proclaimed in the gospel preaching of Luke-Acts is indeed, as Richard Hays has rightly stressed, nothing less than "the one who would redeem Israel" (cf. 24:21): "The two disciples [on the road to Emmaus] are wrong to be discouraged but right to have hoped for Jesus to be the one who would redeem Israel. In their puzzled disappointment, they truly name Jesus's identity without realizing what they are saying, for the Redeemer of Israel is none other than Israel's God."[10] But even this realization—vast and stunning as it is—is still inadequate. The same servant songs that name YHWH as Israel's redeemer (e.g., Isa. 49:7) also insist, in the same breath, that it is "too small a thing" for his servant to restore the tribes of Jacob: "I will also make you a light for the Gentiles, that my salvation may reach to the ends of the earth" (Isa. 49:6). Thus, when Jesus's disciples ask him in Acts 1:6 whether now is the time that he will restore the kingdom to Israel, he responds by telling them that they will be empowered by the Spirit to serve as his witnesses "in Jerusalem, and in all Judea and Samaria, and to the ends of the earth" (1:8).[11]

6. The Gospel Announces a Salvation for Which the Story of Israel Is Paradigmatic

While the restoration of Israel is not the sole content of the gospel that Luke depicts as going out to the ends of the earth, it continues to be part of the hope that the gospel holds out (Jesus's response to the disciples is about the when and the how of Israel's restoration, not the whether)[12] and also functions as a kind of paradigm for the salvation that the gospel announces to the rest of the world.

Thus, for example, the twice-repeated *aphesis* ("freedom . . . free") to which Jesus refers in his reading from Isaiah (Luke 4:18) becomes a key term in the descriptions of salvation that Luke includes in his Gospel. In the Isaiah texts that stand behind Jesus's Nazareth sermon, the word carries multiple layers of meaning, referring in Isaiah 58:6 (a fragment of which Jesus folds into the text that he reads from Isaiah 61) to the liberation of individual Israelites from situations of social and economic oppression, and in Isaiah 61:1 to the total transformation of Israel's fortunes that would mark the end of the "captivity" into which the nation entered as a punishment for its sins (cf. Isa. 5:13; 52:2). Elsewhere in Luke's Gospel (1:71; 3:3; 24:47) the word consistently refers to the "forgiveness of sins" implied by its use in Isaiah 61, suggesting that the images used in Isaiah 61 as metaphors for the condition of the nation ("the poor . . . the brokenhearted . . . the captives . . . the prisoners") can also be applied metaphorically to the individuals within it and beyond its borders (cf. 24:47) to whom the gospel is proclaimed.[13] When Peter preaches the gospel to

10. Hays, *Reading Backwards*, 74.
11. See especially the discussion in Pao, *Isaianic New Exodus*, 91–96.
12. Cf. ibid., 95–96.
13. A similar pattern can be observed in Luke's use of the cognate verb *aphiēmi* (5:20–24; 7:47–49; 11:4; 17:3; 23:34), though note its use in 4:39 to refer to the release from fever experienced by Simon's mother-in-law. On the relationship between individual forgiveness and the end of Israel's exile, see especially Chatraw, "Balancing Out (W)Right"; Treat, *Crucified King*, 133–34.

a gathering of gentiles in the household of Cornelius, he begins by reminding them of "the message God sent to the people of Israel, announcing the good news of peace through Jesus Christ" (Acts 10:36), before telling his hearers that "the prophets testify about him that everyone who believes in him receives forgiveness [*aphesis*] of sins through his name" (10:43).

But this metaphorical sense of Jesus's words in Luke 4:18 does not exhaust the possibilities of meaning that they carry. A little later in the story, when John is in prison and sends messengers to Jesus asking, "Are you the one who is to come, or should we expect someone else?" (7:19–20), Jesus's reply points John's messengers to a series of miracles that he has just performed, describing them in language thick with Isaianic echoes (cf. Isa. 29:18–19; 35:5–6; 42:18; 61:1): "Go back and report to John what you have seen and heard: The blind receive sight, the lame walk, those who have leprosy are cleansed, the deaf hear, the dead are raised, and the good news is proclaimed to the poor" (4:22). Jesus's healing miracles, it seems, are both manifestations in themselves of the saving mercy of God and enacted metaphors that function like the language of Isaiah to symbolize the forgiveness of sins and release from oppression (both human and diabolical) that his kingdom inaugurates.

The salvation that the gospel announces thus includes both the restoration of Israel and the forgiveness of the individual sinner, but neither of these exhausts the scope of what it promises and accomplishes. As Mary's song in Luke 1 celebrates and anticipates, the remembrance of God's mercy to Abraham and his descendants cascades out into a rich plurality of "mighty deeds": scattering the proud, bringing down rulers, lifting up the humble, and filling the hungry (1:51–53).

7. The Gospel Is an Exhortation as well as an Announcement

But the gospel preaching of Luke-Acts does not rain down blessings indiscriminately, irrespective of the responses of the hearers. It announces salvation, but the content of the salvation it announces and the mode in which that salvation is proclaimed are both pregnant with exhortation and command.

In Luke's account of Jesus's Nazareth sermon, one intriguing clue to this exhortative dimension of the gospel can be found in the fragment from Isaiah 58:6 ("to set the oppressed free") that Jesus folds into his reading from Isaiah 61. The most obvious effect of this addition is to reinforce the note sounded earlier in the verse by the reference to "freedom for the prisoners," underlining "freedom" (*aphesis*) as the dominant image of the reading. But for those with ears to hear, the link to Isaiah 58 also functions as a reminder of the original, exhortative function of the words in their first context, where the prophet reminds his hearers that the kind of fasting YHWH has chosen is "to loose the chains of injustice and untie the cords of the yoke, to set the oppressed free and break every yoke" (58:6). In line with the opening notes sounded at the start of Isaiah 56, the final chapters of Isaiah combine a promise, "My salvation is close at hand and my righteousness will soon be revealed," with an exhortation to "maintain justice and do what is right" (56:1), implying a hermeneutic in which the prophet's announcements of salvation are to be heard as implicitly calling the people to repentance and in which his calls to repentance are to be heard as implicitly promising salvation for the repentant.

This close interweaving of announcement and exhortation pervades the gospel proclamation recorded in Luke-Acts. Thus, in the first instance of *euangelizō* reported in Luke's narrative (aside from the angelic announcements of 1:19 and 2:10), the content of John's gospel preaching is explicitly described as including the "many other words" (Luke 3:18)[14] (along the lines of the examples given in 3:7–17) with which he warned of coming judgment, urged repentance, and spelled out in concrete terms the nature of what that repentance would involve. "John's summons to repentance is understood as a way of preaching the gospel, since it showed men the coming way of salvation."[15] In the closing verses of the Gospel, Jesus sums up the message that is to be proclaimed to the nations as a message of "repentance for the forgiveness of sins . . . in [Jesus's] name" (24:47), foregrounding the function of the gospel announcement as a call to repentance.[16] In keeping with this emphasis, the climax of Paul's address to the Athenians refers to the gospel message as a divine command calling on "all people everywhere to repent" (Acts 17:30–31), and his preaching in Lystra gives the content of the good news he brings as a command to "turn from these worthless things to the living God" (Acts 14:15).[17]

14. More literally translated, v. 18 reads: "So also many other things, exhorting he evangelized [*parakalōn euēngelizeto*] the people." Syntactically, the most obvious way to analyze the workings of the sentence is to take the "many other things" as the direct object of *euēngelizeto* (and therefore part of the content of the message proclaimed) and "exhorting" as a description of the mode in which John evangelized. Even if the sentence is translated otherwise (e.g., taking "many other things" as the object of *parakalōn*), the closest of connections is still implied between John's exhorting and his evangelizing.

15. I. H. Marshall, *Gospel of Luke*, 149.

16. The same can of course be said if the alternative reading (represented in codices A, C, and D) is followed, and *kai* is read in place of *eis*; cf. the NRSV's "repentance and forgiveness."

17. Note the way in which the infinitival clause, *apo toutōn tōn mataiōn epistrephein*, functions as the object of *euangelizomenoi*.

8. The Gospel Is an Offer as well as an Exhortation

Hand in hand with the gospel's exhortation and call to repentance is its offer of forgiveness within the preaching of Luke-Acts. As I have argued above, the proclamation of *aphesis* (freedom) in Jesus's sermon is intended not as a bald statement that Israel will be granted freedom, forgiveness, and national restoration, irrespective of its hearers' response to the announcement, but as an offer requiring acceptance. This function of the gospel announcement as an offer requiring acceptance is vividly dramatized in the succeeding narrative: the announcement of "the year of the Lord's favor" (*eniauton kyriou dekton*) comes on the lips of a prophet who is not "accepted" (*dektos*) by the people, and the divine favor extended is repudiated. Jesus's rejection in Nazareth foreshadows his rejection in Jerusalem—the "peace" announced in the gospel (cf. Isa. 52:7; Acts 10:36) is repudiated by a city whose people reject the messenger sent to them (Luke 19:42)—and Jerusalem's rejection of the message is in turn followed by its rejection (for the most part) in the synagogues of the diaspora (e.g., Acts 13:46–47; 24:21–28).

The character of the gospel as an offer to be received is also implied by the language of "repentance for the forgiveness of sins" in the summary of its contents that Jesus gives to his disciples in Luke 24:47. Jesus's language in that verse echoes in the synagogue sermon that Paul preaches in Pisidian Antioch, where—having announced in Jesus's resurrection the fulfillment of God's promises to the ancestors (13:32–37)—he declares to his hearers that "through Jesus the forgiveness of sins is proclaimed to you" (v. 38) and goes on to unpack the statement as an announcement that "through him everyone who believes is set free from every sin, a justification you were not able to obtain under the law of Moses" (v. 39).

While it would be a mistake to conclude that the doctrine of justification by faith *is* the gospel (as if the offer implied in vv. 38–39 could be abstracted from the announcement in vv. 32–37 without damaging both), there are good grounds to argue that it is necessarily entailed by the gospel announcement about the saving lordship of Jesus and the forgiveness offered in his name.[18] (This is why—if we may step momentarily out of Luke-Acts to the letters of Paul—teachers like the Galatian agitators, who agree with Paul about the identity of Jesus as Israel's Messiah and his resurrection from the dead but understand his saving mission in a manner that is incoherent with the free offer of justification to all who believe, are not just disagreeing about a second-order doctrine; they are, Paul implies in Gal. 1:8, preaching "a gospel other than the one [Paul] preached to [them].")

18. Cf. the similar argument in Piper, *Future of Justification*, 83–85.

"Gospel-Centered" Hermeneutics

What can we conclude from our observations about the hermeneutics of the gospel in Luke's Gospel and the book of Acts for the questions with which we began this chapter? First, and most importantly, a survey of Luke-Acts confirms there are good grounds for the evangelical assertion that a proper Christian appropriation of the Old Testament needs to be informed by a gospel-centered hermeneutic: at the climax of salvation history and the center of the canon stands the figure of the risen Jesus, opening the minds of the disciples to understand the Scriptures and commissioning them to play their part in the unfolding story of salvation (cf. Luke 24:25–27, 44–47).[19] But the hermeneutic practiced in Luke-Acts also assists us in clarifying what a properly "gospel-centered" hermeneutic means (and what it does not mean). Three clarifications in particular are worth making.

First, a gospel-centered hermeneutic which follows in the pattern set by the preaching recorded in Luke and Acts is not the kind of unilateral hermeneutic that takes a preformed template of the gospel (whether derived from the confessions of the sixteenth and seventeenth centuries, the revivalism of the nineteenth century, or the popular formulations of our own time) and imposes it from the outside as a grid through which the Scriptures are to be interpreted. The hermeneutic modeled and taught in Luke-Acts not only interprets the Old Testament in light of the gospel but also interprets the gospel in light of the Old Testament,[20] articulating the significance of Jesus's mission, death, and resurrection as the climax of Israel's story and as the fulfillment of the plans and purposes of Israel's God. Even when the gospel announcement is not preceded by an explicit narration of the story of Israel, and the promises of the prophets are not directly in view, the salvation promised in the gospel and the repentance commanded are still deeply informed by the grand narrative of the Old Testament, and the universal promises and commands of the gospel are still warranted by the action of Israel's God in raising from the dead the man Jesus, whom he has appointed as judge of all (cf. Acts 17:30–31).

Second, the rich, multifaceted gospel hermeneutics of Luke-Acts also guards us against the kind of thin, disembodied, individualistic hermeneutic that filters the Old Testament through the sieve of a gospel concerned only with the salvation of individual souls, and appropriates only those aspects of Old Testament Scripture that inform or illuminate that aspect of the gospel's application. The offer of forgiveness to individual sinners and the accompanying call to repentance are certainly prominent in the gospel message preached by

19. Cf. Goldsworthy, *Gospel-Centered Hermeneutics*, 81–82.
20. Cf. Thiselton, *New Horizons in Hermeneutics*, 150.

Jesus and the apostles, but they are attached inseparably to the name and story of the Jesus who is proclaimed in the gospel as Messiah and Lord and are located in the enormous vision of the kingdom of God that was proclaimed by Jesus and confirmed in his resurrection.

Third, the form in which the gospel is proclaimed and the Scriptures appropriated in the Gospel of Luke and the book of Acts contrasts strikingly with the kind of flat-footed hermeneutic that preaches the gospel only in the indicative mood and reads the Old Testament solely as a backdrop to or an anticipation of the gospel's propositional content. Crucial as that propositional content is, and central as the events of Jesus's death and resurrection are to the news that the gospel announces, the gospel preaching of Jesus and his apostles in Luke-Acts does not sit well with one-dimensional propositional accounts of the gospel speech-act, or with overly sharp attempts to pare off the response the gospel calls for and the blessing that it offers from the facts that it announces, as if only the latter were properly part of the gospel.

The gospel proclamation of Jesus and the apostles in Luke-Acts is not only an announcement (and reminder and explanation) of the truth-claims that it asserts but also a summons to repentance and a gracious offer of forgiveness; the Scriptures inform every dimension of the mighty speech-acts of God that the gospel performs and are in turn appropriated via the gospel not merely as a repository of background facts and fulfilled promises but as a living voice that promises, urges, summons, and invites in the "today" of their fulfillment in Jesus. If we pay close attention to the diverse and powerful ways in which Luke records the gospel proclamation of Jesus and the apostles announcing, inviting, offering, warning, reminding, and commanding their hearers, then that proclamation will not only provide us with a model for our own communication of the gospel; it will also help to form us as readers and teachers of the Scriptures at whose center the gospel is proclaimed, so that (to borrow from Paul's words to his apprentice Timothy) our use of the Scriptures might do better justice to their usefulness for all the "teaching, rebuking, correcting and training in righteousness" by which they make us "thoroughly equipped for every good work" (2 Tim. 3:16–17).

9

"That You May Believe"

John and the Hermeneutics of Truth

Truth on Trial

So far in this book, we have mainly focused on the formative dimension of our reading of Scripture—on the work that the biblical writings do to shape us in faith, hope, and love, as we "read, mark, learn, and inwardly digest" their message.[1] But the scope of hermeneutics embraces not only the formative function of texts but also the epistemic responsibilities of readers,[2] even (and perhaps especially) in the case of a book that claims to speak on behalf of God.[3] Part of our task as readers of Scripture is to ask—both of the truth claims asserted in Scripture and of the vision of reality on which its various other speech-acts depend for their legitimacy—"Is it true?"

The truth claims contained in and implied by Scripture are, of course, multitudinous, but they coalesce around a single, central assertion: "that Jesus is the Messiah, the Son of God" (John 20:31). The making and proving of this assertion dominate not only the resurrection narrative within which

---

1. *Book of Common Prayer*, collect for the second Sunday in Advent. Available at https://www.churchofengland.org/prayer-worship/worship/book-of-common-prayer/collects-epistles-and-gospels/the-second-sunday-in-advent.aspx.
2. Cf. Thiselton, *Hermeneutics: An Introduction*, 7–10; Thiselton, *Hermeneutics of Doctrine*, 126–34.
3. Cf. Westphal, *Suspicion and Faith*, 25–29.

it appears but the whole Gospel of John. In this chapter we will focus on this Gospel to explore the hermeneutics of truth.

Perhaps the most famous reference to the problems of epistemology in the Gospel of John is Pilate's question, "What is truth?" asked at the end of the brief conversation that he has with Jesus before sentencing him to be crucified. In its immediate context, the question is not an earnest epistemological enquiry but the cynical, dismissive gesture of a man more interested in the workings of power than in the weight of testimony:

> "What is truth?" [Pilate] asks, and, uninterested in any answer, he leaves the scene of dialogue with the accused to return to the arena in which the play of clashing forces determines the outcome. For both the accusers and the judge, the truth is irrelevant because it works at cross-purposes to their hold on power.[4]

But in the larger context of John's Gospel, thick as it is with the language of "truth," "testimony," and "judgment,"[5] Pilate's question carries resonances immeasurably deeper than the intentions of the man asking it. Matters of truth and testimony may not be of much interest to Pilate, but they are crucial to Jesus, who responds to a question about kingship with an answer about truth: "You say that I am a king. In fact, the reason I was born and came into the world is to testify to the truth" (18:37).

The trial scene in which Jesus's exchange with Pilate is embedded forms part of a larger lawsuit—what Rudolf Bultmann called "the great trial between God and the world"—that is in view across the whole of John's Gospel.[6] The forum in which the Fourth Gospel's claims about Jesus are made and adjudicated is not, of course—in the first instance at least—the forum of twenty-first-century popular opinion or post-Enlightenment academic debate. The bulk of the Gospel (particularly the "Book of Signs" in 1:19–12:50 that comprises most of its first half) is concerned with testimony given to the people and leaders of Israel and with signs performed in their presence. In this trial the rules of evidence

---

4. Volf, *Exclusion and Embrace*, 266.

5. The noun *alētheia* (truth) occurs twenty-five times in John's Gospel, compared with a combined total of seven times in the Synoptic Gospels; the adjective *alēthēs* (true) occurs fourteen times in John, compared with twice in the Synoptics; the related adjective *alēthinos* (genuine) occurs nine times in John, compared with once in the Synoptics. Similarly, with the language of "witness," "testimony," and "judgment": the noun *martyria* occurs fourteen times in John compared with four times in the Synoptics; the verb *martyrein* occurs thirty-three times in John compared with twice in the Synoptics; and the verb *krinein* occurs nineteen times in John compared with twelve in the Synoptics. The pattern is not quite so striking with the noun *krisis*, which occurs eleven times in John compared with twelve in Matthew, zero in Mark, and four in Luke. Cf. the discussion in Lincoln, *Truth on Trial*, 12–13.

6. Bultmann, *Gospel of John*, 655.

and sentencing are set by the Torah (cf. 5:31; 8:13–17; 19:7); a basic axiom is (or ought to be) that "Scripture cannot be set aside" (10:35), and the outcome is a judgment made by Israel "to fulfill the word of Isaiah the prophet" (12:38).

But it is not Israel alone that is called upon to pass judgment in this trial: even in the Old Testament covenant lawsuits between YHWH and Israel that stand behind John's narrative, the nations can be summoned to testify and to pass judgment,[7] and in John's Gospel the decision Israel must make about Jesus manifests and anticipates the judgment that will be made by (and upon) "the world" (e.g., 1:9–13; 12:31, 47; 16:8–11). When Jesus is dragged before Pilate by the leaders of the nation, Pilate attempts to shunt the case back to them for judgment: "Take him yourselves and judge him by your own law" (18:31).[8] His attempts to evade responsibility are futile, however, and he too finds himself required to respond to the Jesus who "came into the world . . . to testify to the truth" (18:37) and take a side for or against the truth that Jesus bears witness to. If the God of Israel is the one by whom, and through whose Word, all things were made (cf. 1:3, 10), then this is a trial in which the whole world must participate.

"If You Believed Moses" (John 5:46)

In the context of that great covenantal and cosmic lawsuit, matters of scriptural testimony and interpretation have a decidedly epistemological and forensic function. Scripture is to be heard and understood in relation to the claims of Jesus and the accusations against him: "If you believed Moses, you would believe me, for he wrote about me" (5:46).

The most extended discussion of this function of Scripture in John's Gospel comes in the second half of chapter 5, in the discourse in which Jesus answers (vv. 19–46) the twin accusations that he has healed a man on the Sabbath and that he has then made things worse by "calling God his own Father, making himself equal with God" (v. 18). Jesus's discourse begins (vv. 19–30) by expounding the meaning of the kind of sonship implied by his reference to Israel's God as "my Father" in verse 17. But in the second half of the discourse (vv. 31–46), the focus shifts from the *meaning* of his claim to its *validity*: "If I testify about myself, my testimony is not true. There is another who testifies in my favor, and I know that his testimony about me is true" (5:31–32).

7. See especially the discussion of Isa. 40–55 in Lincoln, *Truth on Trial*, 38–51.
8. Melba Padilla Maggay comments on the characteristic tendency of worldly power "to dismiss Christianity as an obscure tribal religion mumbling in corners about the meaning of its own symbols." Maggay, "Jesus and Pilate," 31.

Jesus is alert to the fact that people claiming to speak and act on God's behalf can all too frequently turn out to be "thieves and robbers" (10:8), exploiting the people for whom they should be caring or using claims of divine authority to incite hatred and violence: the mere claim, in and of itself, can hardly be received by its hearers as a self-authenticating utterance, floating above the sordid, mundane spheres of human religion and politics in which rival claims of this sort are made and tested. Certainly Jesus's concession in verse 31, "If I testify about myself, my testimony is not true," must be held in tension with his pugnacious insistence in 8:14, "Even if I testify on my own behalf, my testimony is valid, for I know where I came from and where I am going." But for those who (like the Pharisees with whom he is in dialogue in chapter 8, the leaders to whom he is responding in chapter 5, and the readers of the Gospel) have no such knowledge, except as it is given to them, some verification of Jesus's claims is required, and is given in the corroborating testimony of "another who testifies in [his] favor" (5:32).

The referent of "another who testifies" is initially left open, and readers are at first encouraged to assume that Jesus has in mind the testimony of John (vv. 33–35).[9] In verses 36–40 it becomes clear, however, that Jesus has in mind "testimony weightier than that of John," namely, the testimony of the Father himself (cf. 8:16–18), conveyed through the Scriptures that testify about Jesus and the works that the Father has given him to perform. These twin forms of the Father's testimony are interrelated and interdependent: only in light of Scripture's testimony to the works and ways of Israel's God can Jesus's works be recognized as "the works of [his] Father" (10:37), and only in light of Jesus's works can the words of Scripture about the glory of YHWH (and of his Servant and Son) be perceived as having been spoken about Jesus (cf. 12:37–41).

The dynamics of this interrelation can be glimpsed in John's accounts of the first sign performed by Jesus, in Cana (2:1–11), and the clearing of the Jerusalem temple that follows almost immediately (2:13–22). In the former, the closing verse of the paragraph identifies the sign as a revelation of Jesus's glory (v. 11)—glory previously identified as "the glory of the one and only Son, who came from the Father" (1:14). The point of the miracle is not simply the brute fact of the supernatural power that it displays—impressive as that is—but the character of the work in which that power is exercised: the sign echoes and participates in the glorious works of YHWH himself, who waters the earth, clothes the ground with green plants, and brings forth wine

9. Cf. the reading of these verses in Lincoln, *Saint John*, 205–6.

to gladden human hearts.[10] In the temple clearing recounted in John 2:13–22, Jesus's burning zeal for his Father's house is recognized by the disciples as echoing the zeal of the righteous sufferer depicted in Psalm 69; Jesus's reply to the demand of his critics that he give a sign to prove his authority ("Destroy this temple, and I will raise it again in three days"; John 2:19) adds a further layer of significance to the event, but only the subsequent events of his crucifixion and resurrection from the dead give his disciples a retrospective understanding of both "the scripture and the words that Jesus had spoken" (v. 22).[11] The words of Scripture and the works of Jesus (together with the work of his Father in raising him from the dead) combine to interpret one another and testify to the truth of Jesus's claims.

"How Can You Believe?" (John 5:44)

Ample and authoritative as this testimony is, it hardly meets with unanimous acceptance: on the contrary, John tells us (referring to "the crowd" that in the narrative represents the whole nation), "Even after Jesus had performed so many signs in their presence, they still would not believe in him" (12:37). This rejection of Jesus's testimony by his own people is the specter that haunts the whole Gospel of John, from start to finish, as a tragic anomaly crying out for explanation.

At one level, John's explanation appeals to the mysterious, paradoxical purposes of God, foreshadowed in Scripture and fulfilled in the Israel of his own time:

> This was to fulfill the word of Isaiah the prophet: "Lord, who has believed our message and to whom has the arm of the Lord been revealed?" For this reason they could not believe, because, as Isaiah says elsewhere: "He has blinded their eyes and hardened their hearts, so they can neither see with their eyes, nor understand with their hearts, nor turn—and I would heal them." (12:38–40)

At another level, however, John's words in the following verses (about the timidity of those who believed only in secret) suggest a complementary explanation for the unbelief of Israel's leaders, to be found in the murky waters of human fear and desire: "Yet at the same time many even among the

---

10. See especially Ps. 104, itself a meditation on the gloriousness of the works of God on the third day of creation—cf. the "third day" of John 2:1—and in his continuing providential care for the world he has made.

11. Cf. Hays, *Reading Backwards*, 85–86.

leaders believed in him. But because of the Pharisees they would not openly acknowledge their faith for fear they would be put out of the synagogue; for they loved human praise more than praise from God" (12:42–43). Jesus's rhetorical question in chapter 5 implies a similar suggestion: "How can you believe since you accept glory from one another but do not seek the glory that comes from the only God?" (5:44).

Jesus's words in chapter 5 and John's in chapter 12 are a sharp reminder of the extent to which our interpretive decisions are influenced—whether consciously or unconsciously—by our anxieties and aspirations about the social position we wish to maintain (or to escape from) and the reputation we wish to cultivate. Matters of religious belief and unbelief are hardly exempt from such forces; in these matters, as in all things, all of us are biased, prejudiced interpreters.

Of course, not all prejudgment is prejudicial (in the pejorative sense of the word). As readers we never come to a text with an entirely spotless mind, empty of all opinion, motivation, and preunderstanding; and even if we could somehow achieve that feat, it would not make us very good readers.[12] But if we are to be genuinely open to the texts that we read, such preunderstandings and precommitments ought always to be treated as being—in principle at least—capable of being revised or relinquished if that is what is required to do justice to the text and to all the various other claims on us as readers.[13] And because of the characteristic tendency of human hearts to favor beliefs and belief systems that legitimize our own position and privilege, or to defer to the opinions and assumptions of those who exercise social power within the circles in which we move, we ought to be particularly suspicious of the possibility that our own interpretive judgments have been distorted by dynamics of this sort.[14] Those who seek human glory rather than the glory that comes from God (or, to frame the terms even more starkly, in light of Jesus's words in 3:19–20, those who "[love] darkness instead of light" because of the deeds they wish to keep concealed) will inevitably fail to receive the words of Jesus rightly, or to respond to them in a way that does justice to his claims.

12. See especially Gadamer, *Truth and Method*, 268–306.
13. See especially Wolterstorff, "Evidence, Entitled Belief," 452–56.
14. Cf. Volf, *Exclusion and Embrace*, 269–70; Wolterstorff, *Until Justice and Peace Embrace*, 175–76. Because our motivations are not always conscious or transparent, sometimes the *functions* that our beliefs and practices typically perform provide us with the best clues as to what might be the invisible and unconscious motives that underlie them. For a useful discussion of some of the ways in which the respective analyses of Freud, Marx, and Nietzsche (the "masters of suspicion," as Ricoeur dubbed them) can help us from an unexpected quarter in the task of uncovering these clues, see Westphal, *Suspicion and Faith*, 33–289.

"They Will Look on the One They Have Pierced" (John 19:37)

Realistic as John's Gospel is about the subliminal forces of fear and desire that tug on our hearts and bias our interpretations, the story that it tells does not leave us lost in a fatalistic resignation to the vicious interpretive circles which those forces create. Only those "on the side of truth" listen to Jesus (18:37), but John does not close the door on the possibility that a person might change sides—that a person might, in the words of John 5:24, "[cross] over from death to life."

A tantalizing hint in the direction of this possibility is offered by the pair of linked quotations at the end of the second major block of John's narrative (the "Book of the Passion" in 13:1–19:42),[15] which serve as a structural counterpart to the pair of linked quotations in 12:38–40 that John places at the end of the previous block of the narrative (the "Book of Signs" in 1:19–12:50).[16] While the first quotation-pair focuses on Israel's blindness and unbelief (interpreted as a fulfillment of what was foreshadowed in Isaiah), the second points to the events of Jesus's death (once again interpreted as the fulfillment of Scripture) and the witness of the one who "saw [and] has given testimony . . . so that you also may believe":

> When they came to Jesus and found that he was already dead, they did not break his legs. Instead, one of the soldiers pierced Jesus' side with a spear, bringing a sudden flow of blood and water. The man who saw it has given testimony, and his testimony is true. He knows that he tells the truth, and he testifies so that you also may believe. These things happened so that the scripture would be fulfilled: "Not one of his bones will be broken," and, as another scripture says, "They will look on the one they have pierced." (19:33–37)

The original contexts of both texts in the quotation-pair suggest an interpretation of Jesus's death that focuses on its saving significance. It is difficult to say with certainty whether the former quotation is intended to be taken as a reference to Exodus 12:46 or to Psalm 34:20; whichever option is taken,

15. In this account of John's structure, I am following the lead of Hays, *Reading Backwards*, 79; M. Thompson, "'They Bear Witness to Me,'" 268. Hays and M. Thompson both cite C. H. Dodd as the source of the designation "The Book of the Passion," though Dodd included the whole of chs. 13–20 under that heading. Cf. Dodd, *Interpretation of the Fourth Gospel*, 289–91. If the more common account of the narrative structure of John's Gospel is followed, and the second major block is taken as extending from 13:1 to the end of ch. 20, then the twin Scripture quotations of 19:36–37 are still the last explicit Scripture quotations in that section of the Gospel, and the words in 19:35, "he testifies so that you also may believe," anticipate the words of 20:31 with which the section closes.
16. Cf. Hays, *Reading Backwards*, 79.

however, the unbroken bones of Jesus hint at the redemptive significance of his death, either by representing him typologically as a Passover lamb sacrificed for the life of God's people, or by identifying him as the Righteous One whose unbroken bones foreshadow his coming deliverance and the rescue of those who take refuge in him (cf. Ps. 34:19–22).[17]

The second text in the pair is a (slightly reworded) quotation from Zechariah 12:10, an oracle that depicts the rejection of YHWH's servant by the people of Jerusalem and their leaders as an event in which YHWH himself is "pierced." The context, however, suggests a reading in which "they will look" carries as much weight as "pierced."[18] The prophet depicts a moment of dramatically clarified and contrite vision:

> I will pour out on the house of David and the inhabitants of Jerusalem a spirit of grace and supplication. They will look on me, the one they have pierced, and they will mourn for him as one mourns for an only child, and grieve bitterly for him as one grieves for a firstborn son.

The context of the surrounding verses in John 19, with their solemn and emphatic references to the one who "saw" and "has given testimony . . . so that you also may believe," suggests something similar. If verse 37 is read in relation to these twin contexts—the Scripture quotation's original setting in Zechariah 12 and its new setting in John 19—it is not difficult to find in this verse the hope of a hermeneutical conversion in which the blind are given sight and unbelief becomes belief, undoing the vicious cycle of unwillingness and inability depicted in 12:38–40.[19]

Just as the problem of Israel's unbelief is explained in 12:37–43 at two complementary levels—the level of divine hardening and the level of human motive and decision—so also the hermeneutical conversion foreshadowed in 19:35–37 can be described at complementary and interrelated levels of divine and human agency. At one level of explanation, to borrow from the language of Zechariah 12, the "spirit of grace and supplication" that is necessary for such a hermeneutical conversion is a spirit (or Spirit?) poured out by God, as an act of sovereign mercy. At another explanatory level, however, the dynamic in view is the very human dynamic of testimony borne, transmitted,

17. For an argument in favor of taking 19:36 as a reference to Ps. 34:20, see M. Thompson, "'They Bear Witness to Me,'" 278–79.
18. Commentators who argue for the likelihood that John has this broader context of the Zechariah quotation in view include Keener, *Gospel of John*, 1156; Lincoln, *Saint John*, 482; Lindars, *Gospel of John*, 591; Malina and Rohrbaugh, *Gospel of John*, 275; Carson, *John*, 627–28.
19. Notice how the testimony of the singular witness ("the man who saw it," v. 35) enables the many to "look" (v. 37).

evaluated, and received: "The man who saw it has given testimony, and his testimony is true. He knows that he tells the truth, and he testifies so that you also may believe" (19:35).

A similar interplay can be seen in Jesus's words in the farewell discourse about the Advocate and his witness to the world: "When the Advocate comes, whom I will send to you from the Father—the Spirit of truth who goes out from the Father—he will testify about me. And you also must testify, for you have been with me from the beginning" (15:26–27). The twin testimonies that Jesus refers to here are not to be understood as parallel witnesses, operating separately and independently of one another. Rather, as Jesus goes on to explain, the testimony borne by the Spirit of truth will be voiced through the testimony of the disciples, and the disciples will testify by the enabling of the Spirit: "When he, the Spirit of truth, comes, he will guide you into all the truth. He will not speak on his own; he will speak only what he hears, and he will tell you what is yet to come. He will glorify me because it is from me that he will receive what he will make known to you" (16:13–14).

It is in this context that we should understand what is said in the intervening verses about what has traditionally been described as the "convicting" work of the Spirit:

> When he comes, he will prove the world to be in the wrong about sin and righteousness and judgment: about sin, because people do not believe in me; about righteousness, because I am going to the Father, where you can see me no longer; and about judgment, because the prince of this world now stands condemned. (16:8–11)

As most modern commentators correctly argue, and as the NIV translation implies, the work of the Spirit described here is not (immediately and directly) the work of producing a subjective sense of conviction within the hearts of individuals: "Whether those in the world are subjectively convinced of their own guilt does not appear to be in view here. They may or may not be."[20] A good argument can still be made, however, that the work of the Spirit, through the disciples' testimony, to "prove the world to be in the wrong about sin and righteousness and judgment" is *aimed*, in part at least, at evoking the kind of saving contrition that the older interpreters tended to find in these verses. The disciples' testimony (and by implication the Spirit's) is, after all, described elsewhere as being directed toward the goal of eliciting faith (19:35; cf. 1:7; 20:30–31), and the prayer of Jesus at the end of the farewell discourse includes

20. Lincoln, *Saint John*, 419.

a petition "that the world may believe that you have sent me" (17:21). Thus the very message that is, on one level, the word requiring interpretation is, on another level, the means by which the Spirit of truth is at work to overthrow the illegitimate prejudices of human fear and pride and to open the minds of readers to receive the word and interpret it rightly.

Truth, Interpretation, and Continuing Faith

Questions of truth and interpretation do not, of course, arise solely at the threshold of belief. John's Gospel not only narrates the journeys toward faith of people like Nathanael in chapter 1, the Samaritan woman of chapter 4, and the man born blind whose story is told in chapter 9; it also tells about disciples who "turned back and no longer followed him" (6:66), about the frequent perplexity of the disciples as they wrestle with the dark sayings and puzzling actions of Jesus (e.g., 14:5–11; 16:17–18), and about Thomas, who doubted even after the other disciples had met the risen Jesus (20:24–29).[21]

As for the characters in the story, so also for its readers: the question about the truth of Jesus's claims arises not only on the way to faith but also from within faith. This is so in part because of the believer's responsibility to think and live with integrity as a person who is "on the side of truth" (18:37), and in part because of the frailties of faith and distortions of understanding that continue even after the journey of following Jesus begins. The testimony that is gathered, preserved, and transmitted in the Gospel is offered to its readers—whatever stage of the journey they may be at—both as a basis for faith and as a Spirit-enabled means by which their interpretive faculties might be continually revived and renewed. If we are to live up to our hermeneutical duties as a people summoned to make a responsible judgment about the truth claims of the Scriptures and to live out a life of public and private fidelity to the truth that we have become convinced of, reading and rereading the Gospel of John will be an indispensable education for us.

---

21. Even if the aorist verb *pisteusēte* (believe) within the notoriously contested purpose statement that John provides in the following verses is judged to be original, in preference to the well-attested present-tense variant, *pisteuēte* (continue to believe), the aorist form of the verb does not require an exclusive focus on initial faith; and both the verse's immediate context (following directly after a narrative about the doubts of a disciple who, we are told, "believed in [Jesus]" as early as 2:11) and the contents of the Gospel as a whole suggest that the fostering of continuing faith is at least as important as the evocation of initial faith in the purposes of the writer. Cf. the discussions in Michaels, *Gospel of John*, 1020–24; Keener, *Gospel of John*, 1215–16.

❖10❖

"Beyond What Is Written"?

1 Corinthians and the Hermeneutics of Theology

"Beyond the Bible"?

To be an evangelical is, among other things, to be a reader of the Bible. But is reading the Bible enough? Is there a place and a need, as part of the shaping of Christian life and understanding, for us to move "beyond the Bible" to a systematic and organized theology? And if there is, how can this task be performed in a manner that follows the Bible faithfully as authoritative Scripture and does not presumptuously depart from it? What might it look like for our systematic theology to be informed by "ways of interpreting the Bible that are themselves biblical"[1] and apprenticed to the patterns of judgment exemplified within the canon?[2] These were the questions posed in two recent and much-discussed books[3] as part of a larger discussion about the legitimacy of the whole enterprise of systematic theology and the method by which it should be conducted.

For some contributors to the discussion, the issue at stake is whether the whole enterprise of systematic theology is legitimate and useful at all, especially in the post-Christendom times into which the church in the modern

1. I. H. Marshall, *Beyond the Bible*, 32.
2. Vanhoozer, "Into the Great 'Beyond,'" 93–95.
3. I. H. Marshall, *Beyond the Bible*; Meadors, *Moving beyond the Bible*.

West has found itself moving. If, as some have argued, systematic theology is by its very nature the kind of intellectual cathedral-building project that is engaged in by an established church sitting securely on the epistemological high ground of a complacently Christian culture, then surely, barring a miraculous reversal of the trend of secularization, its time has passed (in the West, at least); and the church needs to find new ways of articulating its knowledge of God. Perhaps (one might conclude) the time has come to replace grand strategy with tactical sorties—a kind of intellectual guerrilla warfare. Perhaps the shaping of Christian life in a post-Christendom era would be best served if we abandoned altogether the attempt to construct a coherent, comprehensive system of belief about God, the world, humanity, justice, grace, and so forth, and concentrated instead on narrating the particular story of Israel, Christ, and the church, articulating the various ways in which the bits and pieces of the church's life ought to be informed by that story.[4]

For other contributors to the discussion, the debate is not so much about *whether* the enterprise of theological systematization is legitimate but *how* that task should be undertaken. To what extent should our theological formulations take into account the wisdom of the age we live in and the extrabiblical knowledge that we have access to through the common reason and experience of humanity? Does theology need to be updated to accommodate the developments of history and the advances of human understanding? Does it need to be adapted to the peculiarities of culture and context? Is there any warrant within the Scriptures themselves for an approach to the work of theology that attempts to go beyond the Scriptures in its form and content?

It is tempting to dismiss the discussion as one that can safely be left to the professional theologians—the specialist architects and builders whose whole vocation is to labor in the design and construction of vast theological systems. Certainly, those who do that sort of work for a living have a particular responsibility to take care how they build and to wrestle with the questions that bear directly on their labors. But theology should not be left solely to the theologians; all of us, as readers of Scripture, need to ponder how we relate the particulars of the biblical text to the intuitive (and at times explicit) sense that we have about how the various pieces fit together in the larger picture of our knowledge of God and the world. The discussion about whether (and, if so, how) a big-picture theological system of that sort ought to be assembled and related to the stories and letters and proverbs and

---

4. See, e.g., the brief comments in Hauerwas, *After Christendom?*, 16–19; and the lengthier discussions in Starling, "Not a Wisdom of This Age"; Hauerwas, *Work of Theology*, 11–31.

poems of the Bible—and how it should be related to the common knowledge of humanity and the experiences of our own lives—is of interest and importance to all of us.

This chapter will attempt to make a modest contribution to that discussion by investigating the theological hermeneutic that Paul teaches and models in 1 Corinthians. We will focus not so much on the movement from Scripture to *ethics* (including the much-debated question of whether we should seek to improve on the social ethics of the NT writers), or even on the movement from Scripture to *doctrine* (that is, the question of how the exegesis of Scripture contributes to the pattern of sound teaching that inscribes the boundaries of the church and directs the shape of its life), as on the movement from Scripture to *theology*, and (in particular) the movement from Scripture toward *systematic* theology. Theology, doctrine, and ethics are, of course, closely related, but enough is distinctive about the discipline of systematic theology (including its comprehensiveness of scope; the ordered, systematic shape of its architecture; and the dialectical, academic contexts in which it is typically constructed) to warrant placing it in a category of its own and asking whether this particular movement "beyond the Bible"—the movement to *theology*—is a legitimate one and, if so, how it ought to be made.

Among all the biblical writings, 1 Corinthians is particularly relevant to the question at hand. The language of "wisdom," "speech," and "knowledge" pervades the letter, reflecting a focus on Christian speaking and thinking that commences as early as the opening verses, where Paul thanks God that the Corinthians have been "enriched in every way—with all kinds of speech and with all knowledge" (1:5). It continues throughout the following chapters, with extended explorations of various aspects of the content and function of Christian wisdom and knowledge, and a string of abrasive rhetorical questions—ten in all, across the letter—in which Paul asks the Corinthians, "Do you not know . . . ?" Clearly, this letter is intended as, among other things, a (remedial) education in how to think and speak Christianly. If there is anywhere in the New Testament where it is worth seeking a warrant for doing theology and some guidance on how to do it, 1 Corinthians is that place.

In this chapter we will focus not on the "whether" part of the question but on the "how,"[5] investigating Paul's hermeneutical practices in 1 Corinthians— that is, the ways in which Paul interprets the Corinthians' situation and their world in the light of the Old Testament and its fulfillment in the gospel of Christ—to see what light Paul's interpretive practices within this letter shed

5. For an exploration of the "whether" part of the question, see Starling, "Not a Wisdom of This Age."

on the question of how the movement from Scripture to theology might be faithfully and fruitfully negotiated.

Paul among the Theologians?

If we turn to 1 Corinthians with this sort of question, the first and most obvious observation we must acknowledge is that this is not the work of a "theologian" in the same sense that the word came to carry in later Christian centuries. Even those who compose summations of "Pauline theology" and speak of Paul as "the first and greatest Christian theologian,"[6] or "the great theologian of grace and redemption,"[7] are quick to clarify that he was "not a theologian in our sense of the term."[8]

This is evident in at least three ways when we look even cursorily at 1 Corinthians. First, there is the fact that the text is so manifestly *occasional*. Paul draws our attention to this by the way he organizes its content around references to reports he has received from Corinth (e.g., 1:11; 5:1; 11:18) and to a letter the Corinthians have written to him (e.g., 7:1, 25; 8:1; 12:1; 16:1, 12). What we are reading is self-evidently a letter, not a treatise, and makes no pretense to the contrary.

Second, and relatedly, there is the fact that so much of the letter focuses on *social practices* rather than on what might be regarded as matters of pure doctrinal theory. Across the sixteen chapters of the letter, Paul exhorts and advises the Corinthians on a long list of issues, including factionalism, sexual behavior, predatory litigation, eating and drinking, cultic participation, head coverings, community meals, tongue speaking and prophecy, and the collection for the Christians in Judea. If there is a boundary line worth drawing between the theological and the pastoral or ethical, not much of the content of 1 Corinthians could be placed neatly and simply on the theological side.

Third, and finally, there is the way that Paul asserts his *apostolicity* in the opening verse of the letter and reiterates and defends the claim repeatedly across the following chapters. Although the roles of apostle and theologian need not be regarded as mutually exclusive, there are inevitable and significant differences between the kind of speaking and writing about God done by a theologian who claims to be an authoritative eyewitness of the Lord Jesus, commissioned as a "wise builder" (3:10) to lay foundations for others to build

---

6. Dunn, *Theology of Paul*, 2.
7. Matera, *God's Saving Grace*, 1.
8. Ibid., 6. Dunn similarly stresses that "Paul wrote as a missionary and pastor, and not as an academic theologian." *Theology of Paul*, 53.

on, and the kind done by a theologian in subsequent decades or centuries who seeks to build on those foundations.[9]

None of these observations is fatal to our project, however. A text can be occasional, practical, and apostolic without ceasing to be theological. Even when we have given due regard to the ways in which Paul's project in 1 Corinthians differs from the project of a modern theologian, there is still an abundance of resources within the letter that we can draw upon in our attempt to construct a theological hermeneutic that is faithful to the patterns and purposes of Scripture.

Paul among the *Theologoi*

Although the question motivating our enquiry in this chapter has to do with how Paul's letters might offer a foundation to build on or a paradigm to emulate for subsequent Christian theologians and interpreters, our prior task—if we are to guard against anachronism—is to locate Paul not among the theologians of later generations but among the *theologoi* of his own time. The path toward what eventually came to be known as Christian theology was long and winding, and its beginnings included not only the in-house discussions of the early church and its dialogue with the emerging Judaism of the rabbis, but also its interactions with the vast, sprawling conversation about God and the gods that the Greco-Roman world called *theologia*.

The most famous ancient attempt to offer an account of what was meant by the word *theologia* among the Greeks and the Romans is that of the Roman writer Marcus Terentius Varro, whose treatment of the topic survives in the passages where it is quoted and discussed by Christian writers, including Tertullian and Augustine.[10] Drawing on a tripartite schema most likely developed by others before him, Varro distinguished between three genera of theology: *theologia mythica*, the theology of the poets, as it was presented in the theater; *theologia physica*, the theology of the philosophers, whose locus of operation was "within the walls of a school" and whose domain of study was the whole natural universe; and *theologia civilis*—the theology of the priests, who stood guard over the cultic rituals and sacrifices of the city.[11] Talk about God and the gods in the Greco-Roman world had mythical/dramatic,

9. Related to this point, of course, is the fact that "Scripture" for us refers to a two-testament canon that includes Paul's own writings.

10. See especially Tertullian, *Ad Nationes* 2.1; Augustine, *The City of God against the Pagans* 6.5–12.

11. Augustine, *The City of God against the Pagans* 6.5.

philosophical, and cultic/political dimensions, all interrelated, sometimes in ways that were mutually reinforcing and at other times in ways that exposed awkward and unresolved tensions between them. It was in the context of these swirling currents of story, philosophy, ritual, and politics that Paul undertook his forays in 1 Corinthians from Scripture to *theologia*.

The Hermeneutics of Theology

In this chapter I will touch briefly on three of these forays and the hermeneutic that informs each of them: (1) Paul's words about Scripture, wisdom, and boasting in 1 Corinthians 1–4; (2) his counsel regarding food sacrificed to idols and meals in pagan temples in 1 Corinthians 8–10; and (3) his climactic reminder of the gospel and his response to those who say there is no resurrection of the dead in 1 Corinthians 15.

"Nothing beyond What Is Written" (1 Cor. 1–4)

In 1 Corinthians 1:10–4:21, Paul is responding to reports that have reached him of divisions and quarrels among the Corinthians. For most of the section, however, he focuses not on the divisions themselves but on the arrogant boasting and the false understanding of wisdom that he sees as underlying them. In this section of the letter the topic of "wisdom" first arises in 1:17, where Paul reminds the Corinthians that he was sent "to preach the gospel—not with wisdom and eloquence [*ouk en sophia logou*], lest the cross of Christ be emptied of its power."

Many recent commentators have taken the "wisdom" of 1 Corinthians 1–4 as referring primarily or even exclusively to the specious plausibility and rhetorical flourish of the sophists.[12] There is evidence to support this interpretation in the fact that Paul's first reference to wisdom, in 1:17, occurs in the context of a reminder about Paul's mode of preaching (a theme to which he returns in 2:1–5). Connections can be drawn, too, between Paul's words about wisdom within this chapter and the controversies about rhetoric in 2 Corinthians 10–13, along with the broader cultural context in which rhetorical sophistry was becoming increasingly prominent and highly prized. But the evidence of the following paragraphs suggests that Paul is painting with a somewhat broader brush. Whatever the precise referents Paul had in mind for "the wise person," "the teacher of the law," and "the philosopher of this age" (1 Cor. 1:20), it seems clear that by piling up a list of such

12. See especially Winter, *Philo and Paul*, 180–202.

terms side by side he intends to convey a sense of comprehensiveness: it is "[all] the wisdom of [all] the world" that God has made foolish, not just the fancy talk of the sophists.[13] Paul's concerns about the "wisdom" prized by the Corinthian Christians extend beyond the forms of pagan rhetoric to the content and ethos of pagan philosophy,[14] and his response addresses not only the social power of *sophia* as a demonstration of prestige or a technique of persuasion but also the philosophical and theological claims of *sophia* as a way to "know [God]" (v. 21).

Paul's answer to the arrogant and divisive "wisdom" prized by the Corinthians is studded with frequent citations of Scripture—six in all in this section, in 1:19, 31; 2:9, 16; 3:19, 20. Appeals to Scripture are not Paul's only rhetorical strategy or the sole foundation of his argument, but they contribute crucially to the substance and force of his appeal.

In 1:13–2:5, Paul reminds the Corinthians of the shape of his practice and their experience, pointing out the incompatibility of both with the kind of "wisdom" that the Corinthians prize and seek, and he grounds his account of the way God acted (both in Paul's calling and in the Corinthians' conversion) in the divine wisdom that is summed up in "the message of the cross" (1:18, 20b–25, 27–30). These appeals to example, experience, and the message of the cross are, in turn, pointedly correlated with and explained by citations from Scripture.

Thus, according to the logic of verses 17–19, Christ sent Paul "to preach the gospel—not with wisdom and eloquence," because (*gar*) "the message of the cross is foolishness to those who are perishing" (v. 18), because (*gar*) "it is written: 'I will destroy the wisdom of the wise; the intelligence of the intelligent I will frustrate'" (v. 19). The pronouncement of YHWH through the mouth of Isaiah, in judgment on the foolish craftiness of the Jerusalemite politicians (LXX Isa. 29:14), is taken as paradigmatic of YHWH's ways, confirming and explaining the pattern of divine action that Paul has seen at work in his commissioning as a proclaimer of the gospel and in the content of the message he was given to proclaim.

Similarly, in 1 Corinthians 1:26–31, Paul's reminder of the lowly status of the majority of the Corinthians (v. 26) places that fact within a pattern of God's action "in Christ Jesus, who has become for us wisdom from God" (v. 30). This pattern has a proximate purpose ("to shame the wise . . . to shame the strong . . . to nullify the things that are"; vv. 27–28), which is, in turn, directed toward a larger goal, "so that no one may boast before him" (v. 29).

---

13. Cf. Inkelaar, *Conflict over Wisdom*, 316.
14. See especially Brookins, "Rhetoric and Philosophy"; Brookins, "Wise Corinthians."

The positive correlate of that larger goal recurs at the end of the paragraph in the form of another citation from Scripture: "Therefore, as it is written: 'Let the one who boasts boast in the Lord'" (v. 31, citing LXX Jer. 9:23 [9:24 ET] or 1 Kgdms. 2:10).

In 1 Corinthians 2:6–16, where Paul lays out an account of the wisdom that he "speak[s] . . . among the mature," the two scriptural citations, both from Isaiah, play a similar role, underlining Paul's point about the hiddenness of God's plans and purposes apart from revelation. Paul reiterates his assertion that God's mind is inaccessible to merely human wisdom in the rhetorical question he quotes from Isaiah 40:13 (in an abbreviated form) in the final verse of the chapter: "For, 'who has known the mind of the Lord so as to instruct him?'"

Paul continues to use scriptural citations to humble and chasten his readers as this section of the letter continues in chapter 3, where the two citations come in the final paragraph, as Paul moves from the farming and building metaphors of verses 5–17 toward the warning of verse 21 against "boasting about human leaders." The two citations, paraphrased from Job 5:13 and Psalm 94:11 (LXX 93:11), are sandwiched between that warning in verse 21 and the earlier, ironic, injunction in verse 18: "If any of you think you are wise by the standards of this age, you should become 'fools' so that you may become wise." (The first of these citations perhaps carries an additional edge of irony in that it is taken from the words of the foolish wise man Eliphaz, in his presumptuous advice to Job.)[15]

The thread we have been tracing through chapters 1–3 is highlighted by Paul in 4:6, where he sums up the purpose of the preceding section of the letter: "so that you may learn from us the meaning of the saying, 'Do not go beyond what is written.'" Although various ingenious suggestions have been made for the referent of "what is written," the fact that all thirty other occurrences of *gegraptai* in Paul refer to Old Testament citations strongly supports the simplest and most obvious reading, which takes the word as a reference to Scripture. Given the way that the concerns of 1:31 are reiterated in 3:21–23 and 4:6–7,[16] the particular Scripture that is probably closest to the front of Paul's mind is the citation from Jeremiah 9:24 (LXX 9:23) in 1 Corinthians 1:31. But we need not assume that the saying refers exclusively to a single, particular text; Paul uses the plural *ha gegraptai*, after all, and even in 1:31, as we have seen, his modifications to the citation of Jeremiah summon echoes of a larger choir of scriptural voices. Most likely, then, the whole of Scripture is

15. Cf. Garland, *1 Corinthians*, 123.
16. Wagner, "'Not Beyond.'"

in view, particularly (but not exclusively) the string of texts cited in chapters 1–3.[17] The lesson the Corinthians are to learn is doubly humbling: Paul and Apollos, as their roles have been set forth in 3:5–4:5, model humble dependence on God and submission to the wisdom of the Scriptures; and the contents of the Scriptures themselves, as they have been cited in the preceding chapters, deflate the pretensions of human wisdom, reveal the things that human wisdom could never have uncovered, and summon their readers to boast only in God.[18]

For those who wish to go "beyond the Bible" to theology, the main message of chapters 1–4 is a cautionary one. Those who seek to build anything in God's church (theological systems included) should work in fear and trembling before him, resisting the delusion that they could improve on his plans and specifications by adding some flourish of their own that goes "beyond what is written."

What is less clear at this point of the letter is whether there is any place at all for the particular kind of building work that Paul's Corinthian readers would have recognized as *theologia*—that is, whether the "ten thousand guardians" (4:15; cf. 3:10) who come after Paul should restrict themselves to faithfully preserving and proclaiming the received traditions of Scripture and gospel, or whether there might be a way of constructing something more comprehensive and systematic, in dialogue with the pagan *theologoi*, without falling prey to the hubris against which Paul warns here.

"These Things Occurred as Typoi*" (1 Cor. 8–10)*

Paul's warning in 4:6 against the danger of becoming "puffed up" (*physiousthe*) by a false estimation of human wisdom recurs at the beginning of the next section of the letter that we are examining (8:1). That the same verb also appears in the opening paragraph of chapters 5–6 (5:2: *pephysiōmenoi este*; NIV "you are proud") and in the poem at the center of chapters 12–14 (13:4: *ou physioutai*; NIV "it is not proud") suggests that the warning of 4:6 functions programmatically to indicate the kind of thinking Paul is encouraging in the rest of the letter and that its intention can, in part at least, be gauged from the ways Paul applies the same verb in these subsequent occurrences.

The counsel Paul offers the Corinthians in 1 Corinthians 8–10 concerns their conduct in relation to food sacrificed to idols and meals in pagan temples— topics that Greco-Roman readers would have identified as falling within the

---

17. Cf. Inkelaar, *Conflict over Wisdom*, 62–63.
18. Cf. the argument in P. Marshall, *Enmity in Corinth*, 194–218, that "the idea of hybris underlies the whole passage [1 Cor. 4:6–13]" and particularly the warning against going *hyper ha gegraptai* in v. 6.

realm of *theologia*. Josephus, for example, describes his fellow Jews' pattern of worship and their refusal to participate in the cult of the Egyptian gods as integral to "our theology,"[19] and Emperor Julian mocks the Christians of his day for their anti-idolatrous practices, writing in a letter to a pagan priest: "These two things are the quintessence of their theology, to hiss at demons and make the sign of the cross on their foreheads."[20]

The *theologia* of Christians on these matters, according to Paul, is informed by their knowledge that "an idol is nothing at all in this world," and "there is no God but one" (8:4, probably quoting Corinthian slogans). Paul affirms these slogans, highlighting how they collide with pagan practices and beliefs (v. 5), before rephrasing them in his own tightly constructed but richly allusive formulation: "Yet for us there is but one God, the Father, from whom all things came and for whom we live; and there is but one Lord, Jesus Christ, through whom all things came and through whom we live" (v. 6).

The content of Paul's summary is clearly grounded in the testimony of Scripture (evoking echoes of texts including Gen. 1:1 and Deut. 6:4), refracted through the lens of the gospel's claims about the identity and universal lordship of the risen Jesus, but it is also (and unmistakably) expressed in language that reframes the formulations of Stoic pantheism and Hellenistic Judaism. Obvious comparisons and contrasts can be made, for example, with the wisdom theology of Philo[21] and Stoic formulations such as that of the second-century emperor-philosopher Marcus Aurelius: "From thee [O Nature] are all things, in thee are all things, to thee all things return."[22]

Paul's problem with the Corinthians' "knowledge," it seems, is not with the possession of it, or with the attempt to formulate it in concepts and categories that borrow from or overlap with those of pagan philosophy (after all, his own formulation in v. 6 is far more theologically sophisticated than the Corinthian slogans he appears to be quoting in v. 4), but with the failure to use it in love. What it might look like to use that knowledge in love is elaborated on and illustrated in 8:7–9:27, where love is depicted in terms of practices that involve becoming "a slave to everyone" (9:19), treating one's brother or sister as a person "for whom Christ died" (8:11), and doing all things "for the sake of the gospel" (9:23). Where knowledge—including the knowledge that takes the form of *theologia*—is used in that manner, toward the end of the salvation and upbuilding of others (8:1; 9:19–22), it is to be embraced; where it is not so used, it merely "puffs up" (8:1).

19. *Ag. Ap.* 1.224–25 (my translation).
20. *Letters* 19, trans. Wilmer C. Wright, in Julian, *Letters*, 53.
21. E.g., *Cherubim* 125–26; *Spec. Laws* 1.208.
22. Marcus Aurelius, *Meditations* 4.23, trans. George Long.

The proper use of theological knowledge is further illustrated in chapter 10, where Paul turns from the situations in which love for a brother or sister requires abstaining from something that is permitted in itself to those situations in which the activity itself is out of the question. The passage begins with a variation on the traditional disclosure formula ("I want you to know . . ."), recast into a double negative ("I do not want you to be ignorant . . ."), which may be intended as a subtle dig at the Corinthians' boasts of knowledge. The knowledge Paul urges the Corinthians to take account of in this instance is derived from the Old Testament (with a reflection of Paul's awareness of the rabbinic interpretive tradition in the way that he speaks in v. 4 of the rock that "accompanied" them).[23]

The relevance of this knowledge to the judgments Paul urges the Corinthians to make in their own situation is based on their shared convictions about the oneness and self-consistency of God, which allow them to understand their situation in narrative continuity and typological correspondence with the story of God's actions in the past. Thus, Paul invites the gentile believers in Corinth to view the Israelites of the exodus generation as their own ancestors (10:1) and to understand the things that happened to them as "examples [*typoi*]" for them (10:6, 11),[24] illustrating and reinforcing convictions of permanent validity about enduringly relevant attributes of God (in this instance, according to vv. 13, 22, God's jealousy and faithfulness).

The stability and unity of the grand salvation-historical narrative that Paul evokes in these verses are critical for the hermeneutical bridge that Paul builds across the ditch between historical assertions about unique, particular events and theological truth-claims of universal applicability. The events of which he is reminding the Corinthians line up with their own situation in a single story, with a single, divine protagonist about whom statements can be made that have enduring truth and applicability; on the basis of the narrative logic of that story,[25] Paul is confident that he can commend such statements to the Corinthians as "sensible" people (10:15), asking them to "judge for [them]selves" the implications for their conduct.

Several aspects of Paul's reasoning within this passage (e.g., the assumption that assertions can be made about the divine nature that have universal relevance and applicability; the articulation of *typoi* that govern the speech and conduct of the wise; and the appeal to his readers to exercise a rational judgment about the implications of the divine nature for their conduct as

23. Cf. the discussion in Ciampa and Rosner, *First Letter to the Corinthians*, 450–51.
24. See especially Hays, "Conversion of the Imagination."
25. Cf. Scott, *Paul's Way of Knowing*, 277–88.

a community) suggest obvious affinities with the philosophical theology of the Greco-Roman tradition. An illuminating comparison can be made, for example, with the famous discussion of the *typoi peri theologias* (rules for speech about the divine) in Book Two of Plato's *Republic*,[26] which is the oldest surviving use of the word *theologia* in the works of the Greek philosophers. But there are crucial differences, too. Particularly important for our purposes in this chapter is the role that the Old Testament narrative plays in Paul's *theologia*, which differs strikingly from that of the pagan *mythoi* in Plato's *Republic*. For Plato, the *mythoi* are fictions (*pseudē*), even when they are fictions that teach truth,[27] and their content is plastic in the hands of the poets. The *typoi* that ought to regulate the content of what the poets are permitted to compose are timeless ethical and metaphysical principles supplied by the philosophers: for example, "that God is not the cause of all things, but only of the good" and "that God is altogether simple and true in deed and word, and neither changes himself nor deceives others."[28] For Paul, the Old Testament narrative of God's words and actions is nonnegotiable,[29] and the events of the narrative function as *typoi* for the latter-day reader. The *mythos* is the *typos*, even when it teaches divine attributes like jealousy, which a high-minded reader might be tempted to trim or excise.[30] There is still a place for drawing out implications from the narrative and stating them as ethical norms (e.g., 10:7a, 8a, 9a, 10a) or theological assertions (e.g., 12:13 and, by implication, 10:22). But these derive from the narrative (interpreted and retold in light of the gospel of Christ) rather than standing over it and controlling it.

"In Accordance with the Scriptures" (1 Cor. 15)

In 1 Corinthians 15 we reach the climax of the letter, as Paul reminds the Corinthians of the gospel traditions that were "of first importance" (v. 3) in what he preached to them, and builds on those traditions a response to Corinthian Christians who say "there is no resurrection of the dead" (v. 12).

26. Plato, *Republic* 2.379a.
27. "The fable is, taken as a whole, false, but there is truth in it also." *Republic* 2.377a; cf. 2.382d and the (in)famous "noble lie" of 3.414e–415d.
28. *Republic* 2.380c, 2.382e.
29. The nonnegotiable status of the scriptural narrative for Paul derives both from its presumed historical character ("these things occurred . . . these things happened" [10:6, 11]) and from the divine intention that the events and their inscripturation are seen as serving ("as examples . . . as examples . . . as warnings for us" [vv. 6, 11]).
30. Even I. Howard Marshall seems to make a move of this sort in his discussion (*Beyond the Bible*, 66–67) of the judgment imagery of Jesus's parables and the OT narratives of the slaughter of the Canaanites and the slaying of Achan and his family, in which he pronounces the judgment that "we can no longer think of God like that."

On the surface, an argument for the theological character of this chapter would seem to be swimming against the tide of recent scholarship on 1 Corinthians, which has turned decisively against the older idea that the chapter was written to combat the theological problem of an overrealized eschatology, or the still older idea that the whole letter was occasioned by theological disputes between the factions named in 1:12. As David Garland correctly observes, most recent studies of the letter argue that the problems in Corinth stem "more from the influence of their cultural setting than from specious theological beliefs."[31]

But if *theologia* is understood in an ancient, Greco-Roman sense and not in the sense that it came to have in later Christian usage, then the dichotomy between "the influence of [the Corinthians'] cultural setting" and "specious theological beliefs" loses its neatness. The pagan patterns of belief and practice influencing the Corinthian Christians were in fact deeply theological; Paul's argument in the chapter should be taken not as a theological response to a non-theological problem[32] but as a theological response to a theological problem.

In chapter 15, the problems of deficient (or even overrealized) eschatology and disbelief in future, bodily resurrection can both be understood in terms of the pagan *theologia* of the day, without need for any recourse to speculation about endemically Christian eschatological heresies. Among the various influences that would have encouraged these attitudes among the Corinthian Christians, one particularly powerful one would have been the propaganda of the Roman Empire that emphasized the *pax* and *salus* achieved through the rule of Augustus and his successors.[33] But it was not only the propaganda of the imperial *theologia civilis* that fostered such an attitude; pagan religious practice in general was overwhelmingly (though not exclusively) oriented toward the attainment of prosperity and safety in this present life,[34] and those who achieved these goals—who "ate and drank" in abundance—were able (to some extent at least) to defer uncomfortable thoughts about the fact that "tomorrow we die." The *theologia physica* of the philosophers, likewise, taught an understanding of God and nature that was profoundly incompatible with belief in future, bodily resurrection.[35]

---

31. Garland, "1 Corinthians," 98.

32. This is essentially how Garland reads the letter: "Paul's purpose is not to correct their theology but to get them to think theologically so that they would respond properly to their polytheistic, pluralistic culture." Ibid., 98.

33. See especially the excursus "Roman Imperial Eschatology," in Witherington, *Conflict and Community*, 295–98.

34. Cf. Witherington, "Salvation and Health," 146–50; MacMullen, *Paganism in the Roman Empire*, 53–57.

35. Cf. the survey in N. T. Wright, *Resurrection of the Son of God*, 47–84.

That Paul is consciously conversing with the philosophical speculations of the pagan *theologia physica*—or at least with a pop-philosophical derivative of them—is evident in his reference to "bad company" (or, perhaps better, "bad conversation") in verse 33, and in his response to the scoffing questions of the skeptic, which he invokes in verse 35. Likewise, in the language and imagery of the preceding paragraph he evokes the *theologia civilis* of the imperial propaganda (vv. 20–28).[36]

Citations and echoes of Scripture in 1 Corinthians 15 play a key role in the rhetoric and substance of Paul's response to this multifaceted pagan *theologia*, in line with his repeated assertion in verses 3–4 that the gospel he passed on to the Corinthians was "according to the scriptures." In verse 32, for example, to represent the stance of those who deny the resurrection, he constructs a brief imagined speech ("Let us eat and drink, for tomorrow we die") that simultaneously echoes the Jerusalemites rebuked by the prophet in Isaiah 22:10–13 and the Epicureans of first-century Corinth, as they would have been caricatured by their critics;[37] the prophet becomes a preacher to the pagans, and the force of the prophetic oracle is implicitly generalized and contemporized. Similarly, a few verses earlier, Paul's grand counternarrative to the narratives of pagan and imperial realized eschatology seamlessly integrates modified citations of Ps. 110:1 (LXX 109:1) and 8:6 into his account of the universal triumph of Christ as representative human. The "all" that he inserts into his paraphrase of Psalm 110 in verse 25 is in line with the sense of the original, and has the effect of stitching the two citations of the Psalms even more closely together ("all his enemies . . . everything"; Greek: *pantas . . . ta panta*) and reinforcing the connections between the scriptural roots of Paul's grand narrative and the language of its unmistakably theological finale in verse 28, which points toward a day when God will be "all in all" (*panta en pasin*). Although the language of the grand finale (like that of Paul's summation in 8:6) is noticeably redolent of the language of pagan philosophical theology, Paul locates the passage's depiction of God as "all in all" in a context of scripturally grounded, christocentric eschatological narrative that fills it with distinctively and unmistakably Christian content.

Paul begins his response to the scoffing questions of verse 35 (in vv. 36–44) with a series of analogies between Christian resurrection hope and various phenomena of the natural world. The analogies function, partly, to expose the skeptic's fallacious assumption that the only kind of "bodily" resurrection

---

36. Cf. Witherington, *Conflict and Community*, 305; Thiselton, *First Epistle to the Corinthians*, 1232.

37. E.g., Plutarch, *Moralia* 1098C; cf. 1100D, 1125D.

Paul could have in mind would be one that merely perpetuated into the next life the same mortal, inglorious flesh that our bodies are made of in this life. Bodies, Paul counters, come in all sorts of different forms, with many kinds and degrees of glory; nature itself teaches this much, and Paul does not hesitate to appeal to the natural knowledge of his readers to support his rebuttal of the reductionistic materialism presupposed by his skeptical conversation partner.

The dominant analogy is that of the body as a planted seed (vv. 36–38, 42–44), which (like the analogy of the body as prison in Cicero's "Dream of Scipio") suggests powerful imaginative possibilities—in Paul's case, not of escape from embodiment but of transformation into a radically different form of embodiment. Scripture returns in verse 45, in a citation from Genesis 2:7, which Paul offers in partial support of this picture of transformation from "a natural body" to "a spiritual body." The sequence established in the four parallel assertions of verses 42b–44 (a *psychikon* body is sown in death, in anticipation of a *pneumatikon* body raised in resurrection) is confirmed by the typological relationship between the first Adam (formed by God as a *psychēn zōsan*; NIV "living being") and the last Adam (raised from the dead as a *pneuma zōopoioun*, or "life-giving spirit").

This movement through death to life is celebrated in the final two scriptural citations of the chapter, from Isaiah 25:8 and Hosea 13:14.[38] Paul implicitly invites readers to join with Isaiah's song of victory over death, and, in light of the work of Christ (cf. vv. 56–57), he transforms the summoning of death and hades for judgment in Hosea 13 into a taunt over death, whose penal role has become redundant.[39] The song that Paul makes out of both of these modified scriptural citations reechoes in the explicitly Christian thanksgiving of verse 57, which leads, in turn, to the exhortation of the final verse.

Imitating Paul

This survey of the hermeneutic that underlies Paul's forays into *theologia* in 1 Corinthians 1–4, 8–10, and 15 suggests several conclusions about how we might faithfully move from Scripture to theology, so as to build on the foundations Paul supplies in this letter and imitate the pattern he models.

38. Paul's wording of the citation from Isa. 25:8 probably reflects a version of the Greek text similar to those preserved in the versions of Aquila, Theodotion, and Symmachus. The wording of the citation from Hos. 13:14 also differs from extant versions of the LXX at several points, including the use of *nikos* in place of *dikē* and *thanate* in place of *hadē*.

39. With the ESV and NRSV, and against the NIV, I am reading the first half of Hos. 13:14 as a rhetorical question ("Shall I ransom them from the power of Sheol? Shall I redeem them from Death?"), to which the remainder of the verse implies a negative answer.

The theological hermeneutic that Paul models in 1 Corinthians is a hermeneutic whose disposition is humility and whose purpose is love. As a hermeneutic of humility, it does not attempt to improve on the wisdom of Scripture, even when it converses with the pagan philosophers and borrows concepts and categories from them; nor does it use their axioms and theorems as *typoi*, in Platonic fashion, to censor the portrayal of God in the biblical narratives (cf. 10:1–22; 15:35–50). Similarly, when it orders its ideas in new systems and patterns of arrangement, it does not succumb to the delusion that these intellectual constructions express a greater wisdom than the wisdom already given in Scripture (cf. 4:6). As a hermeneutic of love, it directs its interpretive endeavors and arguments not toward the promotion of its own interests or the display of its own virtuosity but toward the building-up of the church and the promotion of the gospel, in deliberate imitation of Christ (cf. 8:1–9:26); if glory is to be sought in the endeavor, it is not the glory of the theologian in the academy or the church but the glory of Christ and of the lowliest and weakest of his servants (cf. 8:1, 11–13; 10:31–33; 12:21–26).

In terms of the content and mode of interpretation, the hermeneutic that informs Paul's theology in 1 Corinthians is both salvation-historical and apocalyptic. As a salvation-historical hermeneutic, it places the readers and their situation in a single, larger story that includes the story of Israel and its fulfillment in Christ (which is, in turn, placed in the story of God and the world); it interprets that story as a revelation of the character of the one true God; it finds typological correspondences in the story that illuminate the imagination and judgment of Christian readers (cf. 1:17–31; 10:1–22; 15:12–34); and—since the redeemer is also the creator—it seeks coherence between the conclusions drawn from that story and those derived from our natural, human knowledge of the world (cf. 15:35–49). But these convictions regarding the unity and consistency of God's action as creator and redeemer should not be taken as a warrant for a naively positivist epistemology, either in the interpretation of Scripture or in the interpretation of the world—Paul can appeal to his readers "as sensible people" (*hōs phronimois*; 10:15), but he does not encourage them to assume that unaided human reason can make sense of either the Old Testament or the world apart from the undreamt-of revelation of the gospel or the eye-opening work of the Spirit.

The theological hermeneutic that Paul models in 1 Corinthians is as much an apocalyptic hermeneutic as it is a salvation-historical one; it interprets the world and the Old Testament narrative of Israel's election and judgment in light of the *mystērion* made known in the death and resurrection of Jesus (cf. 2:6–16; 10:11; 15:51). This divine in-breaking necessitates a retelling of the story so far-reaching that a judgment oracle summoning death and hades to execute their sentence (Hos. 13:14) is transformed into a victory song that celebrates the way in which they have been swallowed up by life (1 Cor. 15:55); it creates a new community of those "on whom the culmination of the ages has come" (10:11), and it teaches a wisdom that is "not . . . of this age or of the rulers of this age" (2:6).

Where Christian theology is informed and disciplined by a hermeneutic of this sort, Paul's example in 1 Corinthians suggests that theology serves a legitimate and necessary function in the life of the church; where theology pursues a course that seems wiser in its own eyes, 1 Corinthians pronounces a sober warning that theology is likely, at best, to amount to nothing more than empty, puffed-up talk.

❖11❖

"Taken Figuratively"

Galatians and the Hermeneutics of Allegory

Allegory and Appropriation

One of the perpetual challenges faced by Bible readers is the question of how the narratives of the biblical text—so remote historically and so particular (and frequently peculiar) in their content—are to be related meaningfully to the situations and experiences of their readers. It is easy enough to recount the story of how David killed Goliath with a stone—one of five that he took from the riverbed—thrown from his sling at the giant's head; it is possible too, with careful reading and the exercise of appropriate exegetical method, to offer a plausible account of the rhetorical effect that the story might have been intended to have on its original hearers and readers. But what does the story mean *for me*? Am I to place myself somewhere within the scene, identifying perhaps with David, with the watching Israelites, or even, potentially, with the defeated Philistines? Am I to stand outside it altogether? And what (if anything) am I to make of the stones, the sling, the giant, the rejected armor of King Saul, and all the other features of the richly detailed narrative?[1]

For centuries, in late antiquity and the Middle Ages (and on into the modern era too, in portions of the church), the most common solution to that

1. Cf. the discussion in Goldsworthy, *Gospel and Kingdom*, 9–11, 106–11.

predicament was provided by the allegorical method of interpretation. For the allegorical interpreter, the characters, events, and circumstances of the biblical stories could be read as a treasure trove of symbols, carrying meanings and implications that extended far beyond those that could possibly have been understood and intended by their original authors. This approach to interpretation did not go unchallenged: in both antiquity and modernity, critics of the allegorical method protested that this made the Scriptures into a wax nose that the interpreter could twist and stretch into any shape he or she chose, robbing the biblical narratives of their historicity and replacing the literal sense with some new meaning foisted onto the text by the interpreter. The debate continues into our own time, even though the theories of the patristic and medieval allegorists are rarely explicitly invoked as a justification for the reading strategies that are modeled in the preaching and devotional literature of popular evangelical piety.[2]

In the various iterations of this long-running debate, Paul's interpretation of the story of Sarah and Hagar in Galatians 4:21–5:1 has frequently been appealed to as justification for Christian allegorical interpretation. Origen, for example, appeals to the story in support of a sweeping assertion that "all the narrative portion [of Scripture], relating either to the marriages, or to the begetting of the children, or to battles of different kinds, or to any other histories whatever" is to be interpreted as "the forms and figures of hidden and sacred things."[3] Critics of the allegorical method, for their part, have rejected the inference, protesting that Paul's "allegory" is not *really* an allegory but a typology: "Contrary to usage, he calls a type an allegory; his meaning is as follows; this history not only declares that which appears on the face of it, but announces somewhat farther, whence it is called an allegory."[4]

Most recent interpreters of Galatians have rightly pointed out the sterility of this particular war of words. In Paul's time *allēgoreō* had not yet come to be used as a technical term for a particular form of interpretation that finds deeper, timeless meanings hidden behind the details of an ancient narrative. Rather, the verb (and its cognate noun *allēgoria*) could be used to refer to any interpretive strategy that finds figurative elements in a text or, more commonly, to any mode of speech or writing that uses figurative expression.[5] On this

2. Cf. the sharp critique of modern evangelical allegorical interpretation in ibid., 14–18, 112–13.

3. Origen, *De Principiis* 4.9, in *Fathers of the Third Century*, 358, trans. Frederick Crombie, from the Latin of Rufinus. Origen's appeal to the allegory in Gal. 4 is in *De Principiis* 4.13.

4. Chrysostom, *Commentary on Galatians* 4.24, 34, trans. Gross Alexander; similarly (quoting Chrysostom), Calvin, *Epistles of Paul*, 85.

5. Scott, *Paul's Way of Knowing*, 240.

broader definition of allegory as figural reading or writing, "typology" is best regarded not as the opposite of allegory but as a subspecies of it.[6]

More interesting and more complicated than the debate over whether the word "allegory" can properly be used to describe Paul's interpretation and application of the Genesis story is the question of how he goes about constructing the particular allegory (or whatever else we choose to call it) that he offers in these verses, and how he justifies it to his readers. In framing the question this way, we do not aim to defend the indefensible—to press Paul's use of the word "allegory" as if the presence of the mere word in the New Testament could provide a blank check to fund every allegorical adventure of the subsequent centuries. Nor, on the other hand, do we intend to explain away Paul's use of the word as if it told us nothing at all, reinforcing the modern, rationalistic assumption that the only kind of Bible reading that matters is scientific, historical-critical exegesis. Rather, we aim to ask whether (and, if so, how) Paul's mode of applying the Genesis narrative to himself and his readers might serve as a model for us as we attempt a similar task, and teach us something about how we might legitimately and fruitfully perform that task.

Justifying Allegory: An Interpretive Spectrum

Among scholars who have offered an account of how Paul constructs his allegory in Galatians 4:21–5:1 and how he justifies it to his readers, interpretations range across a wide spectrum. At one end are those who represent Paul as bringing to the text of Scripture a set of interpretive warrants derived entirely from outside the text; at the other end are those who represent Paul as deriving the warrants for his interpretation from within Old Testament Scripture itself.

An influential example from one end of the spectrum is the interpretation of Paul's hermeneutic in Galatians 4:21–31 offered by Richard Hays in *Echoes of Scripture in the Letters of Paul.* According to Hays, the reading of the Abraham story and its significance that Paul counterposes to the traditional Jewish readings that his opponents would have relied on is "a strong misreading" based on "the naked assertion (Gal. 4:25b) . . . of a phenomenological correspondence between Law and slavery." The associations that Paul draws here and elsewhere in the letter between law on the one hand and curse (3:10), confinement (3:23–24), and slavery (4:1–11, 24–25) on the other are (Hays

6. Cf. the comments in Gignilliat, "Paul, Allegory," 140.

argues) to be understood as "retrospective judgments . . . grounded upon a new communal experience of freedom in the power of the Holy Spirit."[7]

> Faced with the question of whether the Spirit illumines the text of Scripture or whether Scripture measures and constrains one's experience of the Spirit, Paul's unflinching answer, to the dismay of his more cautious kinsmen then and now, is to opt for the hermeneutical priority of Spirit-experience. This choice leads him, to be sure, not to a rejection of Scripture but to a charismatic rereading, that persuasive power of which would rest precariously on his ability to demonstrate a congruence between the scriptural text and the community summoned and shaped by his proclamation.[8]

An example from the other end of the spectrum can be found in the reading of Paul's argument offered by Ardel Caneday. According to Caneday, readings such as that proposed by Hays convey the impression of a Paul who has nothing but "privileged apostolic insight" or "interpretive dexterity" to warrant his arguments and give authority to his exhortations. "Where, in all his disputations," Caneday asks, "does the apostle Paul assert raw apostolic authority instead of appeal to Scripture as authorization upon which his converts and readers should hang their trust and receive his gospel as true?"[9]

This question launches Caneday into a quest to identify the scriptural warrants for Paul's claim that the Genesis narrative concerning Abraham should be understood as an allegory. It is within the Genesis story itself, Caneday observes, that Paul can point to features such as the promise of blessing to the nations (3:8, quoting Gen. 12:3), the accentuation of faith (in the divine promise of progeny) as what was "credited to [Abraham] as righteousness" (3:6, quoting Gen. 15:6), and the depiction of Sarah's barrenness as an obstacle to God's promises and a spur to faith (Gen. 11:30; 16:2–4; 17:17, alluded to via Isaiah in Gal. 4:27).[10]

On the basis of observations such as these (together with the way he sees Paul's scriptural citations functioning in the logic of his argument in 4:21–31), Caneday concludes that Paul intends his readers to understand that "while Genesis presents the personages and events as real history, also embedded into the text are features that render Abraham, Sarah, Hagar, Ishmael, and Isaac, with their experiences directed by God's actions among them, all symbolically representative of things greater than themselves."[11]

---

7. Hays, *Echoes of Scripture*, 115.
8. Ibid., 108. Cf. the similar approach taken in Fowl, "Who Can Read?"
9. Caneday, "Covenant Lineage Allegorically Prefigured," 51.
10. Ibid., 61–63. Cf. the similar observations in F. Watson, *Hermeneutics of Faith*, 207.
11. Caneday, "Covenant Lineage Allegorically Prefigured," 66.

The Rhetorical Context and Functions of Paul's Allegory

Any attempt to adjudicate between these two contrasting approaches, or to argue for an interpretation that lies somewhere on the spectrum between them, requires careful attention to the context of Paul's allegory in the rhetoric of the letter and the way that rhetoric supports his aims. Three observations in particular are worth making.

Argumentative Rhetoric

First, and perhaps most obviously, our assessment of how the allegory in Galatians 4:21–5:1 is intended to function needs to take into account the argumentative nature of Paul's rhetoric, both here and throughout Galatians.[12] Here, within 4:21–5:1, even the rhetoric of citation with which Paul introduces his references to Scripture is dialogical and argumentative in the connections that it draws between the scriptural citations and the surrounding discourse: "*For* it is written . . ." (4:22, 27); "*But* what does Scripture say?" (v. 30). Similarly, at the end of the paragraph, Paul uses a sequence of logical connectives to link his scriptural citations and the arguments built on them with the concluding imperatives: "*Therefore*, brothers and sisters. . . . Stand firm, *then*" (4:31; 5:1).

Clearly, in this section of the letter, Paul is reading Scripture in order to persuade, in the context of a conflict of interpretations. He is earnestly struggling for the hearts and minds of the Galatians (cf. 4:19), by no means able to assume that his authority will be accepted unquestioningly (cf. 4:15–16, 20). The opening question (4:21) invites the Galatians to enter the interpretive process with him, challenging them to assess the validity of the reading he proposes in the following verses, and the conclusion he states in the penultimate verse (as Hans Dieter Betz observes) implicitly "includes the readers among those who render judgment."[13] In this sort of context, Caneday is correct to stress the inadequacy of interpretations that paint Paul as relying entirely on the trust that his readers must repose in him as a recipient of revelation and an authoritative interpreter of Scripture.

Pathos-Laden and Ethos-Asserting Rhetoric

But logical argumentation is not Paul's sole rhetorical strategy here. Though not in a position to write as a trusted advisor whose counsel has been sought

12. Cf. Longenecker, *Galatians*, cxiv–cxix; contra Martyn, *Galatians*, 22–23.
13. Betz, *Galatians*, 240.

and whose authority is unquestioned, he can still deploy arguments that draw on a deep reservoir of affection and shared experience in his history with the Galatian churches. He addresses his argument to the Galatians not as an expert stranger but as an apostle (1:1), as the missionary from whom they first heard the gospel of Christ (1:8; 3:1; 4:13), and (metaphorically) as a mother who is once more "in the pains of childbirth" because of his concern for the Galatians (4:19). When Paul turns back to argumentation from Scripture in 4:21–5:1, he does not allow his readers simply to forget the shared experiences recalled in 3:1–5 and his pathos-laden appeal in 4:12–20; genuine as the arguments are, they are still addressed not to an impartial public but to "you, brothers and sisters" (4:28; similarly in 4:31), implicitly recalling the content of the preceding appeal. To interpret Paul's allegory as if its sole function were to advance a logical argument is to seriously mishear the tone of his voice.[14]

Deliberative Rhetoric

Third, and crucially, our interpretation of the function of the allegory needs to take into account the deliberative nature of Paul's rhetoric in this portion of the letter.[15] Although it is debatable whether the whole letter can adequately be analyzed as a textbook example of deliberative rhetoric,[16] there are good reasons to assert the practical and ethical aims of Paul's argumentation in 4:21–5:1. Paul's aim here is not only to establish the propositions that he asserts along the way (e.g., in 4:25, 26, 30) but also to persuade the Galatians to act on the imperative that closes the section: "Stand firm, then, and do not let yourselves be burdened again by a yoke of slavery" (5:1b).

To accomplish that goal, Paul seeks not only to convince his readers that being joined to Abraham by a covenant of Torah and circumcision amounts to "be[ing] burdened . . . by a yoke of slavery" but also to spur them into making a decision on the basis of that conviction.[17] Toward that end, the allegory of Hagar and Sarah contributes to a larger pattern of "argument by dissociation" within the letter,[18] dramatizing the Galatians' situation by representing it as a stark choice between two contrasting alternatives. The allegory also enhances the sense of urgency attached to the decision by appropriating Sarah's words

14. Cf. Eastman, *Recovering Paul's Mother Tongue*, 181–84.
15. Deliberative rhetoric, according to the categories of ancient rhetorical theory, was that species of rhetoric that attempted to persuade the hearers of the merits of a particular course of action, within the context of a decision to be made by a community.
16. See especially Kern, *Rhetoric and Galatians*, 90–119.
17. On the motivational function of Paul's rhetoric in this section of the letter, see especially Eastman, *Recovering Paul's Mother Tongue*, 5–7.
18. Cf. Longenecker, *Galatians*, cxvii.

to Abraham as a word of exclusion and banishment that "Scripture" speaks concerning all who are joined to Abraham by a covenant of circumcision and law-keeping.[19]

An awareness of the deliberative and dramatic dimensions of Paul's rhetoric helps to dispel any illusion that Paul's allegory is intended as an objective, context-free exegesis of the original meaning of the Genesis story. It also helps to guard against the false dichotomies between "argument" and mere "illustration" or "ornament" that are sometimes assumed in interpretations of the passage.[20] Paul's allegory may not be a self-contained, logical proof for a doctrinal assertion, but its contribution to his rhetoric is clearly intended to be more than merely ornamental.

The Warrants for Paul's Allegory

With these considerations in mind, what warrants can we find in the allegory and its context to justify how Paul reads the Genesis story and applies it to the circumstances of the Galatians?

Genesis

First, and most importantly, Paul's argument in chapters 3–4 draws his readers' attention to several features of the Genesis story itself that, in his eyes, warrant the kind of applications he is making. Perhaps the most basic element of the Genesis story that fits it to Paul's purposes is the fact that Abraham had "two sons" not one. Paul reminds the Galatians of this in verse 22 as a warrant for the implicit assertion in verse 21 that listening to the law will challenge, not confirm, the Galatians' desire to be subject to it. If the agitators in Galatia are telling Paul's converts that circumcision in their flesh will make them sons of Abraham, Paul reminds them that the Scripture speaks not of one son of Abraham but of two: the one born "according to the flesh" (Ishmael) and the one born "as the result of a divine promise" (Isaac). Paul's point is that there are two ways of being a "son of Abraham"—one of which

19. In support of this reading of how Paul appropriates the words of Sarah in 4:30, see especially Eastman, "'Cast Out.'"

20. Martin Luther, e.g., comments, "Allegories do not provide solid proofs in theology, but, like pictures, they adorn and illustrate a subject. . . . Because he has already fortified his case with more solid arguments . . . now, at the end of the argument, he adds an allegory as a kind of ornament. . . . Just as a picture is an ornament for a house that has already been constructed, so an allegory is a kind of illumination of an oration or of a case that has already been established on other grounds." Luther, *Lectures on Galatians 1535, Chapters 1–4*, 435–36, trans. Jaroslav Pelikan.

leads to freedom (5:1) and inheritance (4:30), the other to slavery (4:24–25) and expulsion (4:30)—and the Galatians need to choose between them.

But the details of the Genesis story offer more to Paul than the bare numerical fact that Abraham had two sons. As we have seen in Caneday's argument, Paul's larger argument from Scripture in chapters 3–4 includes references to the way the Genesis narrative highlights the divine promise of blessing to the nations (3:8, quoting Gen. 12:3), accentuates faith (in the accompanying promise of progeny) as what was "credited to [Abraham] as righteousness" (3:6, quoting Gen. 15:6), and depicts Sarah's barrenness as an obstacle to God's promises and a spur to faith (Gen. 11:30; 16:2–4; 17:17, alluded to via Isaiah in Gal. 4:27).[21]

The extent to which Paul appeals to the Genesis narrative to speak of themes that are native to the Genesis text itself, and constructs his allegory's correspondences from features of the original narrative that are prominent, not incidental, constitutes an important difference from the Alexandrian allegorical interpretations of Philo and his Christian successors.

> The Alexandrian [i.e., Philo] understands Abraham to represent the human soul, Sarah divine Wisdom, and Hagar a merely preparatory education, and the narratives are then read as the saga of the soul's quest for mystical wisdom. . . . Yet none of these ideas even fall within the horizon of the text taken on its own terms. Paul, on the other hand, focuses on the question of how one is included within the heritage of Abraham, on slavery and freedom, and on the difference between the trust in God involved in Isaac's birth and the human effort involved in the birth of Ishmael—all central motifs in the Genesis account.[22]

Isaiah

But the scriptural warrants for Paul's reading of the story of Isaac and Ishmael are not all contained in the Genesis story itself. At the center of the paragraph is a citation from Isaiah 54, which Paul presents as pivotal in justifying his allegory:

> Now Hagar stands for Mount Sinai in Arabia and corresponds to the present city of Jerusalem, because she is in slavery with her children. But the Jerusalem that is above is free, and she is our mother. For it is written:
>
> > "Be glad, barren woman,
> > you who never bore a child;

21. Caneday, "Covenant Lineage Allegorically Prefigured," 61–63. Similarly F. Watson, *Hermeneutics of Faith*, 207.
22. Scott, *Paul's Way of Knowing*, 241–42.

> shout for joy and cry aloud,
>> you who were never in labor;
> because more are the children of the desolate woman
>> than of her who has a husband." (4:25–27)

According to the logic of Paul's argument, the chief function of the citation from Isaiah is to support the way he has assigned the characters and correspondences in his allegory, and in particular to justify his inference in verse 26 that "the other woman corresponds to the Jerusalem above; she is free, and she is our mother" (NRSV).

Interpreters such as Karen Jobes, Joel Willitts, and Martinus de Boer have rightly stressed the vital role of Paul's citation from Isaiah in his argument.[23] Just as the Genesis story contains two sons of Abraham, the Isaianic prophecy speaks of two Jerusalems—one who has a husband and another who is desolate but miraculously fertile. A quick perusal of the original context of the oracle makes it clear that the childless woman being addressed is Jerusalem, bereft of her children in the wake of the Babylonian exile (cf. Isa. 52:1–12), and that the restoration of Jerusalem is linked by Isaiah with the miraculous fertility of the nation's original mother, Sarah (cf. Isa. 51:1–3). To be a true child of Abraham and Sarah is to be among the offspring miraculously given to the Jerusalem that has become, like barren Sarah, the woman who "never bore a child"; it is to be, like Isaac, a child of the promise (Gal. 4:28).

Important as the Isaiah citation is for Paul's argument, it still leaves unanswered the conundrum of how Paul has come to include uncircumcised gentiles in Galatia among these children of promise born to the restored Jerusalem.[24] It is one thing to see an ingathering of gentiles to Jerusalem as one of the *consequences* of the restoration of Israel and the reversal of Israel's exile. It is another thing altogether to say that the gentiles who come to faith in Christ (and remain uncircumcised and living in the diaspora) *are* the returning exiles, the children given to the restored Jerusalem.

The heroic efforts of Jobes and Willitts to locate the warrants for this novel appropriation of Isaiah 54:1 entirely within the book of Isaiah can certainly shed some light on what may have been Paul's own reading of Isaiah (and there is good reason from Paul's other letters to suggest that he was a careful and serious reader of Isaiah who read the book as a unity and with an eye to

---

23. Jobes, "Jerusalem, Our Mother"; Willitts, "Isa 54,1 in Gal 4,24b–27"; de Boer, "Isaiah 54.1 in Galatians 4.27."
24. See especially Starling, "Children of the Barren Woman."

the unfolding story of Israel within it),[25] but Paul does little if anything within Galatians to direct his readers' attention to the phenomena that Jobes and Willitts point out. In the hermeneutical framework that Paul offers his readers in the rest of the letter, the horizon against which the citation of Isaiah 54:1 is to be understood is not a close, detailed reading of the book of Isaiah (as Jobes implies), or even a broader, impressionistic recollection of the story of Israel that Isaiah tells (as Willitts argues), but the story of Israel as it is painted across the wider canvas of "Scripture" in its entirety and reconfigured by Paul in the preceding chapters of the letter.[26]

Israel's Story

The reconfigured story of Israel that Paul constructs for the Galatians in the previous chapters of the letter has two main elements that contribute to the implied justification for Paul's application of Isaiah 54:1 to his readers (as a warrant, in turn, for his allegorical interpretation of the story of Isaac and Ishmael).[27]

The first element is the prominence that Paul gives in Israel's story to the Abrahamic promises and the restoration eschatology of the prophets, and the pointed correlation that he draws between the promise of the outpoured Spirit and the "blessing" promised in Abraham to the nations (Gal. 3:8, 14). Both the righteousness credited to Abraham and the promise of life given through Habakkuk (Gal. 3:6–9, 11b, quoting Hab. 2:4) are not said to be given to those who "[rely] on the law" but to those who believe (3:6–9, 11b). It is, therefore, those "in Christ," joined to him by faith, who receive the blessing of Abraham (3:14) and inherit the promise that properly belongs to "one person . . . Christ" (3:16). The citation of Isaiah in 4:27 reinforces this fusion of the Abrahamic and exilic horizons, suggesting that the true children of Sarah are to be understood as the children of desolate Zion, and the hope for desolate Zion is to be found in the story of the miraculous fertility of barren Sarah.

A second, crucial element of Paul's reconfigured story of Israel is the way he presents the equality of Jew and gentile as having been not only accomplished positively "in Christ" but also anticipated and prepared for negatively in the history of Israel's apostasy and exile under the law of Moses.

25. See especially Wagner, *Heralds of the Good News*, 353–54; Gignilliat, *Paul and Isaiah's Servants*.
26. Cf. especially Scott, *Paul's Way of Knowing*, 159–230; Starling, "Children of the Barren Woman," 97–99; Starling, *Not My People*, 40–46.
27. Cf. Starling, "Children of the Barren Woman," 100–108.

Paul describes this experience of curse, slavery, and death under the law in the strongest possible terms (e.g., 3:10, 13, 22; 4:3; cf. 2:19). The connection Paul draws in verse 25 between Sinai and slavery is not, therefore, merely a "naked assertion";[28] it is anticipated and undergirded by this prior retelling of Israel's story across the preceding chapters of Galatians. Read against the backdrop of this retelling, the promise in Isaiah 54:1 requires to be understood as having been given not to an obedient, Torah-observant Israel but to a disobedient Israel, cast out of the land and living among the gentiles. For Paul, the correct way to hear the story of Sarah and Hagar in the light of that promise and its salvation-historical context is to hear it as a solemn warning that those who are joined to Abraham by means of the law and rely on the covenant in which that law is embedded are "children who are to be slaves," living under the shadow of the words of exclusion and banishment quoted by Paul in 4:30.

Christology and Eschatology

Although Scripture plays a crucial role in Paul's arguments and appeals to the Galatians, he does not make any pretense of attempting to interpret the scriptural story of Israel without reference to its climax in the coming of Christ and the subsequent outpouring of the Spirit. Like his readers in Galatia, Paul reads Scripture from the vantage point of the age in which its promises of salvation have been fulfilled, through "the Lord Jesus Christ, who gave himself for our sins to rescue us from the present evil age" (1:3–4); the apostle depicts the role of the law in God's saving purposes not only in light of the tragic arc of Israel's history under it (e.g., 3:10–12, 21)[29] but also in light of the subsequent coming of Christ (e.g., 3:13–14, 22–25). The present plight of Jew and gentile alike is thus to be understood in a way that fits with the christological solution made known in the gospel (cf. 2:21), and episodes in the story are to be read and interpreted in light of a larger story of divine, saving purposes "for freedom" (5:1). The fact that Paul (in common with his readers in Galatia) interprets the scriptural story of Israel with that christological climax in mind is a crucial factor in establishing the plausibility and coherence of the allegorical schema in which he draws, on the one hand, his positive correspondences between "the free woman," the "promise," and "the Jerusalem that is above," and, on the other hand, the negative correspondences between "the slave woman," "the flesh," and "the present city of Jerusalem."

---

28. Contra Hays, *Echoes of Scripture*, 115.
29. See especially Willitts, "Context Matters"; Sprinkle, *Law and Life*, 163.

The Galatians' Experience

The eschatological events that inform Paul's reading of Scripture include not only the gospel events that Paul proclaimed to the Galatians but also the Galatians' own experiences as hearers of the gospel. The principal experience that Paul has in view is the Galatians' experience of the Spirit—both the phenomena that accompanied and evidenced their initial reception of the Spirit and the ongoing phenomena that continue to take place among them through the Spirit's work. They experience all of these things, Paul reminds them, not "by the works of the law" but "by believing what [they] heard" (3:2, 5). This reminder is crucial in Paul's persuasive strategy. The argument from Scripture into which Paul launches in the following paragraphs does not build from ground zero. Its function is tightly related to the reminder in 3:1–5, interpreting the Galatians' experience of the Spirit and confirming that the conclusions Paul has drawn from it accord with the testimony of Scripture. His claim in 4:28–29 that the Galatians are "children of promise . . . born by the power of the Spirit" is implicitly supported by the combined effect of the reminder in 3:1–5 and its interpretation in the following paragraphs.

The experiences to which Paul is referring in 3:1–5 certainly include the "miracles" worked by God among the Galatians, but his language in the rhetorical question of 3:4 (*tosauta epathete eikē*; "Have you experienced so much in vain?") suggests that he has a broader range of experiences in mind than miracles alone. The close association he draws between the work of the Spirit and the endurance of suffering in the analogous reminders that he gives to other churches (e.g., 1 Thess. 1:5–6; 2 Cor. 12:12) suggests that there is good warrant for interpreting *epathete* as "suffered"[30] or at least for taking the scope of its reference broadly as embracing a range of experiences including the Spirit-empowered endurance of suffering, in solidarity with Paul. In 4:21–5:1, Paul explicitly reminds the Galatians of their sufferings, referring to the "persecut[ion]" that they endured from "the son born according to the flesh," which further warrants Paul's assertion that they are to see themselves as "like Isaac . . . children of promise" (4:28). The allegory, in turn, reframes the sufferings that the Galatians have experienced (and are liable to continue experiencing) so that they will be strengthened to resist the appeals of those who are commending circumcision as a strategy for avoiding persecution (cf. 6:12).

Although Paul's allegory and the exhortation that it supports are framed so as to address a particular set of circumstances in the life of the Galatian churches, the experiences that he focuses on in his framing of the allegory—the

---

30. Cf. Dunne, "Suffering in Vain."

phenomena that accompanied the Galatians' reception of the Spirit and the persecutions that they endured—are not uniquely or peculiarly Galatian experiences. They are, rather, characteristically Christian experiences, manifested in the particularities of the Galatians' situation and calling for an authentically Christian response by them.

Paul's Authority as Apostle and Community Founder

Finally, among the various warrants for Paul's allegory in 4:21–5:1, there is the implicit warrant of Paul's authority as an apostle and community founder. Although he does not explicitly appeal to this in 4:21–5:1, and the argumentative character of the paragraph suggests that he is not assuming that his personal authority alone will carry the day, he still strongly asserts his role in relation to the Galatians immediately before and after the allegory: the Galatians are to hear Paul's argument as one addressed to his "dear children" (4:19) and to respond to the appeals and warnings that the argument supports with an awareness that it is "I, Paul" (5:2), issuing them. By inviting the Galatians into the task of interpreting the scriptural story with him and discerning its implications for their situation, Paul makes it clear that he does not see himself as having a monopoly on the business of hermeneutics, but the terms on which he invites them to join him make it equally clear that they are to learn the art as apprentices from a master, or as children from a father.

Justified Allegory

What might it look like, then, if we were to imitate the kind of interpretive practice that Paul models in his appropriation of the Genesis story for the Galatians? What kind of allegorization (or, if it is too late to rehabilitate that particular word, what kind of figural reading) might we argue for as justified by the precedent of Paul's allegory here?

A careful reading of the hermeneutical rationale and rhetorical function of the allegory that Paul constructs for the Galatians does not provide a license for us to allegorize the biblical text in whatever fashion we wish. It certainly does not point the way toward the kind of speculative allegorization that dissolves the historicity of the original narrative to find a hidden, timeless principle, or that relies on a thin thread of correspondence strung precariously between obscure details of the biblical narrative and the minute peculiarities of the readers' experience. But neither, on the other hand, does Paul's allegory come with an implied warning to modern readers to stick to the safer business of strictly historical-grammatical exegesis and leave the tricky task of figural interpretation to suitably qualified apostolic experts.

The multiple, interrelated warrants of Paul's allegorical interpretation point the way toward a mode of figural reading that is grounded in the phenomena and themes of the original source text, attentive to its intertextual relationships with the rest of canonical Scripture, and directed by the shape of the scriptural story of salvation history. Moved and constrained by these inner-biblical forces, a figural reading of this sort traces patterns of correspondence between the various episodes of the biblical story, their climax in Christ, and the shared circumstances in which we find ourselves as members of Christ's church and bearers of his Spirit. In doing so, figural reading illuminates the particular moment of our own situation in a manner that facilitates faithful and imaginative participation in the drama into which we have been cast.[31]

The fact that figural reading of this sort can function in this way for such a wide variety of readers in such an immense diversity of situations depends on a certain pluripotency in the biblical text (magnified, in many cases, by the multiple ways in which a particular biblical text or motif is echoed and appropriated elsewhere in Scripture). Thus, Martin Luther, for example, can appeal to Hagar on one occasion (drawing on Paul's reading of the story in Gal. 4) as a figure of the Mosaic covenant and on another occasion as a figure of the suffering saints, with whom Christian readers are to identify in their various afflictions.[32]

The twists and turns of Hagar's story and the complexity of her characterization in the Genesis narrative, magnified by the narrative's multiple intertextual connections in the Old Testament and New Testament Scriptures,[33] create space for later readers to find many and various points of imaginative connection between Hagar's story and their own (and between the various

31. See especially Vanhoozer, *Drama of Doctrine*, 223–24; Wells, *Improvisation*, 15–18; Hays, *Conversion of the Imagination*, 5–6.

32. For the former occasion, see Luther, *Lectures on Galatians 1535, Chapters 1–4*, 436–39; for the latter, see Luther, *Lectures on Genesis, Chapters 15–20*, 70–72; Luther, *Lectures on Genesis, Chapters 21–25*, 58–60. See also the discussions in J. Thompson, *Writing the Wrongs*, 87–92; Billings, *Word of God*, 175–79.

33. In addition to the obvious and explicit intertextual connections between the story of Gen. 21 and Paul's allegory in Gal. 4, another important inner-biblical resonance of Hagar's story (particularly the episode recounted in Gen. 16) is with the exodus story of Israel. Note, e.g., the way the description in 16:6 of how Sarah "mistreated" Hagar draws on the language used in 15:13 to foreshadow the way Abram's descendants will be treated by their Egyptian overlords, and note the fact that it is "in the desert . . . beside the road to Shur" (16:7) that the angel finds Hagar and her son, their flight an ironic anticipation of the journey of the oppressed Hebrew slaves on the same road (but in the opposite direction) narrated in Exod. 15:22.

other features in the story and in their own world). Hagar's gender, her servile status, and her experiences of vulnerability, harsh treatment, and exclusion make her story particularly rich with potential points of connection for readers whose situations and experiences include similar elements:

> As a symbol of the oppressed, Hagar becomes many things to many people. Most especially, all sorts of rejected women find their stories in her. She is the faithful maid exploited, the black woman used by the male and abused by the female of the ruling class, the surrogate mother, the resident alien without legal recourse, the other woman, the runaway youth, the religious fleeing from affliction, the pregnant young woman alone, the expelled wife, the divorced mother with child, the shopping bag lady carrying bread and water, the homeless woman, the indigent relying upon handouts from the power structures, the welfare mother, and the self-effacing female whose own identity shrinks in service to others.[34]

The capacity of a character like Hagar to become "many things to many people" does not mean that the original contexts in which the writers, compilers, and readers of Scripture first understood the biblical texts recede into irrelevance for the purposes of theological interpretation. Nor do the many and varied circumstances of biblical readers dissolve the reading community of the church into a cacophony of private interpretations. Figural interpretation that imitates the pattern Paul models in Galatians 4:21–5:1 is still grounded in the phenomena and themes of the source text, constrained by the singularity of the biblical grand narrative and its climax in Christ, and located within the one church composed of all who belong to him.

But within that one church, and constrained by the shape and climax of that one grand narrative, there is still room for a wide diversity of reverent and attentive readings that are alert to the potential of the biblical text to generate imaginative correspondences between the world of the text and the world of the reader.[35] Equally, and vitally, there is ample room (and urgent need) for readers of Scripture to listen to others who read the same texts from within different circumstances—particularly those who read the text from circumstances of exclusion, suffering, and vulnerability—both in order to be alerted to features of the original text they might otherwise have passed over without notice, and in order to be made empathetically aware of the way

---

34. Trible, *Texts of Terror*, 28.

35. Cf. E. D. Hirsch's comments on the way in which the readerly activity of "analogizing to one's own experience" functions almost universally as "an implicit, pervasive, usually untaught response to stories." Hirsch, "Transhistorical Intentions," 553, quoted in Vanhoozer, *Is There a Meaning?*, 422.

Scripture illuminates the circumstances and actions of the brothers, sisters, and neighbors whom God has given to them to love.[36]

Figural reading of this sort has its proper home in the church not the academy (though it is indebted to the academy for the close attention that it pays to the contexts and phenomena of the original texts and their various biblical intertexts, and is assisted by the academy in its efforts to be critically alert and engaged with the social and political forces of its own context and the various other contexts that have informed the reception history of the biblical text). It is a deliberative, imaginative, and dramatic practice, aimed at discerning the implications of the whole biblical story (and the various episodes in it) for the shape of Christian action in the world. This sort of reading and appropriation of biblical narrative does not attempt to deny the historicity of the events in which God's saving activity in the world has taken place, or to dissolve the distance between those events and our own time today. But it does illuminate our imagination, teaching us to see ourselves in the mirror of our forebears, and engage us with the biblical story in a way that goes far beyond merely recounting its contents and analyzing the rhetorical effect that might have been intended for its original hearers. Both the imagination that embraces such a task and the disciplines that constrain it are crucial dimensions of the kind of Bible reading that can inform and motivate faithful Christian understanding and action today.

---

36. See especially the discussions in Wolterstorff, *Until Justice and Peace Embrace*, 173–76; Bauckham, *Bible in Politics*, 142–49.

12

"Today, If You Hear His Voice"

Hebrews and the Hermeneutics of Exhortation

Speaking God's Words

From the earliest days of evangelicalism (regardless of whether those "earliest days" are to be sought in the Reformation of the sixteenth century, the Puritanism of the seventeenth, or the awakenings of the eighteenth), the preached word of God has been central in both the shaping and the enactment of the movement's core convictions. The Protestant Reformation was, in the words of Stephen Webb, "an event in the history of sound": it gave birth to "an outpouring of words in service to the biblical Word of God" and, within that larger outpouring, to a new and distinctive mode of congregational preaching that purposed, with a sense of focused and prophetic occasionality, to "convey grace through sound."[1]

The heirs of the Reformation in the subsequent centuries varied in the forms of preaching that they employed and the ways in which they understood its relation to the common life and organizational structures of the church,[2] but the preached word, in one form or another, remained central in their beliefs

1. S. Webb, *Divine Voice*, 106, 115–16.
2. Note, e.g., the role played by "field preaching" in the emergent evangelicalism of the eighteenth century and the controversies over the "new methods" employed by the revivalists of the nineteenth century.

and practices. The "occasionality" and "prophetic tone," too, which Webb identifies as the twin distinctives of Reformation preaching, were if anything intensified in the developing tradition of evangelical preaching: by the middle of the eighteenth century, under the powerful influence of George Whitefield and John Wesley, a recognizable "evangelical style" of preaching had emerged, a style that borrowed heavily from the idioms of the theater, emphasized the function of the preached word as effecting an encounter with the living God, and summoned the affections and the will of the hearers to respond immediately to what was preached.[3] Preaching of this sort (indeed, preaching of any sort) is hardly the sum total of evangelicalism, but the movement is impossible to imagine without it. Any adequate exploration of "evangelical hermeneutics" needs to give an account of what it means to receive the Scriptures not only as a book to be read and understood but also as a word to be heard and proclaimed.

In our own time, of course, this proclamatory dimension of Scripture's reception and use in the church is widely regarded as problematic. It is one thing to revere a sacred book as an object of private meditation and a resource for spiritual practice; it is another thing altogether to stand in a pulpit and preach its contents to a gathered congregation. In an age that has taught us to be suspicious of power games and authority structures, the right of a preacher to speak from on high, commanding the attention and compliance of an audience, hardly strikes us as self-evident. The gradual migration of the sermon from the pulpit to the microphone stand to the bar stool or to the lounge chair visibly expresses this cultural shift and raises questions that are more than just cosmetic in their implications. Does an elevated pulpit raise the preacher too high, unhelpfully separating preacher from people? Does a bar stool or a lounge chair bring the preacher down too low, implying something inappropriately mundane or casual about the dynamics of the occasion? Should the event of the sermon be staged dramatically as a discrete encounter between the congregation and the voice of God, or should it be framed in a manner that presents it as a contribution to a larger, ongoing conversation within the congregation and between the congregation and God? Underneath (and embedded in) these various pragmatic and symbolic questions lies a fundamental question of a hermeneutical and theological nature: to what extent, and in what sense, should we affirm with the authors of the Second Helvetic Confession that "the preaching of the Word of God is the Word of God,"[4] and—if we do affirm that—what does it imply for our understanding

3. Cf. S. Webb, *Divine Voice*, 96–101; Stout, *Divine Dramatist*, xv–xvi; Noll, *Rise of Evangelicalism*, 123–25.
4. Second Helvetic Confession (1566), as translated in Leith, *Creeds of the Churches*, 133.

of the roles of preacher and congregation in the mediation and reception of God's word?

With questions of this sort we turn to the Letter to the Hebrews, as a canonical example of Christian congregational preaching that is self-conscious and overt in its understanding of its role in mediating God's word to his people.[5] We will particularly focus on *congregational* preaching (i.e., on preaching in the gathered assembly) and on the exhortative function of such preaching,[6] though there will of course be implications for our understanding of the larger dynamic of the gospel's proclamation in the world, and for the various other functions (declarative, explanatory, promissory, etc.) of the preacher's work. We will aim mainly to describe the relationship between the written words of Scripture and the spoken words of the preacher, and describe the kind of interaction between preacher and congregation that this relationship implies.

Hebrews as a "Word of Exhortation"

Among the various books of the New Testament, Hebrews is particularly useful for us in our task in this chapter because it presents itself not as a gospel narrative, an apocalyptic vision, or an apostolic letter, but as a "word of exhortation" (13:22)—a category borrowed by the early Christians from the language of the synagogue (and from Second Temple Judaism more broadly) and used to refer to a preached message expounding and applying a passage of Scripture.[7] Although it came to be collected among the letters of the New Testament, and the closing paragraphs include a few brief prayer requests and greetings (13:18–19, 23–25), Hebrews contains few of the features one would normally expect to see in an ancient letter: the opening verses, for

5. There is of course an additional sense in which the Letter to the Hebrews may be said to be God's word, by virtue of its place in the canon of Scripture. In this chapter, however, we will focus not on what can be said about Hebrews qua Scripture, but on what the letter claims for itself as a Christian sermon and as an exposition of (OT) Scripture in light of God's climactic word spoken in Christ.

6. Cf. the working definition of "preaching" as "the explanation and application of the Word in the assembled congregation of Christ," in Adam, *Speaking God's Words*, 70, and the focus of the Second Helvetic Confession on the word of God as "preached in the church . . . and received by the faithful."

7. Cf. the request for a *logos paraklēseōs* made by the synagogue rulers in Acts 13:15 and the encouragement to Timothy in 1 Tim. 4:13 to devote himself "to the public reading of Scripture, to preaching [*tē paraklēsei*] and to teaching." Noteworthy also is the description in 2 Macc. 15:8–11 of the way in which Judas Maccabeus "exhorted [*parekalei*] his troops . . . encouraging them from the law and the prophets," and so "armed . . . them . . . with the inspiration of brave words [*tēn en tois agathois logois paraklēsin*]" (NRSV).

example, are completely lacking in any of the customary elements with which
a letter traditionally commenced, and while the writer was clearly known to
the recipients (cf. 13:18–25), he nowhere includes his name. Commentators
point to numerous aspects of the letter that have more in common with oral
communication than with letter writing,[8] and most agree that the evidence
of the text suggests that its principal genre (in the mind of its writer and its
first readers) was that of a Christian homily, expounding the Old Testament
Scriptures in light of their fulfillment in Christ and applying their message
to the hearers.[9]

In line with the essentially homiletic genre of Hebrews, as a sermon
preached from a distance, the written words of the text are conveyed to the
readers as an address to be heard as if the writer were present and speaking
to them while they read (e.g., 2:5: "the world to come, about which we are
speaking"; 5:11: "we have much to say about this, but it is hard to make it
clear to you because you no longer try to understand" [more literally: "you
have become sluggish of hearing"]; 11:32: "And what more shall I say? I do
not have time to tell about Gideon, Barak, Samson and Jephthah, about David
and Samuel and the prophets"). Time is short and the message is a weighty
and urgent one; it is therefore of the greatest importance to the writer that
his readers "bear with" the word of exhortation that he has written to them
(13:22) and devote their attention to what he has to say.

"Today, If You Hear His Voice" (Heb. 3:7, 15; 4:7; Ps. 95:7–8)

But it is not only the writer whose voice is conveyed by the text: in the
"today" in which the sermon is read and heard in the congregation, the listeners are encouraged to respond as those who are hearing God's own voice
addressing them (3:7). Thus, as the sermon reaches its rhetorical climax, it
warns listeners, "See to it that you do not refuse him who speaks" (12:25), in
a context suggesting that the warning is to be taken as referring to the writer's
own words, functioning as God's address to his people: as the writer's sermon
is heard in the congregation, God himself is "warn[ing] us from heaven"
(12:25b), with a voice that must not be refused.[10]

8. Cf. Aune, *Literary Environment*, 213; J. Griffiths, *Hebrews and Divine Speech*, 16–24;
Johnson, *Hebrews*, 10; Witherington, *For Jewish Christians*, 20–21.

9. It is therefore (arguably at least—depending on the judgments that we make about the
genre of several other homily-like NT books) "the only example we have in the NT of the text
of a sermon which has been preserved in its entirety." Vanhoye, *Structure and Message*, 3. For the
larger claim that "1 John, James, Hebrews, and probably Jude should [all] be seen as homilies
of one sort or another," see Witherington, *For Hellenized Christians*, 1:43.

10. See especially Koester, *Hebrews*, 552; Smillie, "'One Who Is Speaking.'"

The event of the sermon's reception in the congregation is, therefore, presented as something indisputably dramatic. The voice of the preacher—mediated in this instance by the voice of the person reading the sermon in the assembly—mediates, in turn, the voice of God, experienced in real time by the listening congregation. The divine voice may not on this occasion be accompanied by the same special effects that accompanied it at Sinai—"fire . . . darkness, gloom and storm . . . a trumpet blast . . . [a] sight . . . so terrifying that Moses said, 'I am trembling with fear'" (12:18–21)—but it is still to be heard with reverence and awe, as is fitting for an encounter with a God who is "a consuming fire" (12:28–29).[11]

We must, nonetheless, qualify that assertion in several important ways, based on the larger hermeneutical frame in which the preacher's words mediate God's address. The word's proclamation is indeed dramatic, but the drama of the sermon is not a one-act play, sufficient by itself: its meaning and effect depend on its relation to a series of other words and events that lie behind and beyond it in the history of God's dealings with his people. The "today" in which the preacher's word of exhortation is spoken and heard needs to take into account those various other words and events that precede and follow it, so that the form and content of the preached word are properly related to them and embedded in the larger drama of God's communicative action.

"When . . . He Spoke through David" (Heb. 4:7)

First, and perhaps most obviously, the "today" in which the preacher speaks his words needs to be understood in relation to the earlier "today" in which the words of Scripture were originally given. The very words the writer to the Hebrews uses in 3:7 to implicitly claim that his sermon conveys God's own speech to the hearers are, after all, words that he has borrowed from an earlier human author—a fact that he acknowledges explicitly in the following chapter: "God . . . set a certain day, calling it 'Today.' This he did when a long time later he spoke through David, as in the passage already quoted: 'Today, if you hear his voice, do not harden your hearts'" (4:7).

More than that: the whole sermon, in both its teaching and its exhortation, is permeated with references to Scripture, frequently expounding and commenting on them at length. The opening movement of the letter, in Hebrews 1:1–2:4, is constructed around a catena of texts from the Psalms, 2 Samuel 7, and Deuteronomy 32 (LXX); Hebrews 2:5–18 reflects on Jesus's humanity and humiliation in light of Psalm 8:4–6 (with additional supporting reference to the

---

11. See especially Treier, "Speech Acts."

"brothers and sisters" and "children" of Psalm 22 and Isaiah 8, respectively);
Hebrews 3:6–4:13 discusses Psalm 95:7–11 at length, appropriating the words
of verse 7 to exhort the hearers; Hebrews 5:5–7:28 refers repeatedly to Psalm
110:4 and dwells at length on its key motifs of a Melchizedekan priesthood
and a divine oath; Hebrews 8:1–10:18 includes an extended quotation from
Jeremiah 31:31–34 in chapter 8, and returns to it in chapter 10, with the "new
covenant" concepts of the passage framing the intervening discussion; Hebrews
10:32–12:3 takes a pair of citations from Habakkuk 2:3–4 (LXX) and develops
their theme across the whole of chapter 11 and the opening verses of chapter
12; Hebrews 12:4–13 appropriates and applies a word of exhortation from
Proverbs 3:11–12 (LXX); and Hebrews 12:18–29 draws together a string of
images and phrases from Exodus 18–19 and Haggai 2:6, vividly recalling them
for the readers and drawing out the continuities and contrasts between the Sinai
encounter depicted in Exodus and the situation of the hearers of Hebrews.[12]

Throughout, the sermon repeatedly presents the words of Scripture as
spoken in the present tense by the voice of God, of Christ, or of the Holy
Spirit. In some instances (e.g., 1:6) the present-tense form of the verb dramatically re-presents the words spoken in the narrated past,[13] but in others
(e.g., 3:7: "So, as the Holy Spirit says . . .") the verb of speech clearly refers
to communicative action of God, in the present, addressing the hearers in
the words of Scripture. At times in the sermon Scripture functions as a warrant or vehicle for doctrinal assertions; at other times, however, it is (directly)
paraenetic or hortatory, encouraging or summoning the readers to adopt or
persevere in a particular attitude or mode of conduct.[14] Thus, for example,
in chapter 6, the writer recalls for his hearers the scriptural promise and oath
of God, originally given to Abraham, and applies them to his hearers (as "the
heirs of what was promised"; 6:17): "God [confirmed his promise with an
oath] so that, by two unchangeable things in which it is impossible for God
to lie, we who have fled to take hold of the hope set before us may be greatly
encouraged" (6:18). Similarly, in chapter 12, the hearers of the sermon are
reminded of the words of Proverbs 3:11–12, appropriated as "this word of
encouragement that addresses you as a father addresses his son" (12:5).[15] In-

---

12. Cf. the analysis in Longenecker, *Biblical Exegesis*, 156–65; and its further development
in R. T. France, "Writer of Hebrews."

13. Cf. the discussion of the temporal reference of *legei* and *eisagagē* in 1:6, in Ellingworth,
Epistle to the Hebrews, 116–20.

14. Hughes's assertion that, within Hebrews, "the fundamental role of scripture is a paraenetic one" (Hughes, *Hebrews and Hermeneutics*, 54) needs to be balanced with the rider that
not every citation of Scripture in the sermon is *directly* paraenetic.

15. The focus on the fatherhood of God and readers' status of sonship, both in the subsequent verses (vv. 7–10, 23) and earlier in the letter (e.g., 2:10–14), suggests that the verses from

tegral to the "word of encouragement" that is the sermon as a whole are the
words of Scripture, appropriated as words of divine exhortation addressed to
the congregation (or in the case of the Abrahamic promise and oath referred
to in ch. 6, inherited by them as Abraham's heirs).

This function of Scripture in the sermon as the present address of God to the
hearers does not obliterate the significance of Scripture's original human authorship or collapse the time between Scripture's first context and the situation
of the sermon's hearers: the hermeneutic of Hebrews is still, in an important
sense, a "historical" one that distinguishes between the "old" and the "new"
in the sequence of God's communicative actions, and locates the disjunction
between them in the remembered and attested events of the earthly ministry
of Jesus.[16] Thus, for example, in chapter 12, the recollections of Sinai are
related to the reader via an extended series of contrasts between the situation
in which the divine voice was heard by Israel at the foot of that mountain and
the situation in which the readers now hear God's voice. Rightly hearing the
words of YHWH originally spoken to (and through) Moses requires that the
sermon's hearers be aware that they "have not come" to the same mountain
but have come instead to "Mount Zion . . . , the heavenly Jerusalem," and to
"Jesus the mediator of a new covenant" (12:18, 22–24).

Even when stressing the continuities more than the discontinuities between
the situation of Scripture's original hearers and that of the sermon's address-
ees (as, e.g., in 3:7), the writer still considers the distinction, in principle at
least, worth taking into account. The "today" in which God, through David,
addresses the words of Psalm 95 to Israel can become the "today" in which
the word of God addresses the Christian congregation, but the process of
appropriation is not automatic and unthinking: the assertion of 3:6b, "we
are his house" (combined with the proviso of 3:6c: "if indeed we hold firmly
to our confidence and the hope in which we glory"), gives the writer warrant
to appropriate the words from the psalm in the following verse: "So, as the
Holy Spirit says: 'Today, if you hear his voice, do not harden your hearts'"
(3:7; emphasis added).[17]

Proverbs are to be taken not only as words *about* God as father but also as words spoken *by*
God as father to the readers; the words of the OT sage, addressed to his generic "son," are
being appropriated as words that God speaks in Scripture to the readers *hōs huiois* (NIV: "as
a father addresses his son"). Cf. Peeler, *You Are My Son*, 144–63; Peterson, "Ministry of Encouragement," 247, citing Michel, *Der Brief an die Hebräer*, 438.

16. Cf. Hughes, *Hebrews and Hermeneutics*, 63–66.

17. It is worth noting the similarity—if not a half-echo, then at least a conceptual parallel—
between Heb. 3:6 ("we are his house") and Ps. 95:7 ("we are the people of his pasture, the flock
under his care"), and the continuity implied by the way in which 3:1–6 says both Moses and
Jesus were faithful, in different roles and different times, in the one "house." The "today" in the

"In These Last Days" (Heb. 1:2)

This relationship of distinction-within-connectedness between God's prior speech in Scripture and his contemporary address to the Christian congregation is established in the opening clauses of the carefully composed sentence with which the whole sermon commences: "In the past God spoke to our ancestors through the prophets at many times and in various ways, but in these last days he has spoken to us by his Son, whom he appointed heir of all things, and through whom also he made the universe" (1:1–2).[18] The rest of the sermon makes it clear that, in the writer's understanding, the words of Scripture continue to function as divine address, but they are to be interpreted and appropriated in light of the climactic divine word spoken to us "in these last days . . . by his Son."[19]

One consequence of this which becomes immediately apparent in the first chapter is that texts of Scripture about the sonship and enthronement of the Davidic king (and even texts about worship of YHWH himself) are appropriated retrospectively, in light of Christ's identity as Messiah and Son, as testimonies to Christ's glory and preeminence. The point of the catena is not to prove the sonship and divinity of Christ; rather, with those convictions presupposed, it is to appropriate the words of Scripture to confirm the greater excellence of the one confessed as the divine and messianic Son over the angels through whom the law was given and to prepare the way for the exhortation to the hearers in 2:1–4 to "pay the most careful attention" to the word that was spoken through him.[20]

It is not only in the directly christological portions of the sermon that the word spoken in the Son hermeneutically controls the sermon's appropriation of Scripture and the writer's claim to mediate the word of God to the congregation in his own time. Throughout the sermon this word—the word spoken by God "in these last days . . . to us"—stands at the center of the whole typological scheme through which the writer relates the "rest" promised to

---

psalm is extended also, of course, by the dynamics of the psalm's liturgical use and its inclusion in the Psalter: the words spoken by "David" continue to address the worshiping community of Israel through the repeated use of the psalm in cultic and devotional contexts.

18. The "but" at the beginning of v. 2 in most modern English versions accurately conveys the disjunction implied by the distinction of eras between "the past" (v. 1) and "these last days" (v. 2), and by the descriptions of the differing modes of divine speech in each: "to our ancestors through the prophets at many times and in various ways" (v. 1), and "to us by his Son" (v. 2). But the relationship between the two clauses implies continuity as well as distinction: the one God has spoken in both eras, and in the past he addressed not strangers but "our ancestors" (*tois patrasin*).

19. See especially Schenck, "God Has Spoken."

20. Cf. Hughes, *Hebrews and Hermeneutics*, 54–63; France, "Writer of Hebrews," 255–56.

Israel and the rest to be entered by the hearers, the tabernacle and sacrifices of the old covenant and the tabernacle and sacrifice of the new, the mountain around which the Israelites gathered at Sinai and the mountain to which the hearers have come in Christ. At every point, the writer of the sermon speaks as one who has first heard the decisive and climactic word spoken "to us" (1:2) and frames the content of his exhortation accordingly.[21]

"Yesterday and Today and Forever" (Heb. 13:8)

The writer of Hebrews not only presents his sermon as derivative discourse, dependent on the fundamental and decisive word already spoken in Christ; he also positions his sermon in continuity with all those others, before and (by implication) after, who "spoke the word of God" to his hearers (13:7). Important as is the moment in which the word is presently addressed to the congregation, it is not isolated from all the prior and subsequent exhortation and instruction given to the congregation—and, indeed, to the whole church across the centuries. The "today" which the sermon addresses will have its own particularities, distinguishing it, for example, from the "earlier days" in which the same community originally welcomed the message (10:32; cf. 5:11; 6:10–11), but the substance of the message to be appropriated and applied in all the changing circumstances of the community is the same, "yesterday and today and forever" (13:8).

The writer can call on his hearers not only, therefore, to respond with a decision of the will to the voice of God speaking in the present but also to faithfully and obediently persevere in feeding on the metaphorical food of divine grace (13:9–10), to steadily train themselves and thereby become discerning and mature (5:14),[22] and to continue imitating the faith of their teachers (13:7b). The heart of the hearer needs to be open to the word of God "today" and to be trained and strengthened by the word of God across the years and decades of life, through reminder, encouragement, example, and practice.

Because this is the case, the exhortation of the sermon needs to be embedded not only in the succession of similar exhortations given by the congregation's teachers over time but also within a broader pattern of mutual exhortation among the congregation's members. The hearers of the word are urged to listen receptively and to participate responsibly in a community of faith, speaking as well as receiving the encouragement of the word: "See to it, brothers and sisters, that none of you has a sinful, unbelieving heart that turns away from

21. Cf. O'Brien, *God Has Spoken*, 41: "He speaks of himself first as a listener to whom God has spoken and revealed himself ('to us,' 1:2; 2:3) before he urges them to heed God's word."
22. See especially Treier, "Speech Acts," 344–46.

the living God. But encourage one another daily, as long as it is called 'Today,' so that none of you may be hardened by sin's deceitfulness" (3:12–13; cf. 10:25). It is no accident that so much of the sermon's exhortation is in first person plurals: the preacher understands himself not only as an "I" addressing a "you" but also as a member of an "us" and a "we," receiving the word in solidarity with his fellow believers and exhorting them as one who has come to share in Christ along with them, modeling the same mutuality of concern and encouragement that he urges them to practice among themselves.[23]

"How We May Spur One Another On" (Heb. 10:24): The Drama and Disciplines of Exhortation

What answers, then, should we give to the questions with which we commenced the chapter, about the dramatics of the sermon and its relation to the larger conversation among the members of the congregation and between the congregation and God? It would be foolish to pretend that our brief exploration into the hermeneutics of Hebrews gives a basis for a definitive and unbending set of stipulations about the voice and posture of the preacher or the architecture of the space in which the word is proclaimed. Nothing in Hebrews comes even close to laying down the law on such matters, and even in the era of the New Testament we can point to a wide variety of teaching and preaching practices by Jesus and his first followers, adapting and improvising in response to changing circumstances. The sermon of Hebrews does, however, provide an illuminating and authoritative exemplar for understanding the nature of the drama we are staging when the word is preached; this exemplar ought to shape the disciplines and patterns of judgment that we employ as we attempt to stage it rightly in the peculiarities and constraints of the various situations in which we find ourselves.

Like the tradition of preaching shaped by the convictions of the Reformation of the sixteenth century and the evangelical awakenings of the eighteenth, Hebrews models a practice of congregational exhortation that treats the event of the sermon with deadly seriousness as a form of God's own address to the congregation. This is no casual affair; nor is the occasion a merely horizontal transaction between the preacher and the congregation.

At the same time, though, in several important and interrelated ways, Hebrews reminds us that the event of the sermon must not be enacted or understood as a freestanding drama, isolated from the larger history of God's

---

23. Cf. O'Brien, *God Has Spoken*, 40–41; Peterson, "Ministry of Encouragement," 243–46.

dealings with his people. Behind and beyond the "today" in which the sermon is preached in the congregation stands an indispensable series of other todays, including the "today" in which the words of Scripture were originally spoken (4:7), the "yesterday and today" in which the word of God was earlier spoken to the community (13:7–8), and the daily "today" in which the members of the community are to encourage one another (3:13). Disconnected from these other words and events—and, above all, the decisive word spoken by God "in these last days . . . by his Son" (1:2; 2:3–4)—the preached word has nothing but its own rhetorical bombast or the charismatic power of the preacher to sustain it; rightly connected to them, it is a fully legitimate form of the living and active word of God, at work among God's people for their salvation.

A full-orbed evangelical preaching-hermeneutic needs to take both of these realities into account. On the one hand, it must give full weight to the drama of the sermon as an event in which God is present, speaking by his Spirit to his people, commanding attention and urging a response; on the other, it must take care that the drama of that encounter does not come untethered from the disciplines of biblical exegesis, christocentric canon-sense, and ecclesial commitment that give authenticity to the preached word and durability to its reception among God's people. Only then—when both the drama and the disciplines exemplified in Hebrews are borne in mind—will the ministry of exhortation to which the sermon contributes be characterized by the urgency and the maturity that God's presence among his people calls for.

—⸙13⸙—

"She Who Is in Babylon"

1 Peter and the Hermeneutics of Empire

Reading as Exiles

Across the last few decades in the post-Christendom West, a growing number of Christian writers have challenged their fellow believers to understand themselves as "exiles," no longer even close to the center of the culture. In my own country, Australia—which was never really a stronghold of Christendom in the first place—this view has been particularly prominent and is being expressed with growing vigor and urgency.[1] In a recent and widely read blog post, Western Australian writer Steve McAlpine has urged us to brace ourselves for the transition into "Exile Stage Two"—a new level of cultural estrangement, in which it dawns on us that we are living not in Athens (as cultural oddities on the margins of public life, trying to find an entrée into the cultural conversation) but in Babylon (as the objects of scorn and derision, dragged periodically into the town square to be flayed and humiliated).[2]

---

1. On the "exile" paradigm, see Frost, *Exiles: Living Missionally*. On the peculiarities of the Australian context, see especially Gascoigne, *Origins of European Australia*, 19–34; Frame, *Losing My Religion*.

2. Steve McAlpine, "Stage Two Exile: Are You Ready for It?," Gospel Coalition Australia, June 1, 2015, http://australia.thegospelcoalition.org/article/stage-two-exile-are-you-ready-for-it; see also Nathan Campbell's post in response: "When in Rome: Reframing Our Expectations as the Post-Christendom Church," St. Eutychus, June 2, 2015, http://st-eutychus.com/2015/when-in-rome-reframing-our-expectations-as-the-post-christendom-church/.

If it is true that we are living in Babylon, then we are not the first believers to have lived there. The correspondence between life in the liberal democracies of the modern West and life in the "Babylon" of Ancient Rome (or, for that matter, life for the original Jewish exiles in Babylon itself) is not total, of course. The assumed familiarity of the Christian story in a post-Christendom context, for example, breeds a contempt for Christian claims that is different in kind from the contempt generated by the *un*familiarity of those same claims in the pre-Christendom world of the apostles. The offensiveness of a message about a recently crucified victim of Roman imperial power should not be facilely equated with the offensiveness of a message proclaimed by a church that carries a legacy of twenty centuries of its own abuses of power. Nor—to complicate things still further—do the liberal-democratic values and power arrangements of the culture from which we find ourselves estranged add up to a literal "empire" in the same way as do the values of the Greco-Roman world.[3] Mission after Christendom is not simply a rerun of mission before Christendom.

Nevertheless, as we struggle to negotiate a world in which we find ourselves increasingly alienated from the values of the mainstream culture, and as we try to make sense of its shifting configurations of social power, we can learn much from the way the writers of the New Testament encouraged their readers to interpret the "Babylon" in which they lived and to relate to its power structures and social values. If we are to learn how to read the Bible as exiles, appropriating its stories and promises and commands from an increasingly marginal position in a post-Christian culture, we will find the hermeneutical practices of the New Testament writers, as they appropriated and applied the Old Testament Scriptures to their situation as believers in Christ in a pagan empire, to be an indispensable model.

No New Testament book focuses more explicitly or urgently on this task than 1 Peter. A letter that addresses its readers as "exiles, scattered throughout the provinces" (1:1), and closes with the assurance, "She who is in Babylon, chosen together with you, sends you her greetings" (5:13), clearly invites a reading that relates its injunctions (and the reading of Scripture that informs them) to the recipients' situation in the empire, a reading that interprets that situation in light of the categories and narratives of Scripture.[4]

3. Though in a sense, of course, the pervasive influence of the practices and assumptions of modern, liberal-democratic consumer-capitalism add up to a kind of cultural imperialism; cf. the classic exposition of "cultural hegemony" in Gramsci, *Prison Notebooks*.
4. This is the case regardless of whether the recipients are understood to be Jews or gentiles, and irrespective of whether their identity as "exiles of the Dispersion" is taken to refer primarily to geographical dislocation, social alienation, or eschatological allegiance. On the first of these issues, I incline toward the majority view that sees verses like 1:14, 18; 2:9; 4:3–4 as implying a readership composed primarily of gentile converts from paganism. On the second issue, while

A recent scholarly example of such a reading can be seen in David Horrell's paper, "Between Conformity and Resistance: Beyond the Balch-Elliott Debate toward a Postcolonial Reading of 1 Peter." After briefly surveying the thirty-year history of debates over whether the attitude of 1 Peter's author to the values and power structures of the surrounding culture is essentially "resistant" or "conformist,"[5] Horrell turns to the role of Scripture in shaping the author's rhetoric and understanding,[6] beginning with the language of the letter frame (1:1–2; 5:13), which "evokes a whole narrative, a kind of hidden transcript, one forged in the fire of Jewish experience, and one that reflects the experience of the underside of empire."[7]

Horrell's analysis offers much of value, but his account of how Scripture is read and applied in 1 Peter is somewhat one-sided. When examining the "resistant" elements of the text's ideology, he discusses the influence of scriptural traditions at some length, ascribing a key role to them in explaining the author's alienation from the empire:

> Prior to conversion these people may have been quietly, even contentedly, accommodated to the realities of empire and its local manifestations, keeping the peace and their heads down, paying their dues, financially and religiously. . . . But the call to conversion, a call the author reiterates and amplifies in his letter, is a call to inhabit a narrative, one drawn from the experience of the people of Israel, that puts a different spin on the establishment of empire. Now Rome is Babylon, the oppressor of God's people, who are displaced and homeless in its realm. One might therefore say that the narrative of identity into which 1 Peter invites its readers is one which constructs a form of postcolonial awareness, which challenges positive acceptance or acquiescence and replaces it with a sense of dislocation and distance.[8]

---

it is very likely that some of the recipients would have been among the many in the province who had experienced a literal geographical displacement, the Babylon typology of 5:13 and the reference to "the time of your exile" in 1:17 (read in the light of the eschatological context established in 1:3–7, 13, 21) suggest that the exile language functions primarily as a metaphor for the social alienation experienced by the readers under the powers of the present age, as they wait for the salvation of the age to come.

5. See especially Elliott, "Situation and Strategy"; Balch, "Hellenization/Acculturation."

6. In view of the scholarly debates over the authorship of 1 Peter, I will refer to "the author" of the letter when describing the views of interpreters who are not persuaded that the author is Peter, and to "Peter" when offering my own reading of the letter. For an assessment and rebuttal of the argument that 1 Peter should be read as a pseudonymous text, see Michaels, *1 Peter*, lxii–lxvii; I. H. Marshall, *1 Peter*, 21–24; Schreiner, *1, 2 Peter, Jude*, 21–36. Although I read the letter on the assumption of Petrine authorship, I will restrict myself to statements about the readers' experience of life in the empire that could have applied equally under Nero, Domitian, or Trajan.

7. Horrell, "Between Conformity and Resistance," 126.

8. Ibid., 128.

When discussing the more socially conformist dimensions of the letter, however, Horrell makes no reference at all to the influence of Scripture, content to explain the author's injunctions as nothing more than "a kind of survival strategy . . . a common and understandable response to the pressures and threats of imperial domination."[9] A picture emerges of a kind of halfway house between readings of 1 Peter that emphasize its "socially resistant" elements and readings that highlight its "socially conformist" dimensions: Horrell characterizes the letter's stance toward its imperial context as one of "polite resistance," in which the "resistance" derives (in part, at least) from a scripturally grounded identity narrative and the "politeness" derives from the survival instincts of the author.

While an account of this sort may fit neatly enough with the sensibilities of modern readers, most of whom will likely find the elements of resistance in the letter more interesting and attractive than the elements of social conformity, it does not do full justice to Scripture's nuanced and multidimensional role in the letter, or to the extent to which the various strands of the social ethic advocated in the letter cohere.[10] Whatever conclusions we may draw about the social motivations for the author's injunctions, the rhetoric with which he voices and justifies them (including both the "resistant" and the "conformist" injunctions) is soaked in Scripture and in recollections of the story of Christ. Furthermore, the elements which we tease out from each other in our analysis and assign to the categories of "resistance" and "conformity" respectively are, within the letter itself, closely interrelated and undergirded by appeals to the same scriptural sources.

There is room, then, for a more careful examination of how the language and categories of Scripture contribute to the interpretation of empire in 1 Peter. In the exploration of that question that I will offer in this chapter, I will focus on the forces of fear, patronage, and honor as dimensions of the imperial context that shaped the social experience of the letter's original readers, and investigate some of the ways in which Peter's interpretation and appropriation of Scripture contribute to what he says about each of these dimensions.

Scripture, Empire, and Fear

Perhaps the most obvious dynamic of empire that contributed to the shaping of the sociopolitical context of 1 Peter was that of the fear elicited by the use and threat of force. Relations of fear and intimidation were integral and essential to the workings of empire, from the very bottom of the structure (in the coercive force that the master of a household could exert to keep his slaves

9. Ibid., 134–35.
10. Cf. Volf, "Soft Difference," 22.

in their servile position)[11] to the very top (in the threats of exile and execution that emperors could marshal against their critics and rivals);[12] such relations were experienced both by the subject peoples who yielded to the force of the Roman armies[13] and by the soldiers who served in them.[14] Without fear, there would have been no empire.

Within that context, it is not surprising that 1 Peter often refers to fear, in the context of both his instructions about attitudes toward God and his instructions about how the readers are to respond to the bearers of power in their social context. In 1:17, it is the word *phobos* (reverent fear) that Peter uses to summarize how his readers should conduct their lives while in exile. Slaves, according to 2:18, are to accept the authority of their masters "in reverent fear" (*en panti phobō*). Wives are to accept their husbands' authority, so that husbands who do not obey the word might be won over by "the purity and reverence of [their wives'] lives" (*tēn en phobō hagnēn anastrophēn hymōn*; 3:2).[15] When required to give account for their hope, the readers of the letter are to offer their answer "with gentleness and respect" (*praytētos kai phobou*; 3:16).

Hand in hand with these injunctions to the readers to demonstrate "reverence" and "respect" in their social relationships, other exhortations counsel *against* fear. The paragraph directed to wives, for example, ends by encouraging them to "do what is right and . . . not give way to fear" (3:6), and the carefully worded summary statement in 2:17 draws what appears to be a principled distinction between the command to "fear" (*phobeisthe*) God and

11. Cf. Saller, *Patriarchy, Property*, 133–54.

12. Cf. Tacitus, *Agricola* 1–2; Tacitus, *Histories* 1.2–3, and the discussion in MacMullen, *Enemies of the Roman Order*, 18–45.

13. Cf. Tacitus's shrewd observations in *Agricola* 14–38 on the necessity (and limitations) of fear as a motive for subjection to imperial domination.

14. Cf. the speech that Tacitus puts in the mouth of Calgacus, which describes the "fear and panic" that function as the "sorry bonds of love" binding the Gauls and Germans and Britons in the Roman army to their superiors: "Take these away, and those who have ceased to fear will begin to hate." *Agricola* 32.2, 85, trans. M. Hutton.

15. Peter's injunctions to wives in 3:1–6 are premised, in part, on the patriarchal social arrangements of the day, in which the authority of husbands over their households was comprehensive and legally sanctioned; hence, the *homoiōs* (in the same way) that links the instructions of 3:1–6 with the words to slaves in 2:18–25, framing both as particular applications of the general exhortation in 2:13 that believers should "submit . . . for the Lord's sake to every human authority." In the husband-wife relationship, however, the rationale for Peter's instructions is somewhat more complex than that general principle, as evidenced by the presence of the complementary word to husbands in 3:7 (also commencing with *homoiōs*), which urges on husbands a way of relating to their wives that takes into account both their equality with their husbands before God as "heirs with [their husbands] of the gracious gift of life" and the vulnerabilities to which they are exposed because of the differences between men's bodies and women's ("as the weaker partner"; Greek: *hōs asthenesterō skeuei*).

the commands to "show proper respect" (*timēsate*) to all people and "honor" (*timate*) the emperor. Fear, it seems, is both prescribed and prohibited in the readers' social relationships, sometimes within almost the same breath.

The best clue to how the language of "fear" can function in the letter both to warrant and to limit the deference readers are to give to masters, husbands, governors, and emperors can be found in the Old Testament roots that undergird the exhortations. The place to start in tracing those roots is with the summary injunction in 1:17, "Live out your time as foreigners here in reverent fear," which precedes all the specific instructions of the household code. This injunction is predicated, according to verse 17a, on the assumption that the readers "call on a Father who judges each person's work impartially"—a basic axiom of Old Testament faith (cf. Prov. 24:12; Ps. 62:12; Deut. 10:17; the wording of these verses is echoed in the phraseology of v. 17a) that calls for a response of reverence and humility before God and confidence that present injustices will in the future be reversed. That expectation of future divine judgment evoked in 1:17a is further recalled in the reference in 2:12 to "the day he visits us" (*en hēmera episkopēs*), which echoes the expression used in Isaiah 10:3 to speak of a judgment in history on the nation of Israel and echoes the similar language used in later Jewish literature (e.g., Sir. 18:20; Wis. 3:7) to speak of a divine judgment on individuals.

The fear of YHWH that is evoked by this consciousness of divine judgment has complex implications for social relationships. On the one hand, the Old Testament Scriptures speak of the fear of YHWH as engendering a general disposition of humility (e.g., Prov. 8:13; 15:33; 22:4; cf. Sir. 1:27, 30; 2:17) and a particular response of respect and deference toward God's servants (e.g., Ps. 2:11–12; cf. Sir. 7:29–31), toward one's elders (e.g., Lev. 19:32),[16] and toward the bearers of civil authority (Prov. 24:21). Accordingly, the Scriptures can speak of "fear" as the appropriate way to relate to one's parents (Lev. 19:3) and as the attitude one would expect a slave to have toward a master (Mal. 1:6).

But an inclination of this sort toward humility and deference to authority is just one of the many social implications of the fear of YHWH, as the idea is articulated and applied in Scripture. Leviticus 19, for example, speaks of the fear of God as engendering respect not only for one's elders (v. 32) but also for the deaf and the blind (v. 14); later, the same book ties this fear to the compassionate treatment of the landless poor (25:36, 43; cf. Neh. 5:15). According to Psalm 34:13–14 (verses that are quoted as part of an extended citation of

16. See also LXX Prov. 3:34, which does not explicitly mention the fear of YHWH but does warn that he "opposes the proud" and "gives grace to the humble," and is cited in 1 Pet. 5:5 in support of a call for humility and submission to elders.

Ps. 34:13–16 in 1 Pet. 3:10–12, and preceded in the original context of the psalm by an invitation to "come" so that the psalmist might "teach [them] the fear of the LORD"), learning the fear of YHWH involves being taught a whole cluster of social behaviors: "Whoever . . . loves life and desires to see many good days, keep your tongue from evil and your lips from telling lies. They must turn from evil and do good; they must seek peace and pursue it."[17]

While the didactic content of the second half of Psalm 34 and its emphasis on "the fear of the LORD" (vv. 9, 11; vv. 10, 12 in LXX) suggest affinities with the wisdom tradition, the first half of the psalm reads like the opening of an individual thanksgiving, inviting the community to join with the psalmist in praising God for delivering him, and urging them to learn from his example to seek refuge in YHWH in the midst of their troubles. The psalm first refers to the fear of YHWH in verse 7, in an assurance that "the angel of the LORD encamps around those who fear him, and he delivers them," and the second half of the psalm depicts the righteous as a beleaguered and suffering people. If this is wisdom literature, it is wisdom under pressure; with its invitation to come and learn the fear of YHWH is also a promise that "the angel of the LORD . . . deliver[s] . . . those who fear him" (v. 7) and a story of how "the LORD . . . delivered [the psalmist] from all [his] fears" (v. 4). This, too, is a pervasive Old Testament theme (e.g., Pss. 33:18–19; 85:9; 111:5; 115:11; 145:19; Prov. 14:26–27; 19:23) and would have been obviously relevant to the original vulnerable and suffering recipients of 1 Peter.

Thus, the traditional, scriptural language of "the fear of the LORD" on which Peter is drawing when he calls his readers to a life of "reverent fear" (1:17; 2:18) carries implications for their social relationships that include not only a disposition of humility and deference to authority but also a broader set of social virtues including integrity, benevolence, and peaceableness, and a certain fearlessness in the face of the threats and terrors of life.

The Old Testament speaks in at least two ways of the fear of YHWH driving out other fears, both of which are relevant to how 1 Peter employs "fear" language and to the imperial context of the letter. First, as in Psalm 34, the fear of YHWH involves confidence in his power to protect his people and defeat their enemies. Second, and pervasively in the Old Testament (e.g., Deut. 10:12; 13:4), the fear of YHWH is depicted as exclusive, incompatible with idolatry. These two dynamics are interrelated, since the worship of a god can involve

---

17. The reminder in the following verses of the psalm (quoted in 1 Pet. 3:12) that "the eyes of the LORD are on the righteous, and his ears are attentive to their cry," but "the face of the LORD is against those who do evil" may also help to explain the basis on which husbands are warned a few verses earlier (in 3:7) that a failure to "be considerate" of their wives and "treat them with respect" will "hinder [their] prayers."

both a fear of that god's own hostility and an exercise of trust in that god to keep at bay the other things one is afraid of. Thus, in Isaiah 8:12–13 (the first verse of which is quoted in 1 Pet. 3:14) the command, "Do not fear what [these people] fear, and do not dread it," is followed immediately by a summons to the exclusive fear of YHWH: "The LORD Almighty is the one you are to regard as holy; he is the one you are to fear, he is the one you are to dread."

For the readers of 1 Peter, then, the summons to a life of "reverent fear" during the time of their exile is both a call to humility and social deference, on the one hand (including a willingness to defer to the authority of emperors, governors, masters, husbands, and elders), and a strict limit on the proper motivation and expression of that deference, on the other. Wives must "not give way to fear" (3:6); slaves are to live "as free people" (2:16), submitting to earthly masters *dia syneidēsin* ("because they are conscious of God"; 2:19) and not because of a servile terror of punishment; members of the church are to relate to the emperor and his servants (and, by implication, to the practices of the imperial cult) in a way that maintains a distinction between the "fear" that belongs to God alone and the "honor" due the emperor (2:17),[18] even where that involves the risk of suffering and death.

The complex texture of that "fear" and its social implications cannot adequately be explained as deriving simply from a tension between a scripturally generated alienation from the empire and a social conformity motivated by the survival instincts of the author. Both the reverence and respect to be shown to the bearers of earthly authority and the fearlessness with which those authorities are to be resisted when their claims overreach their divine mandate are grounded by Peter in the same set of interconnected scriptural patterns and traditions.

Scripture, Empire, and Grace

Important as it is to understand the role of fear and intimidation in the social arrangements of life in the empire, fear alone was not the only force that held the empire together, or the only way the imperial context shaped the daily lives of those who lived within its borders. Seneca's depiction of

---

18. If, as I think likely, the second half of the formulation in 2:17 (*ton theon phobeisthe, ton basilea timate*) involves an intended echo of Prov. 24:21 (*phobou ton theon, huie, kai basilea*), then the alteration of the original suggests even more strongly that the distinction between *phobeisthe* and *timate* is deliberate and emphatic. Cf. Horrell, "Between Conformity and Resistance," 134–35, for a succinct and lucid critique of Warren Carter's argument that the author of 1 Peter is counseling his readers, where necessary, to honor the emperor by (outward) participation in the rituals of the imperial cult.

the benevolent ruler—so well "protected by his own good deeds" that he "needs no bodyguard"—painted as a contrast to the tyrant in his treatise *On Mercy*, is clearly exaggerated and idealized; no real Roman emperor ever wore his arms "for adornment only."[19] But it is still, in its own way, grounded in shrewd observations of the workings of power, from a writer who had ample opportunity to observe both the brittleness of an allegiance that rests on fear alone and the power that could be exerted by benefaction and reciprocal obligation in the value system of the Romans.[20] As modern historians since Anton von Premerstein have increasingly agreed, the Roman Empire was as much an empire of patronage as it was an empire of fear.[21]

Within the context of an empire in which patronage played such a crucial role as a mechanism for social integration, the heavy emphasis of 1 Peter on the language of "grace," "mercy," "goodness," and "good deeds" has powerful social and theological resonances.

First (principally in the opening and closing sections of the letter—i.e., in 1:1–2:10 and 4:12–5:14),[22] the letter draws on the resources of the Old Testament, interpreted in a framework of christological fulfillment (1:10–12), to direct its readers' gratitude toward God in Christ as the supreme and incomparable benefactor. Thus (after the greeting and a blessing that wishes the readers "grace and peace . . . in abundance"; 1:2) the letter opens in 1:3–5 with a eulogy that blesses God for his "great mercy" in granting them new birth through Christ's resurrection into a living hope and an imperishable inheritance—"the salvation that is ready to be revealed in the last time." These themes of rebirth and future salvation remain in view throughout the rest of the chapter and continue to be tied explicitly to the gracious activity of God in Christ. The prophets are spoken of in verses 10–12 as pointing forward to "this salvation . . . the grace that was to come" to them, and the readers are urged in verse 13, "Set your hope on the grace to be brought to you when Jesus Christ is revealed"—the word *teleiōs* (NRSV "*all* your hope") implying not only fullness of assurance but also singleness of loyalty to Christ as patron and benefactor, preparing the way for the exhortations to holiness in the following verses.

---

19. Seneca, *On Mercy* 1.13.5, trans. John W. Basore in Seneca, *Moral Essays*, 399.

20. Cf. Seneca's observations on the dangerous effects of "fear that is constant and sharp and brings desperation" (*On Mercy* 1.12.4, trans. John W. Basore in Seneca, *Moral Essays*, 395) and the comments that Dio Cassius puts into the mouth of Augustus (*Roman History* 53.4.1, 201, trans. Earnest Cary and Herbert B. Foster) about how "those who were on my side have been made devoted by my reciprocating their friendly services."

21. Cf. Premerstein et al., *Vom Werden*; and the discussions in Wallace-Hadrill, "Patronage in Roman Society"; Lendon, *Empire of Honour*, 11–13.

22. I am following the analysis of the letter's structure that is proposed in Achtemeier and Epp, *1 Peter*, 73–74.

The readers are exhorted in the following verse to obey because they are "children" who owe obedience to their Father, and they are reminded in verses 18–19 that their salvation was accomplished "not with perishable things such as silver or gold . . . but with the precious blood of Christ"—a contrast that simultaneously emphasizes the costly generosity of God as their heavenly benefactor and deprecates the value of the "perishable things such as silver and gold" that earthly patrons might offer. The chapter closes by reminding readers in verses 23–25 that they have been "born again . . . through the living and enduring word of God"; the "word" through which they have been reborn is specified in verse 24 as the merciful summons to return from exile spoken by the prophet in Isaiah 40. This word is appropriated in verse 25 as an announcement or anticipation of the gospel of Christ.

The opening paragraph of the second chapter maintains the focus on the twin gifts of new birth and future salvation. The injunctions of verse 1 are supported by an appeal to the readers in verse 2 as "newborn babies" to "crave pure spiritual milk, so that by it [they] may grow up in [their] salvation." This experience of drinking from the milk of God's kindness is depicted in 2:3, in an echo of Psalm 34:8, as one of "tast[ing] that the Lord is good [*chrēstos*]." As when he appropriated Isaiah 40:8 in the previous paragraph, Peter understands readers to have experienced this gracious activity of God when they encountered Christ—the "him" of 2:4 implicitly identifying the psalm citation's reference to "the Lord" as a reference to Christ.

The catena of scriptural citations and allusions in verses 6–10 that concludes this first section of the letter closes with the words of the prophet Hosea about apostate and restored Israel, appropriated and applied to the readers of the letter so as to ground their salvation and their very identity as a people in the mercy of God: "Once you were not a people, but now you are the people of God; once you had not received mercy, but now you have received mercy" (2:10; cf. Hosea 1:6–10). It is not surprising, therefore, that in the previous verse Peter speaks of the readers' calling as being directed toward the purpose that they might "declare the praises [*tas aretas*] of him who called [them] out of darkness into his wonderful light"—language reminiscent of the honorific inscriptions praising the generosity of a benefactor.[23]

The closing chapters of the letter, too (4:12–5:14), emphasize the grace of God in Christ. God is depicted in 5:5 as the one who "shows favor to the humble" (drawing on the language of LXX Prov. 3:34) and in 5:10 as "the God of all grace," who "will himself restore" them and make them "strong, firm and steadfast." Finally, 5:12 uses similar language to summarize the

23. Cf. Danker, *Benefactor*, 319, 452.

purpose of the whole letter: "I have written . . . encouraging you and testify-
ing that this is the true grace of God. Stand fast in it." In the absence of any
suggestion in the letter that it is occasioned by internal theological debates
over the place of divine grace and works of the law, this solemn injunction is
best taken as urging trust in the generosity and faithfulness of God as against
trust in earthly resources and defenders.

If the opening and closing sections of the letter frame its contents with
the reminder that God is the great benefactor, the middle (2:11–4:11) calls on
believers to imitate and participate in the generosity of God by being benefactors themselves, both within and beyond the community of the church.

Within the church, readers must, according to the closing verses of the
section, act toward one another as "faithful stewards of God's grace in its
various forms" (4:10); they are to minister to one another in word and deed,
extending and embodying the grace of God, so that their actions function as
his actions and their words as his words (4:11). The "steward" imagery of verse
10, together with the injunction to practice hospitality in verse 9, underlines
how these expressions of grace in the Christian community connect with the
metaphor of the church as a home for the homeless. Faithfulness to Christ
may alienate readers from patronage networks that might otherwise have offered them some degree of advancement or protection, but the church's own
practices of hospitality and benefaction offer an alternative source of security,
as a present and visible expression of the kindness of God.[24]

But the "good works" that the letter encourages in the readers are not limited to these intramural expressions of mutual benevolence—they are also part
of the way members of the church are to relate to their wider community. The
opening verses of the middle section point strongly in this direction—believers
are not only to "declare the praises" of God (2:9) by their words: "Live such
good lives among the pagans that, though they accuse you of doing wrong,
they may see your good deeds and glorify God on the day he visits us" (2:12).

The "good deeds" (*kala erga*) that are immediately in view here are not to
be taken exclusively or even primarily as works of active, public benevolence;
the verse is flanked on either side by a call to "abstain from sinful desires"
and an injunction to "submit . . . to every human authority," suggesting that
a life of "good deeds" should be read as embracing a wide range of actions
and abstentions. Nevertheless, the reference in the very next verse to governors
as being sent not only "to punish those who do wrong" but also "to commend those who do right" (2:14) gives good support to the theory that acts of
public benefaction (by those who had the resources to perform them) should

---

24. Cf. Elliott, *1 Peter*, 753.

be included in the scope of the expression. It is, after all, almost impossibly difficult to imagine situations in which the Roman civic authorities would have singled out particular citizens to "praise" them for exemplary marital fidelity or submission to authority, but public praise for notable acts of benefaction was widespread and well documented.[25]

Verse 15 explicitly states one intended function of such "good deeds": "that by doing good you should silence the ignorant talk of foolish people." The visibly virtuous lifestyle of the church's members, including their abstention from "sinful passions," their public benefaction, and their submission to authority, is envisaged as rebutting the slanders of their critics. This expectation, however, should not be read as nothing more than a pragmatic strategy to improve the church's public reputation. Even here the apologetic function of believers' good works is articulated as being "God's will"—consistent with an emphasis on the will and pleasure of God that continues throughout the middle section of the letter (2:16, 20, 21; 3:4, 12, 17; 4:2). The readers must do "good deeds" not only, or ultimately, to be praised by the governor or to silence the ignorant but to fulfill God's own will and purpose.

In the verses immediately surrounding the author's assurance in 2:15, he does not state the source of his confidence that good works of this character are "God's will" and that their divinely intended effect includes the silencing of the ignorant critics of the Christian community. Elsewhere in the letter, however, he gives explicit scriptural grounds for his exhortations to good works and his confidence about their apologetic effect. The most obvious place where he does this is in 3:8–13, where the exhortations of verses 8–9 and the reassurance of verse 13 wrap around an extended citation from Psalm 34:12–16 (LXX Ps. 34:13–17). In those verses, the psalmist urges his hearers to "turn from evil and do good" and to "seek peace and pursue it," presenting this path not only as a way of duty but as a path of blessedness for those who "[love] life and [desire] to see many good days" (Ps. 34:12). In addition to this explicit and unmistakable citation from Psalm 34, it is also possible (as Bruce Winter has argued) that Peter expected his readers—whose lives he was depicting as a metaphorical time of exile (1:17)—to hear the language of "do[ing] good" and "seek[ing] peace" as echoing the letter to the exiles in Jeremiah 29, with its advice, "Seek the peace and prosperity of the city to which I have carried you into exile . . . because if it prospers, you too will prosper" (v. 7).[26]

In an empire in which patronage and benefaction were powerful forces of social integration, and exclusion from patronage networks could mean painful

25. Cf. the arguments in Winter, *Seek the Welfare*, 21–23, 26–40.
26. Cf. ibid., 15–17.

alienation, 1 Peter's reminders about the "grace," "mercy," and "goodness" of God and its exhortations to believers to "do good" and act as "stewards of God's grace"—drawing, in both cases, on deep wells of scriptural tradition—performed important social functions. In pointing to God as the great benefactor of his people and urging believers to act as agents of his benefaction toward one another, these reminders loosened the ties of dependence and obligation that readers would have felt to pagan patronage networks and compensated for some of the alienation from them that they would have experienced; at the same time, in urging believers themselves to be active in outwardly directed, publicly visible good works, these reminders encouraged the letter's readers to maintain positive social linkages with the wider community, extending blessing to their neighbors and combating the slanders of their enemies.

Scripture, Empire, and Glory

The bonds of patronage and reciprocity that were so vital to the workings of the empire did not function crudely or mechanistically, like a "colossal back-scratching scheme."[27] The ideals and practices of patronage (along with those of fear and intimidation, discussed above) played their part in a wider, interconnected ecology of economic, aesthetic, ethical, and religious systems. In that larger, imperial ecology, a third crucial dimension of empire—sometimes reinforcing the dynamics of fear and patronage, and sometimes in tension with them—was the system of honor that functioned as a currency for evaluating people and communities, and as a code for measuring and directing conduct. Honor could be amassed by virtuous conduct and exercises of mastery (in battle or some other analogous contest), and it was displayed in visible, public manifestations of glory.[28] It was no accident that the language of "preciousness" was cognate with the language of "honor"[29] since the system was simultaneously ethical, economic, and aesthetic; representations of what was considered splendid and glorious (and, by way of contrast, what was considered shameful and ugly) both drew upon and reinforced the empire's moral codes and its social and economic order.

The imperial code of honor and its omnipresent visual representations are a crucial background against which to read the language of "glory," "honor,"

---

27. Lendon, *Empire of Honour*, 13.
28. Cf. MacMullen, *Roman Social Relations*, 62–63, 109–13.
29. Cf. the analysis of "the Latin and Greek lexicon of honour" in Lendon, *Empire of Honour*, 272–79.

and "preciousness" that is so prevalent in 1 Peter. For readers who understood themselves to be "exiles" in the empire of "Babylon," the reminder in 1:24 that "all flesh is like grass and all its glory like the flower of grass" (NRSV) was not just an ornamental flourish or an unfocused truism; in its new context in 1 Peter, as in its original context in Isaiah 40, it would have carried obvious and weighty implications for how the readers were to view the particular "flesh" and the particular "glory" of the empire under which they lived (cf. Isa. 40:6–8, 23–24). Along with this reminder of the passing glory of empire, there is also a string of references to the transitoriness of the empire's "perish[able]" and "fad[ing]" commodities (1:4, 7; 3:4).

While the bearers of earthly power may be greedy for glory and insistent that they receive it, the readers of the letter are reminded that the one to whom all glory properly belongs is God (4:11). The readers' vocation is to "declare the praises of him who called you out of darkness into his wonderful light" (2:9), and Peter articulates his desire for the conversion of their pagan neighbors in terms of a hope that the neighbors will "see [their] good deeds and glorify God on the day he visits [his people]" (2:12).

Although the letter describes God's glory in unmistakably imperial terms, it does not call on readers simply to mimic the codes of honor and value that pertained within the empire of Rome and to transfer them to the empire of God. By including the shamed and suffering figure of the crucified Jesus in the identity of God, 1 Peter radically recalibrates the scale of values on which honor and preciousness are to be measured.

This emphasis emerges early in the letter and is given an explicitly hermeneutical grounding in 1:10–11, where the readers are told that "the Spirit of Christ" testified through the prophets to "the sufferings of the Messiah and the glories that would follow" (v. 11). Although the connection between suffering and glory is thus expressed in 1:11 as sequential, its representation takes on more complexity in 1:18–19, which depicts the blood of Christ's crucifixion—through Roman eyes, a badge of almost unutterable shame and ugliness—as "precious" (timios) in the retrospective light of the divine verdict of glorification referred to in verse 21. The same language of "precious[ness]" recurs in the following paragraph, which describes the crucified and resurrected Jesus as "the living Stone—rejected by humans but chosen by God and precious to him" (2:4)—a description supported by a citation in verse 6 from LXX Isaiah 28:16 that speaks of "a chosen and precious cornerstone," laid by God in Zion.[30] The language of Scripture also

30. The fact that the crucifixion of Christ took place at the hands of the Romans would have given the readers of the letter warrant for connecting the "builders" depicted in Isa. 28 and Ps. 118 with the imperial authorities under whom they suffered.

echoes, to similar effect, in 3:22, which depicts the risen Christ as seated "at God's right hand—with angels, authorities and powers in submission to him" (cf. Ps. 110:1).

This representation of the crucified Christ as "chosen and precious" to God implies chosenness, beauty, and preciousness for those associated with him—including the humble, the powerless, and the persecuted. This connection is anticipated as early as 1:1, which addresses the readers as "elect," and 1:7, which depicts their faith in the midst of sufferings as "of greater worth than gold." The link between "living Stone" and "living stones" is made explicit in 2:4–5, and its implication for the "precious[ness]" of the readers is spelled out in 2:7 (reading *hymin . . . hē timē* as referring not to the status of Christ in the estimation of the readers [cf. NIV "to you who believe, this stone is precious"] but to the status of the readers in their association with Christ [cf. ESV "the honor is for you who believe"]).[31]

The most obvious inference the letter draws from this line of connection is for the way readers are to regard the sufferings they undergo—the pattern of "sufferings" and subsequent "glory" established in 1:11 recurs across the rest of the letter (cf. 4:13–16; 5:1, 10) and is extended to the sufferings and disgrace of those who "bear that name" (4:16). But suffering and persecution are not the only points at which the readers' social experience is to be interpreted and evaluated according to a scale of honor that has been recalibrated in the light of the story of Christ. Peter tells wives in 3:4 that "a gentle and quiet spirit" constitutes "unfading beauty" that is "very precious [*polyteles*] in God's sight"[32] and urges husbands to give "honor" (*timē*) to their wives (3:4) precisely on account of their wives' weaker position. He depicts unjust punishments experienced by slaves not only as shame and suffering that will one day be reversed by the honor they will share with Christ but also as expressing their decision to defer to their masters' authority—a stance of submission and endurance that is valorized in 2:20 as carrying great *kleos* (credit) in God's sight.[33] Peter presents the extended citation of Isaiah 53 that follows not only as showing an example to be imitated but also as giving proof that such conduct is "commendable before God" (v. 20)—presumably a conclusion drawn from the references to divine exaltation and glorification that frame the fourth servant song (cf. Isa. 52:13; 53:3–4, 12).

31. Cf. Achtemeier and Epp, *1 Peter*, 160–61.
32. Cf. the comments on *polyteles* and its function in the discourse of status and honor in Elliott, *1 Peter*, 568; B. Campbell, *Honor, Shame*, 157.
33. Cf. Lendon, *Empire of Honour*, 277, for a discussion of the heroic connotations of *kleos* and its function in the lexicon of honor.

The letter's depiction of God as not the private deity of Christians but the creator of all the world (cf. 2:13; 4:19) helps to explain the author's confidence that the values of the church and those of the surrounding culture can be understood as, to some extent, commensurable.[34] If beauty, honor, and preciousness are ultimately to be measured by how things appear "in God's sight" (3:4; cf. 2:4, 5, 20), then the countercultural value system according to which the readers are encouraged to measure things throughout the letter is being commended not merely as the private morality and aesthetics of a sectarian community but as the way things really are. What is beautiful in the sight of God can—at least in principle—be found beautiful by all who have eyes to see (cf. 2:12; 3:1–2).

A Hermeneutic for Exiles

The words and themes of Scripture, interpreted in the light of the sufferings and glorification of Christ, are therefore pervasively present and fundamentally important within Peter's interpretation of life in the empire. Both the socially "conformist" and the socially "resistant" dimensions of the letter's injunctions, applied to the dynamics of fear, patronage, and honor that shaped the social experience of the readers, are expressed in terms of scriptural categories and grounded in scriptural patterns of judgment. Scripture, interpreted christologically, gave Peter a language and a rationale for an argument that included *both* a warrant for deference to secular authority *and* a limit to its claims; for exhortations that fostered *both* a willingness to accept alienation from pagan patronage networks *and* a readiness to engage in works of public benevolence; and for a vision of what was beautiful and glorious that embraced *both* a radical recalibration of the empire's system of values *and* a hope that some at least among the empire's citizens and magistrates would see glimpses of beauty and glory in that vision's social embodiment.

Christians in our own time, learning how to read the Bible in the "Babylon" of the late-modern West, can learn much from Peter's perspective on life in the Roman Empire. His letter reminds us of the deep scriptural roots we will need if we are to preserve a faithful Christian identity in the midst of an increasingly post-Christian culture, resisting the pressure to conform our values and lifestyle to those of the cultural mainstream, without succumbing to the temptations to disengagement and defeatism that lie in the opposite direction. In the story of the sufferings and glory of Christ, and in the Scriptures that

34. Volf, "Soft Difference," 26.

continue to address us as the living and enduring word of God, we have the resources for a distinctive, gracious, and hope-filled existence, even in Babylon; the exilic hermeneutics of 1 Peter offer us a powerful example of how to mine those resources and use them to build a faithful Christian community in a post-Christian world.

—— ✽14✽ ——

"Take It and Eat"

Revelation and the Hermeneutics of Apocalyptic

Apocalypse and Interpretation

The book of Revelation is notorious for the challenges that it poses to interpreters; introductions to the book generally start by acknowledging its bewildering complexity and surveying the various competing approaches (preterist, futurist, historicist, idealist, etc.) that have been taken to interpret it.[1] Books offering guidance in interpreting the visions and prophecies of Revelation are plentiful, and with good reason.

But the apocalyptic genre is not just a hermeneutical challenge; it is itself a hermeneutic, offering its readers an interpretation of the puzzling and perplexing realities of history and experience and telling them how to relate those realities to the Scriptures and the story of Jesus. David deSilva neatly summarizes this aspect of the book's intended function:

> More than needing to be interpreted, Revelation interprets the reality of the
> audience, showing them the true character of the emperor, the ruler cult,
> and the city that has enslaved the world, the true struggle behind the scenes
> of the visible world, the true stakes of the choices believers make, the true

1. See, e.g., the survey in Beale, *Book of Revelation*, 44–49.

193

nature of the character and message of other prophets in the communities John addresses.[2]

One way in which John represents this hermeneutical function is through the recurring image of a scroll, which appears repeatedly and at pivotal points in the visions recounted in Revelation. The climax of the heavenly vision in chapters 4–5 is the announcement of the Lamb who is worthy to open the seals on the scroll in the hands of the one seated on the throne. John's recommissioning as a prophet in chapters 10–11 takes the form of a vision in which he is given an open scroll, commanded to eat it, and told to prophesy. And the final chapter of the book depicts the contents of his own prophecy as an unsealed scroll, whose words are to be kept by all who hear them. Sealed and unsealed; tasted, swallowed, and inwardly digested; prophesied, heard, and kept—at each point John's vision focuses on a scroll and its contents.

In none of these instances are the contents of the scroll to be directly identified with the words of Scripture per se, if by "Scripture" we mean the collection of Old Testament books that John and his first readers would have referred to by that name. Simply to equate the image of the scroll with the category of Scripture is to smooth over the complexities of John's visions. Nor, strictly speaking, does Revelation offer itself as an explicit contribution to scriptural interpretation. Though saturated from start to finish with words, phrases, images, and ideas from the Scriptures (indeed, Revelation has more scriptural references of this sort than any other NT book),[3] Revelation does not contain a single scriptural quotation that is overtly identified and introduced as such.

Nevertheless, as we will see, John's visions clearly imply that his book is to be received just as Scripture is to be received; that its contents are consistent with and permeated by the contents of Scripture; and that the difficulties it poses to those who receive and propagate its contents are the same as the difficulties posed by Scripture more generally. The help that Revelation offers its readers in the task of interpreting their world and their experience is also, indirectly, help in the task of living as faithful readers of Scripture in a time when its message is widely disbelieved and fiercely opposed and its central promises remain, as yet, unconsummated.

This final chapter, then, will not so much interpret Revelation as investigate how it forms its readers as interpreters; we will focus on how John's visions encourage those who hear them to make sense of their experience and their

---

2. DeSilva, *Introduction to the New Testament*, 889.
3. Cf. Smalley, *Revelation to John*, 9; the discussion in Swete, *Apocalypse of John*, cxl–cliii. Swete catalogs no less than 278 verses in Revelation that allude to particular OT texts.

observations of the world, in light of what has been revealed to them about
the story of salvation, its climax in the death and resurrection of Jesus, and
its divinely intended culmination in the things that are yet to take place. And
because the task of reading the Bible can never be separated from the task of
making sense of the world and of our lives, the question we pose here will
also conclude this whole book's exploration of what it means to be readers
of Scripture who keep its words with a persevering faith and an earnest quest
for understanding.

Opening the Sealed Scroll (Rev. 4–5)

After the opening vision of Jesus as "someone like a son of man" in Revelation 1:9–20, and the letters to the churches that John is commanded to
write in chapters 2–3, the first great heavenly vision that John records for his
readers is of a throne on which God himself is seated, surrounded by living
creatures giving glory to him in words adapted from those of the seraphim
of Isaiah 6. Unlike Isaiah's vision, however, this vision does not climax with
a prophetic commissioning; John was already commissioned in the vision of
Christ recounted in 1:9–20. In this later vision, God is not waiting to speak
a word and asking who will go as his messenger; rather, he is holding in his
hand a scroll full of words—with writing on both sides—and the question is
whether anyone is qualified to take charge of those words, interpreting and
implementing them so as to fulfill them.

The image of a sealed scroll is familiar to readers of Scripture. Isaiah, for
example, shortly after the commissioning scene in chapter 6, is given a dreadful
word of judgment, then told: "Bind up this testimony of warning and seal up
God's instruction among my disciples," because "the LORD . . . is hiding his
face from the descendants of Jacob" (Isa. 8:16–17). Daniel, similarly, is given
words of revelation about the coming judgments of God, then told to "roll up
and seal the words of the scroll until the time of the end" (Dan. 12:4). When
a figure in his vision inquires, "How long will it be before these astonishing
things are fulfilled?" he is answered in terms that Daniel finds cryptic and
confusing; Daniel in turn is reminded, when he asks for something clearer,
that "the words are rolled up and sealed" (12:5–9). At a time when wickedness seems to rule the earth and the face of God is hidden from his people,
the image of the sealed scroll speaks of details and timings in the purposes
of God that are known to him but still veiled to his people.

The question asked by the figure in Daniel's vision ("How long will it
be . . . ?")—echoing the question of Isaiah (6:11) and the psalmists (e.g., 6:3;

13:1–2; 35:17; 74:9–10; 89:46) and echoed in turn by the martyred souls under the altar in Revelation 6:10—is not asked in idle curiosity or theoretical speculation. It is a question that articulates the anguish and concern of a faith that is being tested by the delay of God's promised acts of justice. Hence, in John's vision, he weeps when "no one in heaven or on earth or under the earth [can] open the scroll or even look inside" (5:3). Even the most glorious vision of the splendors of heaven is occluded by tears and accompanied by questions that John cannot simply shake off or screen out, concerning the as-yet-unfulfilled promises of God to vindicate his people and restore his world. John's tears, and the question that provokes them, do not interrupt the narrative of his heavenly vision; they are integral to it. A god whose worship did not evoke such questions would be vastly different from the God of the Bible, and a mode of apocalyptic that did not make room for such matters of mundane justice would be radically distinct from the apocalyptic of the Old and New Testaments.

The answer given to the question (and the response to John's weeping) is not, in the first instance at least, an immediate unfolding of the words written on the sealed scroll; it is, rather, an announcement of the one who is able (Rev. 5:5; cf. v. 3) and worthy (v. 9; cf. vv. 2, 4) to do so. Closely related as they are, the questions of ability and worthiness are not treated in the rhetoric of the vision-report as if they were identical and interchangeable.[4] It is in his capacity as "the Lion of the tribe of Judah, the Root of David, [who] has triumphed" (v. 5), that the one who steps forward to take the scroll is announced as being able to open the scroll and its seals, but it is (repeatedly and emphatically) in his capacity as "a Lamb, looking as if it had been slain" (v. 6), that he is worshiped and honored as worthy (vv. 9, 12).

The question represented by the sealed scroll of God's plans and purposes is a question of God's faithfulness and justice as much as one of his omnipotence. Similarly, the answer given about the one who can understand and enact those purposes focuses less on his sheer power to accomplish those tasks than on the legitimacy with which he exercises that power: if anyone has the right to wield that sort of "power and wealth and wisdom and strength" or to be given the "honor and glory and praise" that are offered up to him for doing so, it is the one who was slain like a lamb and who shed his blood to purchase men and women for God. Given the dark clouds that obscure God's purposes and the long delay in their consummation, believers are not wrong to seek a warrant for their continuing decision to trust that the God they worship is sovereign and well intentioned. The warrant that they are given is the death and resurrection of Jesus—his worthiness as the slain lamb and his triumph

4. Contra Smalley, *Revelation to John*, 129.

over death as the Lion of the tribe of Judah. The events that ensue as the seals on the scroll are broken are terrifying and opaque, but John and his hearers are assured in the knowledge that these events are within the control and understanding of the Lamb.

Eating the Open Scroll (Rev. 10–11)

After the seven seals have been opened (6:1–8:1) and the first six of the seven trumpets that follow them have been sounded (8:2–9:21), John is given a second vision of a scroll, described this time as a "little scroll" (10:2) and held in the hand of "another mighty angel" (10:1; cf. 5:2). Despite the multiple and close connections between this vision and the vision of chapter 5, the two scrolls are not described in terms that suggest they are to be taken as identical, as if the scroll in chapter 10 were simply the unsealed version of the one in chapter 5.[5] Unlike the scroll of chapter 5, this is an open one, unrolled and held aloft for all to see (10:2, 8), and its description as a "little scroll" (*biblaridion*; a diminutive of *biblarion*, which is in turn a diminutive of *biblion*, the term used in ch. 5) suggests something markedly less comprehensive in its contents than the larger, double-sided scroll that the earlier vision focuses on. This scroll, it seems, contains not the secret counsels of God but a word that is to be published and made known, through the prophecy of his servant John.

Whereas the earlier scroll is entrusted into the hands of the Lamb, this scroll is handed over directly to John. More than that: he is told, "Take it and eat it. It will turn your stomach sour, but 'in your mouth it will be as sweet as honey'" (10:9). This instruction clearly echoes the similar instruction to Ezekiel, and the promise that the scroll will be sweet in John's mouth is expressed in words taken from the description of the prophet's experience when he ate the scroll he was given (cf. Ezek. 3:1–3). But the words on this scroll are not only sweet to the mouth; they are also sour to the stomach—a reality that John immediately experiences when he eats the scroll as he has been instructed.[6] In the context of a prophetic call narrative (cf. Rev. 10:11), and against the background of the intertext in Ezekiel, the contrast in the metaphor between the "mouth" (in which the words are sweet) and the "stomach" (in which they turn sour) does not imply a distinction between the (superficial and temporary) taste of the words' sweetness and the (lasting and real) sourness that they bring about

---

5. Contra Osborne, *Revelation*, 393–95.

6. While there is no direct equivalent in Ezek. 3 for the sourness in the stomach that John is promised and experiences, something similar is implied by the description in Ezek. 2:10 of the message written on the scroll as "words of lament and mourning and woe."

when ingested. For the prophet, the mouth is not only the organ of taste but also, and more importantly, the organ of speech (cf. Ezek. 3:1, 4; Jer. 1:9; 5:14); the contrast is between the sweetness of the justice and salvation that the prophet is given the task of proclaiming and the sourness of the sufferings that must go before that salvation as its inescapable prelude—a sourness that the prophet must ingest and endure within his very self.[7]

After John is commissioned to prophesy in chapter 10, he sees a vision in chapter 11 of the whole company of God's people, in solidarity with whom he is called to bear witness. The image of the "two witnesses" in that chapter is clearly intended to symbolize a group far more numerous than just two individuals. Their testimony antagonizes all the inhabitants of the earth (vv. 9–10) and extends across the whole period (1,260 days) during which "the holy city" is trampled by the gentiles (v. 3; cf. vv. 1–2); interpreted against the background of the vision of the measured temple in verses 1–2 and the earlier pattern of lampstand imagery in the visions and letters of Revelation 1–3, the vision of the twin lampstands (v. 4) suggests an image of the church, bearing witness to both Israel and the nations (cf. 11:8–10), in the power of Moses and Elijah (cf. 11:6).[8]

John's image of the lampstands has another, earlier antecedent, of course: the single golden lampstand of Zechariah 4. Zechariah's vision is also the source of the parallel image of the two witnesses as "the two olive trees" and of the statement that "they stand before the Lord of the earth" (Rev. 11:4; cf. Zech. 4:3, 14). The allusion to Zechariah's vision of the two olive trees (along with the allusions to Moses and Elijah in v. 6) suggests a strong sense of continuity between the testimony of the two witnesses in John's vision and that of the prophets of the Old Testament.[9] The scroll that John is given to eat in the vision of chapter 10 may not, formally speaking, be a symbol for the books of the Old Testament, but the prophecies that he is to speak when he has eaten the scroll, along with the prophecies that all of his fellow witnesses are to proclaim,[10] are clearly to be understood as extending the message and ministry of their Old

7. Cf. Koester, *Revelation*, 483.

8. Cf. Beale, *Book of Revelation*, 574–75; Aune, *Revelation 6–16*, 631; Bauckham, *Book of Revelation*, 84–88; Koester, *Revelation*, 497–98.

9. Zechariah's image of the two olive trees (interpreted in Zech. 4:14 as standing for "two sons of oil who stand before the Lord of all the earth" [my translation]) is traditionally taken as referring to Zerubbabel and Joshua as anointed servants of YHWH, but Anthony Petterson has made a convincing case for reading them as prophetic figures—not anointed office-bearers but agents of anointing—which appears to be the sense in which the image is interpreted and appropriated in Rev. 11. Petterson, *Behold Your King*, 63–83; also Petterson, *Haggai, Zechariah and Malachi*, 155–57.

10. I am reading the "two witnesses" of the vision as a collective representation for all of John's readers.

Testament forebears. Their fate, too, is depicted in terms that suggest strong continuity with the fate of the prophets who went before them: like them, and like the Lord Jesus himself, the two witnesses are destined to die in "the great city—which is figuratively called Sodom and Egypt—where also their Lord was crucified" (11:8; cf. Luke 13:33). The only difference is that Jerusalem has now, it seems, become a figure for the whole world,[11] and human beings from "every people, tribe, language and nation" (11:9) walk through the public square of the city and gaze upon the dead bodies of the two witnesses.

According to this vision, the privilege of receiving the words of God's revelation goes with the command to eat them, internalizing their message, and with the commission to speak them, however unwelcome their contents may be to those who hear them. The church, as John's visions depict it, is a prophetic community: a lampstand in a dark time, in a temple whose courts are besieged by the enemies of God. John is aware, of course, that not every single believer, in every place and time, will end up martyred for the testimony that he or she bears; John himself, after all, has been exiled not executed. But if John's hearers are to see themselves as collectively represented by the figures of the two witnesses in the vision of Revelation 11, they can be under no illusions about what the ultimate cost of fidelity to the word could be.

Bloody and confronting as the vision of Revelation 11 is, it can hardly be described as defeatist: the two witnesses are kept alive until the time when they have finished their testimony (v. 7), and after the brief season in which their enemies have gloated over their dead bodies and celebrated their defeat, the witnesses are brought back to life by the breath of God, stood on their feet, and raised up to heaven in a cloud (vv. 11–12). Their victory is a victory of the powerless over the powerful, accomplished not only in their eventual resurrection but also, proleptically, in the moral victory of the testimony and martyrdom that precede it: like the faithful witnesses whose triumph is celebrated in the following chapter, they overcome "by the blood of the Lamb and by the word of their testimony, [because] they did not love their lives so much as to shrink from death" (12:11).

Keeping the Unsealed Scroll (Rev. 22)

The final scroll in John's visions is the one referred to in the words of the angel who speaks to him in the final chapter of the book (22:6–11), a reference John

---

11. Paul Minear speaks in terms of a "transhistorical model" in which all five "cities"— Sodom, Egypt, Babylon, Jerusalem, and Rome—have been merged into a single apocalyptic symbol of the world in its rejection of God. Minear, "Ontology and Ecclesiology," 98.

himself takes up in the warning of 22:18–19. This time, the scroll is an image not for the secret counsels of God, nor for the words that John is to ingest and prophesy, but for the words that he has completed writing and is now to deliver to their intended readers. The passage focuses, accordingly, not on the speaking of God's words but on their reception, not on the church as a prophetic community but on the church as a hearing community that accepts John's words and keeps them as a revelation from the Lord Jesus.

Two things stand out among the various pronouncements in the final chapter of Revelation about the words written in the scroll of John's prophecy. The first is the command in verse 10 that the words of the prophecy must be left unsealed. In a deliberate contrast with Daniel, whose words were "rolled up and sealed until the time of the end" (Dan. 12:4, 9), John represents his prophecies as a text that speaks with an urgent immediacy to its own time. What was predicted in Daniel 12:10 about the reception of Daniel's words in the time of the end ("Many will be purified, made spotless and refined, but the wicked will continue to be wicked. None of the wicked will understand, but those who are wise will understand") is reiterated by John in the form of a prophetic imperative about the reception of his own words, in his own time: "Let the one who does wrong continue to do wrong; let the vile person continue to be vile; let the one who does right continue to do right; and let the holy person continue to be holy" (Rev. 22:11).

The fact that John holds out his words to his readers as an open scroll does not mean that nothing is left hidden in the counsels of God, or that the ideal reader of John's prophecies is represented as capable of a complete, Godlike understanding. Along the way it has been made abundantly clear that the great, double-sided scroll of the divine plans and purposes is entrusted to the Lamb alone; John may witness the opening of its seals, but he does not pretend to read its words or to master its contents. Not even all that John has been told is written down to be passed on to his readers: the words of the seven thunders, for example, are to be "seal[ed] up" and not committed to writing (10:4). But the things that John has been given to write are to be received as a word with urgent and present relevance: "The time is near" (22:10).

The second thing that stands out is the repeated references to John's words (first in the words of Jesus, then in the words of the angel who has given the revelation to John) as a message that those who hear it are to "keep" (22:7, 9; cf. 1:3). At one level the language stands out for how much it claims about the significance of John's words: what is said elsewhere about the commandments of God (12:17; 14:12) is said here about John's own prophecies. At another level, though, the language stands out for how modest it is in the demand that it makes: in the first instance, at least, the duty of the hearer is simply to "keep" the word that has been spoken. It is true, of course, that "keeping" a word from God implies a long string of other duties—reading, meditating, studying, believing, obeying—and "keep" can sometimes be used (e.g., Prov. 3:1; LXX 1 Kgdms. 15:11 [ET 1 Sam. 15:11]) to speak directly of such tasks and dispositions. But the first duty implied by "keep," and the one that appears to be in the center of the frame here, is simply the faithful retention of the message that has been received, neither adding to nor taking away from its contents (cf. Rev. 22:18–19).

Keeping the message—the whole message, and nothing but the message—turns out to be not so easy. Because of the various other duties that "keeping" a message as a word from God implies, and because of the intense pressures and the competing voices and visions that the church is exposed to, it is no small thing that the church in Philadelphia, with its "little strength," has continued to keep the word of the Lord Jesus and his "command to endure patiently" (3:8, 10). The Philadelphian believers become an exemplar of the kind of fidelity to the word that all of John's hearers are called to, and the promise given to them functions, by implication, as a promise to all who have ears to hear it: "I will also keep you from the hour of trial that is going to come on the whole world to test the inhabitants of the earth" (3:10b).

A Hermeneutic for Our Time?

What are we to make of the apocalyptic hermeneutics of the book of Revelation, as twenty-first-century evangelical readers of Scripture? It would be tempting to push the book to the margins of the biblical canon, dipping into its strange, symbolic world only occasionally and confining the relevance of its dark visions and strenuous demands to those times and places in which Christians are the victims of savage persecution. For many of us, as wealthy and comfortable inhabitants of the late-modern West, integrity surely demands that we acknowledge a certain level of dissonance between our own circumstances and the scenes of suffering and tribulation that occupy so much of John's vision.

Valid as such acknowledgment may be, John's address to his readers does not encourage us to conclude that his book is written for someone other than us. According to the apocalyptic calendar by which the book measures time, we live in the same days as its original readers: for us, as for them, "the time is near." Nor should we assume that John intends the book to speak only to readers who are in situations of extreme suffering and bloody persecution. If the letters in chapters 2–3 are anything to go by, John sees himself

as addressing an audience of churches who find themselves in a wide variety
of circumstances and is aiming as much to warn the comfortable against the
dangers of assimilating to the prevailing social order as he is to encourage
the oppressed to bear up faithfully under it.[12] Richard Hays's summary of
the intended function of the letters to the churches in Revelation 2–3 is apt:

> The overall message of the seven letters is to call for sharper boundaries between
> the church and the world. Those who advocate eating idol-food apparently
> think that they can blend in as "normal" members of their society; perhaps
> some even argue that Christians can accommodate the emperor cult as a civic
> obligation without betraying their faith in Jesus. Against such thinking, John
> sounds an alarm. It is no accident that the letter to Laodicea comes as the
> climax of this section. There can be no compromise, John insists, and the
> church that thinks it can live comfortably within the empire's economic system
> is in spiritual danger.[13]

For Bible readers in the culturally accommodated evangelicalism that is the
norm in much of the modern West, John's urgent summons to faithful retention of God's revelation and persevering obedience to his commandments is
a message that could not be more relevant. The pressures to add or subtract
from God's word, or to let go of it altogether, are as strong for us as for any
of John's original readers. We do not find it easy to continue trusting that
the God whom we hear addressing us in the pages of the Bible will honor
the promises he has given, or to ingest his words without remainder and bear
faithful witness to them in the public square of the great city of the world.
If we have ears to hear, we will do well to heed the message that the Spirit
speaks to the churches through the words of John's visions.

As we near the end of a book about how to interpret and appropriate the
words of Scripture, it is fitting that John has the last word, inviting us to come,
drink, and live, warning us against the perils of adding to or subtracting from
the words that God has given, pointing us forward to the coming of the Lord
Jesus, and commending us to his grace:

> The Spirit and the bride say, "Come!" And let the one who hears say, "Come!"
> Let the one who is thirsty come; and let the one who wishes take the free gift
> of the water of life.
>   I warn everyone who hears the words of the prophecy of this scroll: If anyone
> adds anything to them, God will add to that person the plagues described in this

---

12. Cf. the summary of the rhetorical situation implied by the letters in deSilva, *Seeing
Things John's Way*, 34–63; Koester, *Revelation*, 99–103.
13. Hays, *Moral Vision*, 177.

scroll. And if anyone takes words away from this scroll of prophecy, God will take away from that person any share in the tree of life and in the Holy City, which are described in this scroll. He who testifies to these things says, "Yes, I am coming soon." Amen. Come, Lord Jesus. The grace of the Lord Jesus be with God's people. Amen. (Rev. 22:17–21)

Epilogue

Always Apprentices

Let the wise listen and add to their learning,
 and let the discerning get guidance—
for understanding proverbs and parables,
 the sayings and the riddles of the wise. (Prov. 1:5–6)

Some things are best learned by taking a course. If I want to become proficient in calculus, for example, I can purchase a textbook, enroll in a class, memorize some rules, and practice some examples. Over time, with the right rules and sufficient practice in applying them, I can gain mastery of the subject and pass an examination to prove it.

But not everything is best learned that way. If I want to become an electrician, I cannot simply read a book about it, take a written exam, and then start tearing into electrical boxes. One mistake could create a horrible outcome. The challenge is magnified because there are so many real-life applications of electricity; the variety of permutations seems incalculable. Hence, we put anyone who wants to become an electrician into an apprenticeship program. The program will likely involve some formal class instruction. But mostly it involves working side by side with a master electrician as he or she encounters one situation after another, solving problems by drawing on a combination of theory and practice, knowledge and experience, and learning the kind of courage and patience and carefulness and skill that a good electrician requires.

If one wants to learn how to interpret the Bible, there is no simple set of rules to follow, no easily cataloged set of techniques to master. This is especially so if the kind of "interpretation" we have in mind includes not only the exegetical practices that work toward establishing the original meanings of the words and sentences and books of the Bible for their first hearers but also the hermeneutical practices that receive those texts as Scripture and seek to live and make sense of the world in light of them.

If we are to learn to read the Bible like that, then we need something more like an apprenticeship program. It may involve some formal instruction. It will certainly—in all but the most exceptional of circumstances—involve participation in the flesh-and-blood community of the church and learning from the (imperfect) examples of mothers, fathers, brothers, and sisters in the faith. If we are wise, it will also involve extending our horizons beyond the parochialism of our own particular generation and place, to learn from others who have read the same Scriptures at different times and in different situations. But the deepest springs of hermeneutical wisdom are to be found in the Scriptures themselves, and the interpretive practices of the canonical writers ought to play a uniquely formative and authoritative role in shaping us as readers of the Bible.

This book has attempted, across fifteen short chapters, to offer a sample of what it might look like to apprentice ourselves in this manner to the biblical writers, watching them at work as they read, appropriate, and apply biblical texts and traditions in their own contexts, and asking what we can learn if we approach our own questions and predicaments in light of the wisdom embedded in their practices and patterns of judgment. The sample I have offered is very small, of course, leaving vast tracts of the canon untouched and addressing only a tiny selection of the issues raised in books we have examined. Nor is the kind of learning process attempted in this book one that could ever terminate with an exam and a diploma that certified our mastery of the task and allowed us to graduate to some new endeavor: even if a comprehensive curriculum of this sort could be constructed, it would be foolishness to think that we could complete the course and emerge as fully formed biblical interpreters, with nothing more to learn. The wisdom God has given us to learn in Christ is an unbounded and infinite wisdom, and the combination of our human finitude and the ever-changing world in which we are to learn it means that the lessons we learned once, we will need to relearn over and over again. In the getting of that wisdom that begins with the fear of the Lord, we are always apprentices. But the apprenticeship is still richly worth the effort that it requires, and the labors we expend in learning will also be joys in themselves and acts of service offered up to God. So take and read, and keep taking and keep reading, so that the Spirit may be our teacher as we seek within the Scriptures the wisdom that we need to receive and interpret and apply them as we ought.

Bibliography

Abadie, Philippe. "From the Impious Manasseh (2 Kings 21) to the Convert Manasseh (2 Chron. 33): Theological Rewriting by the Chronicler." In *The Chronicler as Theologian: Essays in Honor of Ralph W. Klein*, edited by M. Patrick Graham et al., 89–104. JSOTSup. London: T&T Clark, 2003.

Achtemeier, Paul J., and Eldon Jay Epp. *1 Peter: A Commentary on First Peter*. Hermeneia. Minneapolis: Fortress, 1996.

Ackroyd, Peter R. "The Chronicler as Exegete." *JSOT* 2 (1977): 2–32.

Adam, Peter. *Speaking God's Words: A Practical Theology of Expository Preaching*. Downers Grove, IL: InterVarsity, 1996.

Alt, Albrecht. "The Origins of Israelite Law." In *Essays on Old Testament History and Religion*, 79–132. Oxford: Blackwell, 1966.

Alter, Robert. *The Art of Biblical Poetry*. New York: Basic Books, 1985.

Arnold, Bill T. "The Love-Fear Antinomy in Deuteronomy 5–11." *VT* 61 (2011): 551–69.

Ash, Christopher. *Bible Delight: Heartbeat of the Word of God: Psalm 119 for the Bible Teacher and Bible Hearer*. Fearn, Scotland: Christian Focus, 2008.

Augustine. *On Christian Teaching*. Translated by R. P. H. Green. Oxford: Oxford University Press, 1999.

———. *Selected Writings*. Translated by Mary T. Clark. London: SPCK, 1984.

———. *Sermons on Selected Lessons of the New Testament*. Translated by R. G. MacMullen. In *St. Augustine: Sermon on the Mount, Harmony of the Gospels, Homilies on the Gospels*, 237–545. NPNF 1.6. Grand Rapids: Eerdmans, 1956.

Auld, A. Graeme. "What Was the Main Source of the Books of the Chronicles?" In *The Chronicler as Author: Studies in Text and Texture*, edited by M. Patrick Graham and Steven L. McKenzie, 91–99. JSOTSup. Sheffield, UK: Sheffield Academic, 1999.

Aune, David Edward. *The New Testament in Its Literary Environment*. Philadelphia: Westminster, 1987.

———. *Revelation 6–16*. WBC. Nashville: Nelson, 1998.

Austin, J. L. *How to Do Things with Words*. Oxford: Clarendon, 1962.

Balch, David L. "Hellenization/Acculturation in 1 Peter." In *Perspectives on First Peter*, edited by Charles H. Talbert, 79–101. Macon, GA: Mercer University Press, 1986.

Barker, Paul A. *The Triumph of Grace in Deuteronomy: Faithless Israel, Faithful Yahweh in Deuteronomy*. Milton Keynes, UK: Paternoster, 2004.

Bauckham, Richard. *The Bible in Politics: How to Read the Bible Politically*. 2nd ed. Louisville: Westminster John Knox, 2011.

———. "The Book of Ruth and the Possibility of a Feminist Canonical Hermeneutic." *BibInt* 5 (1997): 29–45.

———. *The Theology of the Book of Revelation*. Cambridge: Cambridge University Press, 1993.

Bayer, Oswald. *Martin Luther's Theology: A Contemporary Interpretation*. Grand Rapids: Eerdmans, 2008.

Beale, G. K. *The Book of Revelation: A Commentary on the Greek Text*. NIGTC. Grand Rapids: Eerdmans, 1999.

Ben Zvi, Ehud. "The Concept of Prophetic Books and Its Historical Setting." In *The Production of Prophecy: Constructing Prophecy and Prophets in Yehud*, edited by Diana V. Edelman and Ehud Ben Zvi, 73–95. London: Equinox, 2009.

Betz, Hans Dieter. *Galatians: A Commentary on Paul's Letter to the Churches in Galatia*. Hermeneia. Philadelphia: Fortress, 1979.

Billings, J. Todd. *The Word of God for the People of God: An Entryway to the Theological Interpretation of Scripture*. Grand Rapids: Eerdmans, 2010.

Blocher, Henri. "The 'Analogy of Faith' in the Study of Scripture: In Search of Justification and Guidelines." *SBET* 5 (1987): 17–38.

Block, Daniel Isaac. *Deuteronomy*. NIVAC. Grand Rapids: Zondervan, 2013.

Bock, Darrell L. *Luke*. 2 vols. BECNT. Grand Rapids: Baker, 1994.

Boda, Mark J. *Haggai, Zechariah*. NIVAC. Grand Rapids: Zondervan, 2004.

———. "Terrifying the Horns: Persia and Babylon in Zechariah 1:7–6:15." *CBQ* 67 (2005): 22–41.

Bonhoeffer, Dietrich. *Meditating on the Word*. Cambridge, MA: Cowley, 1986.

Bovon, François. *Luke 1: A Commentary on the Gospel of Luke 1:1–9:50*. Hermeneia. Minneapolis: Fortress, 2002.

Braude, William Gordon. *The Midrash on Psalms*. 2 vols. YJS. New Haven: Yale University Press, 1959.

Bretzke, James T. *Consecrated Phrases: A Latin Theological Dictionary*. Collegeville, MN: Liturgical Press, 1998.

Briggs, Richard. *The Virtuous Reader: Old Testament Narrative and Interpretive Virtue*. Grand Rapids: Baker Academic, 2010.

Brookins, Timothy. "Rhetoric and Philosophy in the First Century: Their Relation with Respect to 1 Corinthians 1–4." *Neot* 44 (2010): 233–52.

———. "The Wise Corinthians: Their Stoic Education and Outlook." *JTS* 62 (2011): 51–76.

Brown, Jeannine K. *Scripture as Communication: Introducing Biblical Hermeneutics*. Grand Rapids: Baker Academic, 2007.

Bruns, Gerald L. "Midrash and Allegory: The Beginnings of Scriptural Interpretation." In *The Literary Guide to the Bible*, edited by Robert Alter and Frank Kermode, 625–46. Cambridge, MA: Harvard University Press, 1987.

Bultmann, Rudolf Karl. *The Gospel of John: A Commentary*. Oxford: Blackwell, 1971.

Bush, Frederic W. *Ruth, Esther*. WBC. Dallas: Word, 1996.

Calvin, Jean. *The Epistles of Paul the Apostle to the Galatians, Ephesians, Philippians and Colossians*. CNTC. Grand Rapids: Eerdmans, 1965.

———. *Institutes of the Christian Religion*. 2 vols. Edited by John T. McNeill. Translated by Ford Lewis Battles. Philadelphia: Westminster, 1960.

Campbell, Barth L. *Honor, Shame and the Rhetoric of 1 Peter*. Atlanta: Scholars Press, 1998.

Campbell, Edward F. *Ruth: A New Translation with Introduction, Notes and Commentary*. AB. Garden City, NY: Doubleday, 1975.

Campolo, Anthony. *Red Letter Christians: A Citizen's Guide to Faith and Politics*. Ventura, CA: Regal, 2008.

Caneday, Ardel B. "Covenant Lineage Allegorically Prefigured: 'Which Things Are Written Allegorically' (Galatians 4:21–31)." *SBJT* 14 (2010): 50–77.

Carson, D. A. *The Gospel according to John*. Grand Rapids: Eerdmans, 1991.

———. *Love in Hard Places*. Wheaton: Crossway, 2002.

Chatraw, Josh. "Balancing Out (W)Right: Jesus' Theology of Individual and Corporate Repentance and Forgiveness in the Gospel of Luke." *JETS* 55 (2012): 299–321.

Chaucer, Geoffrey. *The House of Fame*. In *The Riverside Chaucer*, edited by Larry D. Benson, 347–74. Oxford: Oxford University Press, 2008.

Childs, Brevard S. *Introduction to the Old Testament as Scripture*. Philadelphia: Fortress, 1979.

Chrysostom, John. *Commentary on Galatians*. Translated by Gross Alexander. In *Homilies on Galatians, Ephesians, Philippians, Colossians, Thessalonians, Timothy, Titus and Philemon*, 1–48. NPNF 1.13. Grand Rapids: Eerdmans, 1988.

Ciampa, Roy E., and Brian S. Rosner. *The First Letter to the Corinthians*. PNTC. Grand Rapids: Eerdmans, 2010.

Clines, David J. A. *Job 1–20*. WBC. Dallas: Word, 1989.

———. *Job 21–37*. WBC. Nashville: Nelson, 2006.

———. *Job 38–42*. WBC. Nashville: Nelson, 2011.

Cosgrove, Charles H. *Appealing to Scripture in Moral Debate: Five Hermeneutical Rules*. Grand Rapids: Eerdmans, 2002.

Coxhead, Steven R. "Deuteronomy 30:11–14 as a Prophecy of the New Covenant in Christ." *WTJ* 68 (2006): 305–20.

Curtis, Byron G. *Up the Steep and Stony Road: The Book of Zechariah in Social Location Trajectory Analysis*. AcBib. Atlanta: SBL, 2006.

Danker, Frederick W. *Benefactor: Epigraphic Study of a Graeco-Roman and New Testament Semantic Field*. St. Louis: Clayton, 1982.

de Boer, Martinus C. "Paul's Quotation of Isaiah 54.1 in Galatians 4.27." *NTS* 50 (2004): 370–89.

deSilva, David Arthur. *An Introduction to the New Testament: Contexts, Methods and Ministry Formation*. Downers Grove, IL: InterVarsity, 2004.

———. *Seeing Things John's Way: The Rhetoric of the Book of Revelation*. Louisville: Westminster John Knox, 2009.

Dio Cassius. *Roman History*. Vol. 6, *Books 51–55*. Translated by Earnest Cary and Herbert B. Foster. LCL 83. Cambridge, MA: Harvard University Press, 1917.

Dodd, C. H. *The Interpretation of the Fourth Gospel*. Cambridge: Cambridge University Press, 1953.

Doob, Penelope Reed. *The Idea of the Labyrinth from Classical Antiquity through the Middle Ages*. Ithaca, NY: Cornell University Press, 1990.

Driver, S. R. *A Critical and Exegetical Commentary on Deuteronomy*. ICC. Edinburgh: T&T Clark, 1895.

Dunn, James D. G. *The Theology of Paul the Apostle*. Grand Rapids: Eerdmans, 1998.

Dunne, John Anthony. "Suffering in Vain: A Study of the Interpretation of ΠΑΣΧΩ in Galatians 3.4." *JSNT* 36 (2013): 3–16.

Eastman, Susan Grove. "'Cast Out the Slave Woman and Her Son': The Dynamics of Exclusion and Inclusion in Galatians 4.30." *JSNT* 28 (2006): 309–36.

———. *Recovering Paul's Mother Tongue: Language and Theology in Galatians*. Grand Rapids: Eerdmans, 2007.

Edelman, Diana V. "From Prophets to Prophetic Books: The Fixing of the Divine Word." In *The Production of Prophecy: Constructing Prophecy and Prophets in Yehud*, edited by Ehud Ben Zvi and Diana V. Edelman, 29–54. London: Equinox, 2009.

Ellingworth, Paul. *The Epistle to the Hebrews: A Commentary on the Greek Text*. NIGTC. Grand Rapids: Eerdmans, 1993.

Elliott, John H. *1 Peter: A New Translation with Introduction and Commentary*. AB. New York: Doubleday, 2000.

———. "1 Peter, Its Situation and Strategy: A Discussion with David Balch." In *Perspectives on First Peter*, edited by Charles H. Talbert, 61–78. Macon, GA: Mercer University Press, 1986.

Fischer, James A. "Ruth." In *The Collegeville Bible Commentary: Old Testament*, edited by Dianne Bergant, 797–803. Collegeville, MN: Liturgical Press, 1992.

Forde, Gerhard O. "The Normative Character of Scripture for Matters of Faith and Life: Human Sexuality in Light of Romans 1:16–32." *WW* 14 (1994): 305–14.

———. "*Scriptura Sacra Sui Ipsius Interpres*: Reflections on the Question of Scripture and Tradition." In *A More Radical Gospel: Essays on Eschatology, Authority, Atonement, and Ecumenism*, edited by Gerhard O. Forde et al., 68–74. Grand Rapids: Eerdmans, 2004.

Fowl, Stephen E. "Virtue." In *Dictionary for Theological Interpretation of the Bible*, edited by Kevin J. Vanhoozer, 837–39. Grand Rapids: Baker Books, 2005.

———. "Who Can Read Abraham's Story? Allegory and Interpretive Power in Galatians." *JSNT* 55 (1994): 77–95.

Fowl, Stephen E., and L. Gregory Jones. *Reading in Communion: Scripture and Ethics in Christian Life*. Grand Rapids: Eerdmans, 1991.

Frame, T. R. *Losing My Religion: Unbelief in Australia*. Sydney: University of New South Wales Press, 2009.

France, R. T. *The Gospel of Matthew*. NICNT. Grand Rapids: Eerdmans, 2007.

———. "The Writer of Hebrews as a Biblical Expositor." *TynBul* 47 (1996): 245–76.

Frost, Michael. *Exiles: Living Missionally in a Post-Christian Culture*. Peabody, MA: Hendrickson, 2006.

Gadamer, Hans-Georg. *Truth and Method*. 2nd ed. London: Continuum, 2004.

Garland, David E. *1 Corinthians*. BECNT. Grand Rapids: Baker Academic, 2003.

———. "1 Corinthians." In *Theological Interpretation of the New Testament: A Book-by-Book Survey*, edited by Kevin J. Vanhoozer, 97–107. Grand Rapids: Baker Academic, 2008.

Gascoigne, John. *The Enlightenment and the Origins of European Australia*. Cambridge: Cambridge University Press, 2002.

Gignilliat, Mark S. "Paul, Allegory, and the Plain Sense of Scripture: Galatians 4:21–31." *JTI* 2 (2008): 135–46.

———. *Paul and Isaiah's Servants: Paul's Theological Reading of Isaiah 40–66 in 2 Corinthians 5:14–6:10*. LNTS. London: T&T Clark, 2007.

Gilbert, Greg. *What Is the Gospel?* Wheaton: Crossway, 2010.

Goldingay, John. *Psalms*. Vol. 3, *Psalms 90–150*. Baker Commentary on the Old Testament Wisdom and Psalms. Grand Rapids: Baker Academic, 2008.

Goldsworthy, Graeme. *Gospel and Kingdom: A Christian Interpretation of the Old Testament*. Exeter, UK: Paternoster, 1981.

———. *Gospel-Centered Hermeneutics: Foundations and Principles of Evangelical Biblical Interpretation*. Downers Grove, IL: InterVarsity, 2006.

Goodman, Lenn Evan. *Love Thy Neighbor as Thyself*. Oxford: Oxford University Press, 2008.

Gramsci, Antonio. *Prison Notebooks*. Translated by Joseph A. Buttigieg. New York: Columbia University Press, 1992.

Green, Joel B. *The Gospel of Luke*. NICNT. Grand Rapids: Eerdmans, 1997.

Greenstein, Edward L. "Jeremiah as an Inspiration to the Poet of Job." In *Inspired Speech: Prophecy in the Ancient Near East: Essays in Honor of Herbert B. Huffmon*, edited by John Kaltner and Louis Stulman, 98–110. JSOTSup. London: T&T Clark, 2004.

Griffiths, Jonathan I. *Hebrews and Divine Speech*. LNTS. London: T&T Clark, 2014.

Griffiths, Paul J. *Religious Reading: The Place of Reading in the Practice of Religion*. New York: Oxford University Press, 1999.

Guthrie, Stan. "When Red Is Blue: Why I Am Not a Red-Letter Christian." *Christianity Today*, October 11, 2007.

Hagner, Donald Alfred. *Matthew 1–13*. WBC. Dallas: Word, 1993.

Hahn, Scott W. *The Kingdom of God as Liturgical Empire: A Theological Commentary on 1–2 Chronicles*. Grand Rapids: Baker Academic, 2012.

Hauerwas, Stanley. *After Christendom? How the Church Is to Behave If Freedom, Justice, and a Christian Nation Are Bad Ideas*. Nashville: Abingdon, 1991.

———. *The Work of Theology*. Grand Rapids: Eerdmans, 2015.

Hauerwas, Stanley, and Charles Robert Pinches. *Christians among the Virtues: Theological Conversations with Ancient and Modern Ethics*. Notre Dame, IN: University of Notre Dame Press, 1997.

Hays, Richard B. *The Conversion of the Imagination: Paul as Interpreter of Israel's Scripture*. Grand Rapids: Eerdmans, 2005.

———. "The Conversion of the Imagination: Scripture and Eschatology in 1 Corinthians." *NTS* 45 (1999): 391–412.

———. *Echoes of Scripture in the Letters of Paul*. New Haven: Yale University Press, 1989.

———. *The Moral Vision of the New Testament: Community, Cross, New Creation: A Contemporary Introduction to New Testament Ethics*. San Francisco: Harper, 1996.

———. *Reading Backwards: Figural Christology and the Fourfold Gospel Witness*. Waco: Baylor University Press, 2014.

Hirsch, E. D. "Transhistorical Intentions and the Persistence of Allegory." *New Literary History* 25 (1994): 549–67.

Holmgren, F. "Barking Dogs Never Bite, Except Now and Then: Proverbs and Job." *AThR* 61 (1979): 341–53.

Hood, Jason B. *Imitating God in Christ: Recapturing a Biblical Pattern.* Downers Grove, IL: InterVarsity, 2013.

Horrell, David G. "Between Conformity and Resistance: Beyond the Balch-Elliott Debate towards a Post-Colonial Reading of First Peter." In *Reading First Peter with New Eyes: Methodological Reassessments of the Letter of First Peter*, edited by Robert L. Webb and Betsy Bauman-Martin, 111–43. LNTS. London: T&T Clark, 2007.

Horton, Michael Scott. *Christless Christianity: The Alternative Gospel of the American Church.* Grand Rapids: Baker Books, 2008.

Hughes, Graham. *Hebrews and Hermeneutics: The Epistle to the Hebrews as a New Testament Example of Biblical Interpretation.* SNTSMS. Cambridge: Cambridge University Press, 1979.

Hugh of St. Victor. *Selected Spiritual Writings.* New York: Harper and Row, 1962.

Huxley, Aldous. *Brave New World.* London: Vintage Books, 2008.

Inkelaar, Harm-Jan. *Conflict over Wisdom: The Theme of 1 Corinthians 1–4 Rooted in Scripture.* CBET. Leuven: Peeters, 2011.

Jacobs, Alan. *A Theology of Reading: The Hermeneutics of Love.* Boulder, CO: Westview, 2001.

Janzen, J. Gerald. "'He Makes Peace in His High Heaven': Job and Paul in Resonance." In *Reading Job Intertextually*, edited by Katharine J. Dell and Will Kynes, 246–58. LHBOTS. New York: T&T Clark, 2013.

Japhet, Sara. "Chronicles: A History." In *From the Rivers of Babylon to the Highlands of Judah: Collected Studies on the Restoration Period*, 399–415. Winona Lake, IN: Eisenbrauns, 2006.

———. *I & II Chronicles: A Commentary.* Louisville: Westminster John Knox, 1993.

Jobes, Karen H. "Jerusalem, Our Mother: Metalepsis and Intertextuality in Galatians 4:21–31." *WTJ* 55 (1993): 299–320.

Johnson, Luke Timothy. *Hebrews: A Commentary.* Louisville: Westminster John Knox, 2006.

Jones, L. Gregory. "Formed and Transformed by Scripture: Character, Community and Authority in Biblical Interpretation." In *Character and Scripture: Moral Formation, Community and Biblical Interpretation*, edited by William P. Brown, 18–33. Grand Rapids: Eerdmans, 2002.

Julian. *Letters. Epigrams. Against the Galilaeans. Fragments.* Translated by Wilmer C. Wright. LCL 157. Cambridge, MA: Harvard University Press, 1923.

Kant, Immanuel. *Kant's gesammelte Schriften.* Berlin: G. Reimer, 1902.

Keener, Craig S. *A Commentary on the Gospel of Matthew.* Grand Rapids: Eerdmans, 1999.

———. *The Gospel of John: A Commentary.* 2 vols. Peabody, MA: Hendrickson, 2003.

Kelly, Brian E. *Retribution and Eschatology in Chronicles.* JSOTSup. Sheffield, UK: Sheffield Academic, 1996.

Kern, Philip. *Rhetoric and Galatians: Assessing an Approach to Paul's Epistle.* SNTSMS. Cambridge: Cambridge University Press, 1998.

Kierkegaard, Søren. *For Self-Examination.* Minneapolis: Augsburg, 1940.

Kingsbury, Jack Dean. *Matthew: Structure, Christology, Kingdom.* 2nd ed. Philadelphia: Fortress, 1989.

Knoppers, Gary N. "Images of David in Early Judaism: David as Repentant Sinner in Chronicles." *Bib* 76 (1995): 449–70.

Koester, Craig R. *Hebrews: A New Translation with Introduction and Commentary.* AB. New York: Doubleday, 2001.

———. *Revelation: A New Translation with Introduction and Commentary.* AB. New Haven: Yale University Press, 2014.

Kraus, Hans-Joachim. *Die biblische Theologie: Ihre Geschichte und Problematik.* Neukirchen-Vluyn: Neukirchener Verlag des Erziehungsvereins, 1970.

Kynes, Will. "Job and Isaiah 40–55: Intertextualities in Dialogue." In *Reading Job Intertextually,* edited by Katharine J. Dell and Will Kynes, 94–105. LHBOTS. New York: T&T Clark, 2013.

———. *My Psalm Has Turned into Weeping: Job's Dialogue with the Psalms.* BZAW. Berlin: De Gruyter, 2012.

Lacocque, André. *Ruth: A Continental Commentary.* Continental Commentaries. Minneapolis: Fortress, 2004.

Lapsley, Jacqueline E. "Feeling Our Way: Love for God in Deuteronomy." *CBQ* 65 (2003): 350–69.

Leith, John H. *Creeds of the Churches: A Reader in Christian Doctrine from the Bible to the Present.* Rev. ed. Richmond: John Knox, 1973.

Lendon, J. E. *Empire of Honour: The Art of Government in the Roman World.* Oxford: Clarendon, 1997.

Linafelt, Tod, and Timothy K. Beal. *Ruth and Esther.* Berit Olam. Collegeville, MN: Liturgical Press, 1999.

Lincoln, Andrew T. *The Gospel according to Saint John.* BNTC. London: Continuum, 2005.

———. *Truth on Trial: The Lawsuit Motif in the Fourth Gospel.* Peabody, MA: Hendrickson, 2000.

Lindars, Barnabas. *The Gospel of John.* NCBC. Grand Rapids: Eerdmans, 1981.

Longenecker, Richard N. *Biblical Exegesis in the Apostolic Period.* 2nd ed. Grand Rapids: Eerdmans, 1999.

———. *Biblical Exegesis in the Apostolic Period.* Grand Rapids: Eerdmans, 1974.

———. *Galatians.* WBC. Dallas: Word, 1990.

Longman, Tremper. *Proverbs.* Baker Commentary on the Old Testament Wisdom and Psalms. Grand Rapids: Baker Academic, 2006.

Lortz, Joseph. *The Reformation in Germany.* 2 vols. London: Darton, 1968.

Luther, Martin. *Assertio Omnium Articulorum M. Lutheri per Bullam Leonis X. novissimam damnatorum.* In *D. Martin Luthers Werke, kritische Gesamtausgabe,* 7.91–151. Weimar: Hermann Böhlaus, 1883–1966.

———. *The Bondage of the Will.* Translated by Philip S. Watson. In *Luther's Works,* 33.3–295. St. Louis: Concordia, 1957–1986.

———. *Daß diese Wort Christi "Das ist mein Leib" noch fest stehen wider die Schwärmgeister.* In *D. Martin Luthers Werke, kritische Gesamtausgabe,* 23.38–320. Weimar: Hermann Böhlaus, 1883–1966.

———. *Lectures on Galatians 1535, Chapters 1–4.* Translated by Jaroslav Pelikan. In *Luther's Works,* 26.3–461. St. Louis: Concordia, 1957–1986.

———. *Sermon on John 6:27.* Translated by Martin H. Bertram. In *Luther's Works,* 23.12–19. St. Louis: Concordia, 1957–1986.

MacIntyre, Alasdair C. *Three Rival Versions of Moral Enquiry: Encyclopaedia, Genealogy, and Tradition.* Notre Dame, IN: University of Notre Dame Press, 1990.

MacMullen, Ramsay. *Enemies of the Roman Order: Treason, Unrest, and Alienation in the Empire.* 2nd ed. London: Routledge, 1992.

———. *Paganism in the Roman Empire.* New Haven: Yale University Press, 1981.

———. *Roman Social Relations, 50 B.C. to A.D. 284.* New Haven: Yale University Press, 1974.

Maggay, Melba Padilla. "Jesus and Pilate: An Exposition of John 18:28–40." *Transformation* 8 (1991): 31–33.

Malina, Bruce J., and Richard L. Rohrbaugh. *Social-Science Commentary on the Gospel of John.* Minneapolis: Fortress, 1998.

Marcus Aurelius. *The Meditations of Marcus Aurelius.* Translated by George Long. HC 2. New York: Collier, 1909.

Marshall, I. Howard. *Beyond the Bible: Moving from Scripture to Theology.* With essays by Kevin J. Vanhoozer and Stanley E. Porter. ASBT. Grand Rapids: Baker Academic, 2004.

———. *1 Peter.* IVPNTC. Downers Grove, IL: InterVarsity, 1991.

———. *The Gospel of Luke: A Commentary on the Greek Text.* NIGTC. Exeter, UK: Paternoster, 1978.

Marshall, Peter. *Enmity in Corinth: Social Conventions in Paul's Relations with the Corinthians.* WUNT. Tübingen: Mohr-Siebeck, 1987.

Martyn, J. Louis. *Galatians: A New Translation with Introduction and Commentary.* AB. New York: Doubleday, 1997.

Mason, Rex. *The Books of Haggai, Zechariah and Malachi.* CBC. Cambridge: Cambridge University Press, 1977.

———. "Why Is Second Zechariah So Full of Quotations?" In *The Book of Zechariah and Its Influence,* edited by Christopher Tuckett, 21–28. Aldershot, UK: Ashgate, 2003.

Matera, Frank J. *God's Saving Grace: A Pauline Theology*. Grand Rapids: Eerdmans, 2012.

Matthews, Victor Harold. *Judges and Ruth*. NCBC. Cambridge: Cambridge University Press, 2004.

Mays, James Luther. *Psalms*. Interpretation. Louisville: Westminster John Knox, 1994.

McCann, J. Clinton. "Wisdom's Dilemma: The Book of Job, the Final Form of the Book of Psalms, and the Entire Bible." In *Wisdom, You Are My Sister: Studies in Honor of Roland E. Murphy, O. Carm., on the Occasion of His Eightieth Birthday*, edited by Michael L. Barré, 18–30. CBQMS. Washington, DC: Catholic Biblical Association of America, 1997.

McKnight, Scot. *The King Jesus Gospel: The Original Good News Revisited*. Grand Rapids: Zondervan, 2011.

Meadors, Gary T., ed. *Four Views on Moving beyond the Bible to Theology*. Counterpoints. Grand Rapids: Zondervan, 2009.

Meeks, Wayne A. *The Moral World of the First Christians*. Philadelphia: Westminster, 1986.

Meier, John P. *Law and History in Matthew's Gospel: A Redactional Study of Mt. 5:17–48*. AnBib. Rome: Biblical Institute Press, 1976.

———. *Matthew*. NTM. Wilmington, DE: Michael Glazier, 1980.

Michaels, J. Ramsey. *1 Peter*. WBC. Waco: Word, 1988.

———. *The Gospel of John*. NICNT. Grand Rapids: Eerdmans, 2010.

Michel, Otto. *Der Brief an die Hebräer*. 13th ed. KEK. Göttingen: Vandenhoeck & Ruprecht, 1975.

Milbank, John. *Theology and Social Theory: Beyond Secular Reason*. Cambridge, MA: Blackwell, 1991.

Minear, Paul S. "Ontology and Ecclesiology in the Apocalypse." *NTS* 12 (1966): 89–105.

Mitchell, Basil. *The Justification of Religious Belief*. Oxford: Oxford University Press, 1981.

Moloney, Francis J. *The Living Voice of the Gospels*. Peabody, MA: Hendrickson, 2006.

More, Thomas. *The Dialogue concerning Tyndale by Sir Thomas More*. London: Eyre and Spottiswoode, 1927.

Nielsen, Kirsten. "Whose Song of Praise? Reflections on the Purpose of the Psalm in 1 Chronicles 16." In *The Chronicler as Author: Studies in Text and Texture*, edited by M. Patrick Graham and Steven L. McKenzie, 327–36. JSOTSup. Sheffield, UK: Sheffield Academic, 1999.

Nissinen, Martti. "Spoken, Written, Quoted, and Invented: Orality and Writtenness in Ancient Near Eastern Prophecy." In *Writings and Speech in Israelite and Ancient Near Eastern Prophecy*, edited by Ehud Ben Zvi and Michael H. Floyd, 235–72. Atlanta: SBL, 2000.

Noll, Mark A. *The Rise of Evangelicalism: The Age of Edwards, Whitefield and the Wesleys*. Nottingham, UK: Inter-Varsity, 2004.

O'Brien, Peter T. *God Has Spoken in His Son: A Biblical Theology of Hebrews*. NSBT. Downers Grove, IL: InterVarsity, 2016.

O'Donovan, Oliver. "Again: Who Is a Person?" In *Abortion and the Sanctity of Human Life*, edited by J. H. Channer, 125–38. Exeter, UK: Paternoster, 1985.

―――. "The Reading Church: Scriptural Authority in Practice." Fulcrum Anglican, 2009. http://www.fulcrum-anglican.org.uk/articles/the-reading-church-scriptural -authority-in-practice/.

Olson, Roger E. *Arminian Theology: Myths and Realities*. Downers Grove, IL: InterVarsity, 2006.

Origen. *De Principiis*. Translated by Frederick Crombie. In *Fathers of the Third Century: Tertullian, Part Fourth; Minucius Felix; Commodian; Origen, Parts First and Second*. ANF 4. Grand Rapids: Eerdmans, 1982.

Orwell, George. *Nineteen Eighty-Four*. Anniversary ed. London: Penguin, 2009.

Osborne, Grant R. *The Hermeneutical Spiral: A Comprehensive Introduction to Biblical Interpretation*. 2nd ed. Downers Grove, IL: InterVarsity, 2006.

―――. *Revelation*. BECNT. Grand Rapids: Baker Academic, 2002.

Pao, D. W. C. *Acts and the Isaianic New Exodus*. WUNT 2. Tübingen: Mohr Siebeck, 2000.

Peeler, Amy L. B. *You Are My Son: The Family of God in the Epistle to the Hebrews*. LNTS. London: T&T Clark, 2014.

Pelikan, Jaroslav. *Luther the Expositor: Introduction to the Reformer's Exegetical Writings*. Luther's Works. St. Louis: Concordia, 1959.

Peterson, David. "The Ministry of Encouragement." In *God Who Is Rich in Mercy*, 235–53. Homebush West, Australia: Lancer, 1986.

Petterson, Anthony R. *Behold Your King: The Hope for the House of David in the Book of Zechariah*. LHBOTS. London: T&T Clark, 2009.

―――. *Haggai, Zechariah and Malachi*. AOTC. Downers Grove, IL: InterVarsity, 2015.

Piper, John. *The Future of Justification: A Response to N. T. Wright*. Wheaton: Crossway, 2007.

Premerstein, Anton von, et al. *Vom Werden und Wesen des Prinzipats*. München: Bayerischen Akademie der Wissenschaften, 1937.

Pressler, Carolyn. *Joshua, Judges, and Ruth*. Louisville: Westminster John Knox, 2002.

Rainey, Anson F. "The Chronicler and His Sources—Historical and Geographical." In *The Chronicler as Historian*, edited by M. Patrick Graham et al., 30–72. JSOTSup. Sheffield, UK: Sheffield Academic, 1997.

Robson, James. *Honey from the Rock: Deuteronomy for the People of God*. Nottingham, UK: Inter-Varsity, 2013.

Rosner, Brian. *Paul and the Law: Keeping the Commandments of God*. NSBT. Downers Grove, IL: InterVarsity, 2013.

Rowe, Christopher Kavin. *Early Narrative Christology: The Lord in the Gospel of Luke*. BZNW. Berlin: De Gruyter, 2006.

Sailhamer, John. *Introduction to Old Testament Theology: A Canonical Approach*. Grand Rapids: Zondervan, 1995.

Saller, Richard P. *Patriarchy, Property, and Death in the Roman Family*. Cambridge: Cambridge University Press, 1994.

Sanders, James A. "From Isaiah 61 to Luke 4." In *Christianity, Judaism and Other Greco-Roman Cults; Part 1, New Testament*, edited by J. Neusner, 75–106. Leiden: Brill, 1975.

Schenck, Ken. "God Has Spoken: Hebrews' Theology of the Scriptures." In *The Epistle to the Hebrews and Christian Theology*, edited by Richard Bauckham et al., 321–36. Grand Rapids: Eerdmans, 2009.

Schleiermacher, Friedrich. *Hermeneutics: The Handwritten Manuscripts*. Missoula, MT: Scholars Press, 1977.

Schreiner, Thomas R. *1, 2 Peter, Jude*. NAC. Nashville: Broadman & Holman, 2003.

Scott, Ian W. *Paul's Way of Knowing: Story, Experience, and the Spirit*. Grand Rapids: Baker Academic, 2009.

Seitz, Christopher R. *The Character of Christian Scripture: The Significance of a Two-Testament Bible*. Grand Rapids: Baker Academic, 2011.

———. *Prophecy and Hermeneutics: Toward a New Introduction to the Prophets*. Grand Rapids: Baker Academic, 2007.

Selman, Martin J. *1 Chronicles: An Introduction and Commentary*. TOTC. Leicester, UK: Inter-Varsity, 1994.

Seneca. *Moral Essays*. Vol. 1, *De Providentia. De Constantia. De Ira. De Clementia*. Translated by John W. Basore. LCL 214. Cambridge, MA: Harvard University Press, 1928.

Sloane, Andrew. *At Home in a Strange Land: Using the Old Testament in Christian Ethics*. Peabody, MA: Hendrickson, 2008.

———. "Love and Justice in International Frame." *Case* 22 (2010): 14–19.

Smalley, Stephen S. *The Revelation to John: A Commentary on the Greek Text of the Apocalypse*. Downers Grove, IL: InterVarsity, 2005.

Smillie, Gene R. "'The One Who Is Speaking' in Hebrews 12:25." *TynBul* 55 (2004): 275–94.

Smith, Christian. *The Bible Made Impossible: Why Biblicism Is Not a Truly Evangelical Reading of Scripture*. Grand Rapids: Brazos, 2011.

Smith, Christian, and Melinda Lundquist Denton. *Soul Searching: The Religious and Spiritual Lives of American Teenagers*. Oxford: Oxford University Press, 2005.

Smith, James K. A. *The Fall of Interpretation: Philosophical Foundations for a Creational Hermeneutic*. 2nd ed. Grand Rapids: Baker Academic, 2012.

Soll, William Michael. *Psalm 119: Matrix, Form, and Setting*. Washington, DC: Catholic Biblical Association of America, 1991.

Sprinkle, Preston M. *Law and Life: The Interpretation of Leviticus 18:5 in Early Judaism and in Paul*. WUNT. Tübingen: Mohr Siebeck, 2007.

Starling, David I. "The Analogy of Faith in the Theology of Luther and Calvin." *RTR* 72 (2013): 5–19.

―――. "The Children of the Barren Woman: Galatians 4:27 and the Hermeneutics of Justification." *JSPL* 3 (2013): 93–110.

―――. "Not a Wisdom of This Age: Theology and the Future of the Post-Christendom Church." In *Theology and the Future*, edited by Trevor H. Cairney and David I. Starling, 81–98. London: T&T Clark, 2014.

―――. *Not My People: Gentiles as Exiles in Pauline Hermeneutics*. BZNW. Berlin: De Gruyter, 2011.

Stead, Michael R. *The Intertextuality of Zechariah 1–8*. LHBOTS. London: T&T Clark, 2009.

―――. "Sustained Allusion in Zechariah 1–2." In *Tradition in Translation: Haggai and Zechariah 1–8 in the Trajectory of Hebrew Theology*, edited by Mark J. Boda and Michael H. Floyd, 144–70. London: T&T Clark, 2008.

Stevenson, James. *Creeds, Councils and Controversies: Documents Illustrative of the History of the Church, A.D. 337–461*. London: SPCK, 1966.

Stout, Harry S. *The Divine Dramatist: George Whitefield and the Rise of Modern Evangelicalism*. Grand Rapids: Eerdmans, 1991.

Swete, H. B. *The Apocalypse of John*. 3rd ed. London: Macmillan, 1908.

Tacitus, Cornelius. *Agricola. Germania. Dialogue on Oratory*. Translated by M. Hutton. LCL 35. Cambridge, MA: Harvard University Press, 1914.

―――. *Histories: Books 1–3*. LCL 111. Cambridge, MA: Harvard University Press, 1925.

Thiselton, Anthony C. *The First Epistle to the Corinthians: A Commentary on the Greek Text*. NIGTC. Grand Rapids: Eerdmans, 2000.

―――. *Hermeneutics: An Introduction*. Grand Rapids: Eerdmans, 2009.

―――. *The Hermeneutics of Doctrine*. Grand Rapids: Eerdmans, 2007.

―――. *New Horizons in Hermeneutics*. Grand Rapids: Eerdmans, 1992.

Thompson, John Lee. *Writing the Wrongs: Women of the Old Testament among Biblical Commentators from Philo through the Reformation*. Oxford: Oxford University Press, 2001.

Thompson, Marianne Meye. "'They Bear Witness to Me': The Psalms in the Passion Narrative of the Gospel of John." In *The Word Leaps the Gap: Essays on Scripture and Theology in Honor of Richard B. Hays*, edited by J. Ross Wagner et al., 267–83. Grand Rapids: Eerdmans, 2008.

Tollington, Janet E. *Tradition and Innovation in Haggai and Zechariah 1–8*. JSOTSup. Sheffield, UK: JSOT Press, 1993.

Treat, Jeremy R. *The Crucified King: Atonement and Kingdom in Biblical and Systematic Theology*. Grand Rapids: Zondervan, 2014.

Treier, Daniel J. "Speech Acts, Hearing Hearts, and Other Senses: The Doctrine of Scripture Practiced in Hebrews." In *The Epistle to the Hebrews and Christian Theology*, edited by Richard Bauckham et al., 337–50. Grand Rapids: Eerdmans, 2009.

Trible, Phyllis. *God and the Rhetoric of Sexuality*. Philadelphia: Fortress, 1978.

———. *Texts of Terror: Literary-Feminist Readings of Biblical Narratives*. Philadelphia: Fortress, 1984.

Tuell, Steven S. *First and Second Chronicles: Interpretation: A Bible Commentary for Teaching and Preaching*. Louisville: Westminster John Knox, 2012.

Tyndale, William. *A Pathway into the Holy Scripture*. In *The Work of William Tyndale*, edited by G. E. Duffield, 2–24. Appleford, UK: Sutton Courtenay, 1964.

van der Toorn, Karel. "From the Oral to the Written: The Case of Old Babylonian Prophecy." In *Writings and Speech in Israelite and Ancient Near Eastern Prophecy*, edited by Ehud Ben Zvi and Michael H. Floyd, 219–34. Atlanta: SBL, 2000.

Vanhoozer, Kevin J. *The Drama of Doctrine: A Canonical-Linguistic Approach to Christian Theology*. Louisville: Westminster John Knox, 2005.

———. "Into the Great 'Beyond': A Theologian's Response to the Marshall Plan." In *Beyond the Bible: Moving from Scripture to Theology*, edited by I. Howard Marshall, 81–95. Grand Rapids: Baker Academic, 2004.

———. *Is There a Meaning in This Text? The Bible, the Reader, and the Morality of Literary Knowledge*. Leicester, UK: Apollos, 1998.

Vanhoye, Albert. *Structure and Message of the Epistle to the Hebrews*. Rome: Editrice Pontificio Istituto Biblico, 1989.

Van Leeuwen, Raymond C. "Proverbs." In *Theological Interpretation of the Old Testament: A Book-by-Book Survey*, edited by Kevin J. Vanhoozer, 171–78. Grand Rapids: Baker Academic, 2008.

———. "Wealth and Poverty: System and Contradiction in Proverbs." *HS* 33 (1992): 25–36.

Vesco, Jean-Luc. *Le psautier de David: Traduit et commenté*. 2 vols. Paris: Cerf, 2006.

Volf, Miroslav. *Exclusion and Embrace: A Theological Exploration of Identity, Otherness, and Reconciliation*. Nashville: Abingdon, 1996.

———. "Soft Difference: Theological Reflections on the Relation between Church and Culture in 1 Peter." *ExAud* 10 (1994): 15–30.

Wagner, J. Ross. *Heralds of the Good News: Paul and Isaiah "in Concert."* NovTSup. Leiden: Brill, 2002.

———. "'Not beyond the Things Which Are Written': A Call to Boast Only in the Lord (1 Cor. 4.6)." *NTS* 44 (1998): 279–87.

Wallace-Hadrill, Andrew. "Patronage in Roman Society: From Republic to Empire." In *Patronage in Ancient Society*, edited by Andrew Wallace-Hadrill, 63–87. London: Routledge, 1989.

Walton, John H. *Ancient Near Eastern Thought and the Old Testament: Introducing the Conceptual World of the Hebrew Bible.* Nottingham, UK: Apollos, 2007.

Watson, Francis. *Paul and the Hermeneutics of Faith.* London: T&T Clark, 2004.

Watson, Wilfred G. E. *Classical Hebrew Poetry: A Guide to Its Techniques.* 2nd ed. London: T&T Clark, 2005.

Webb, Barry G. *Five Festal Garments: Christian Reflections on the Song of Songs, Ruth, Lamentations, Ecclesiastes, Esther.* NSBT. Downers Grove, IL: InterVarsity, 2000.

———. *The Message of Zechariah: Your Kingdom Come.* BST. Downers Grove, IL: IVP Academic, 2003.

Webb, Stephen H. *The Divine Voice: Christian Proclamation and the Theology of Sound.* Grand Rapids: Brazos, 2004.

Webster, John B. *Barth's Earlier Theology: Four Studies.* London: T&T Clark, 2005.

Wells, Samuel. *Improvisation: The Drama of Christian Ethics.* Grand Rapids: Brazos, 2004.

Wenham, Gordon J. *Psalms as Torah: Reading Biblical Song Ethically.* Grand Rapids: Baker Academic, 2012.

Wenzel, Heiko. *Reading Zechariah with Zechariah 1:1–6 as the Introduction to the Entire Book.* Leuven: Peeters, 2011.

Westphal, Merold. *Suspicion and Faith: The Religious Uses of Modern Atheism.* Grand Rapids: Eerdmans, 1993.

Wilch, John R. *Ruth.* St. Louis: Concordia, 2006.

Williams, Daniel H. *Tradition, Scripture, and Interpretation: A Sourcebook of the Ancient Church.* Grand Rapids: Baker Academic, 2006.

Williamson, H. G. M. "Eschatology in Chronicles." In *Templum Amicitiae: Essays on the Second Temple Presented to Ernst Bammel*, edited by William Horbury and Ernst Bammel, 15–31. JSNTSup. Sheffield, UK: JSOT Press, 1991.

———. "History." In *It Is Written—Scripture Citing Scripture: Essays in Honour of Barnabas Lindars, SSF*, edited by D. A. Carson and H. G. M. Williamson, 25–38. Cambridge: Cambridge University Press, 1988.

———. *Israel in the Books of Chronicles.* Cambridge: Cambridge University Press, 1977.

Willimon, William H. *The Intrusive Word: Preaching to the Unbaptized.* Grand Rapids: Eerdmans, 1994.

Willitts, Joel. "Context Matters: Paul's Use of Leviticus 18:5 in Galatians 3:12." *TynBul* 54 (2003): 105–22.

———. "Isa 54,1 in Gal 4,24b–27: Reading Genesis in Light of Isaiah." *ZNW* 96 (2005): 188–210.

Wilson, Lindsay. "Job." In *Theological Interpretation of the Old Testament: A Book-by-Book Survey*, edited by Kevin J. Vanhoozer, 148–56. Grand Rapids: Baker Academic, 2008.

Winter, Bruce W. *Philo and Paul among the Sophists: Alexandrian and Corinthian Responses to a Julio-Claudian Movement*. 2nd ed. Grand Rapids: Eerdmans, 2002.

———. *Seek the Welfare of the City: Christians as Benefactors and Citizens*. Grand Rapids: Eerdmans, 1994.

Witherington, Ben, III. *Conflict and Community in Corinth: A Socio-Rhetorical Commentary on 1 and 2 Corinthians*. Grand Rapids: Eerdmans, 1995.

———. *Letters and Homilies for Hellenized Christians*. 2 vols. Downers Grove, IL: InterVarsity, 2006.

———. *Letters and Homilies for Jewish Christians: A Socio-Rhetorical Commentary on Hebrews, James and Jude*. Downers Grove, IL: InterVarsity, 2007.

———. *Matthew*. SHBC. Macon, GA: Smyth & Helwys, 2006.

———. "Salvation and Health in Christian Antiquity: The Soteriology of Luke-Acts in Its First Century Setting." In *Witness to the Gospel: The Theology of Acts*, edited by I. Howard Marshall and David Peterson, 145–66. Grand Rapids: Eerdmans, 1998.

Wolterstorff, Nicholas. *Divine Discourse: Philosophical Reflections on the Claim that God Speaks*. Cambridge: Cambridge University Press, 1995.

———. "Evidence, Entitled Belief, and the Gospels." *Faith and Philosophy* 6 (1989): 429–59.

———. *Justice in Love*. Grand Rapids: Eerdmans, 2011.

———. *Until Justice and Peace Embrace: The Kuyper Lectures for 1981 Delivered at the Free University of Amsterdam*. Grand Rapids: Eerdmans, 1983.

Work, Telford. *Living and Active: Scripture in the Economy of Salvation*. Sacra Doctrina. Grand Rapids: Eerdmans, 2002.

Wright, Christopher J. H. *Deuteronomy*. NIBCOT. Peabody, MA: Hendrickson, 1996.

Wright, N. T. *The New Testament and the People of God*. Minneapolis: Fortress, 1992.

———. *The Resurrection of the Son of God*. London: SPCK, 2003.

Zagzebski, Linda Trinkaus. *Virtues of the Mind: An Inquiry into the Nature of Virtue and the Ethical Foundations of Knowledge*. New York: Cambridge University Press, 1996.

Index of Subjects

Index of Scripture and Other
Ancient Literature

232